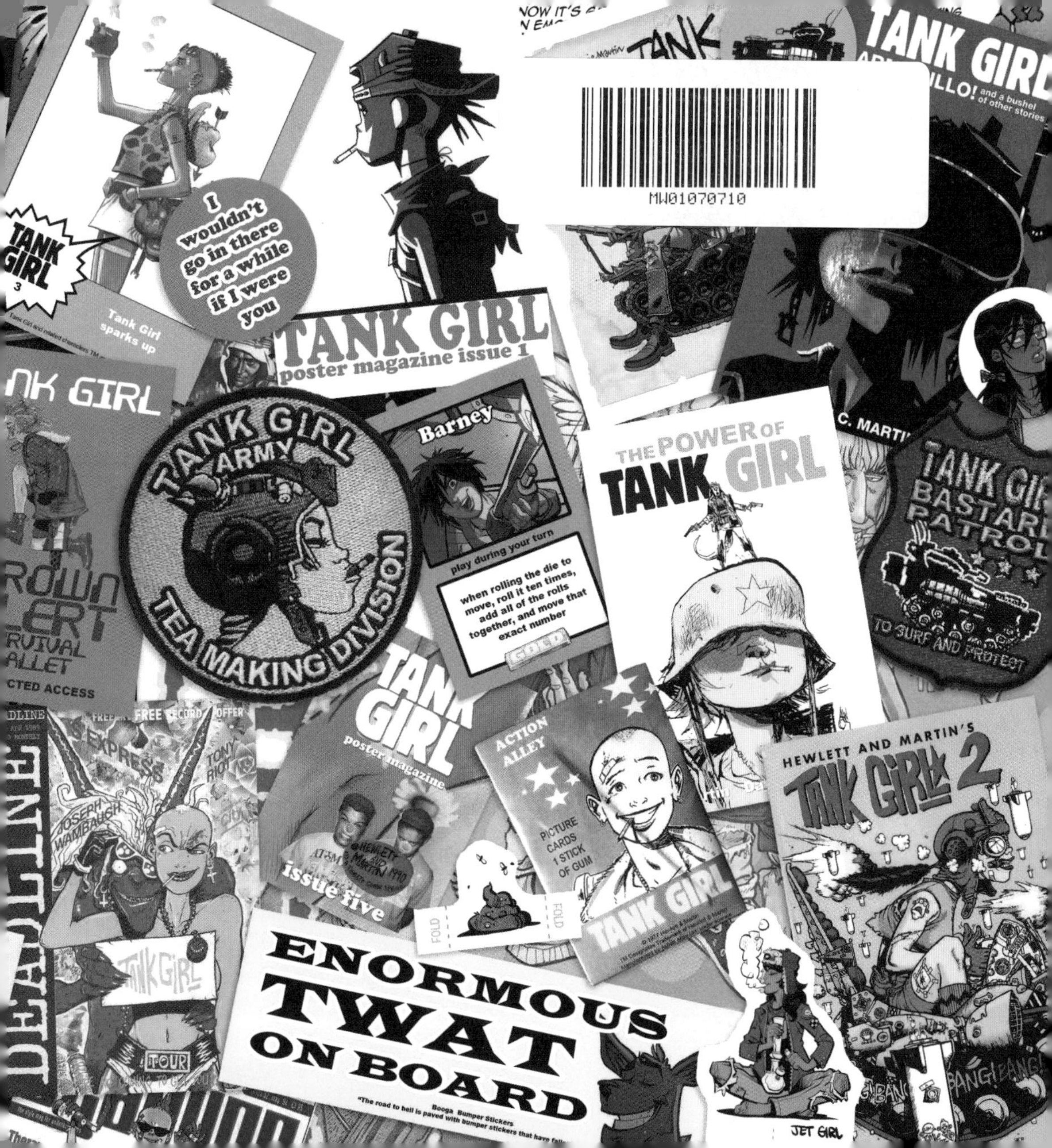

TANK GIRL
ARMADILLO! and a bushel of other stories
TANK GIRL 3
I wouldn't go in there for a while if I were you
Tank Girl sparks up
TANK GIRL poster magazine issue 1
TANK GIRL ARMY
TEA MAKING DIVISION
Barney
play during your turn
when rolling the die to move, roll it ten times, add all of the rolls together, and move that exact number
GOLD
THE POWER OF TANK GIRL
C. MARTIN
TANK GIRL BASTARD PATROL
TO SURF AND PROTECT
TANK GIRL poster magazine
issue five
ACTION ALLEY
PICTURE CARDS 1 STICK OF GUM
TANK GIRL
HEWLETT AND MARTIN'S TANK GIRL 2
DEADLINE
FREE RECORD OFFER
EXPRESS
TONY RIOT
JOSEPH WAMBAUGH
TANK GIRL
TOUR
FOLD
ENORMOUS TWAT ON BOARD
Booga Bumper Stickers
"The road to hell is paved with bumper stickers that have fallen
JET GIRL
BANG! BANG!

THE WAY OF
TANK GIRL

Titan
COMICS

THE WAY OF TANK GIRL

FRONT COVER ARTWORK
BY JAMIE HEWLETT

BACK COVER ARTWORK
BY BRETT PARSON

INTERIOR ARTWORK
BY JAMIE HEWLETT, BRETT PARSON, AND ASHLEY WOOD

WORDS AND DESIGN
BY ALAN MARTIN

TITAN COMICS

EDITOR
LAUREN MCPHEE

SENIOR DESIGNER
ANDREW LEUNG

MANAGING EDITOR
ANDREW JAMES

SENIOR PRODUCTION CONTROLLER
JACKIE FLOOK

PRODUCTION SUPERVISOR
MARIA PEARSON

PRODUCTION CONTROLLER
PETER JAMES

PRODUCTION ASSISTANT
NATALIE BOLGER

ART DIRECTOR
OZ BROWNE

SENIOR SALES MANAGER
STEVE TOTHILL

PRESS OFFICER
WILL O'MULLANE

MARKETING MANAGER
RICKY CLAYDON

ADVERTISING MANAGER
MICHELLE FAIRLAMB

ADS & MARKETING ASSISTANT
TOM MILLER

HEAD OF RIGHTS
JENNY BOYCE

PUBLISHING MANAGER
DARRYL TOTHILL

PUBLISHING DIRECTOR
CHRIS TEATHER

OPERATIONS DIRECTOR
LEIGH BAULCH

EXECUTIVE DIRECTOR
VIVIAN CHEUNG

PUBLISHER
NICK LANDAU

WAY OF TANK G
ISBN: 97817858646

PUBLISHED BY TITAN COMICS, A DIVISION OF TITAN PUBLISHING GROUP,
144 SOUTHWARK STREET, LONDON, SE1 0

A CIP CATALOGUE FOR THIS TITLE IS AVAILABLE FROM THE BRITISH LIBRA

1 0 9 8 7 6 5 4 3

WWW.TITAN-COMICS.CO
BECOME A FAN ON FACEBOOK.COM/COMICSTITAN | FOLLOW US ON TWITTER @COMICSTI
VISIT THE OFFICIAL TANK GIRL WEBSITE AT WWW.TANK-GIRL.C

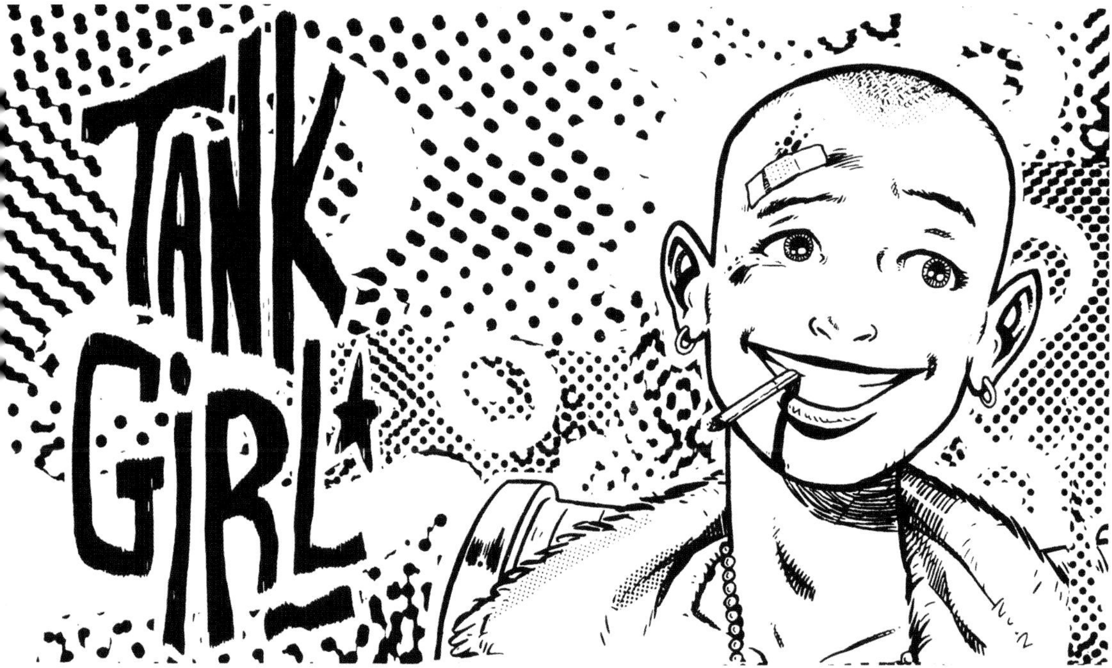
TANK GIRL

In these days of memes, avatars, and social media, the worth of an image can be evaluated instantaneously - Did it go viral? How many likes? Did it meet the criteria of the algorithm? Did my Aunty Mary comment that it wasn't really her cup of tea?

Tank Girl burst onto the scene in 1988, a time of no smart phones, no personal computers, no glowing screen in every direction you look. She became an anti-hero for extroverts and reclusives alike, and most of her fans didn't give a shit if anybody else liked her or not. Since then, technology and media have changed into unrecognisable forms, and when Tank Girl enters into cyberspace, she is judged by the same yardstick as all other cultural icons, whether old or new, underground or overground, or Wombling free.

I spend a great deal of my time running her website and certain social media pages, and it has become a constant fascination to me to watch which images travel far and wide into the universe, and which ones fall flat on their faces at the starting line. Through this process, I have gained a hitherto useless knowledge of which images from Tank Girl's chequered publishing career are best loved.

The initial idea for this book came to me a few years ago; I wanted to distil Tank Girl's essence - boil her down into a phial of bitter-sweet, sticky-brown syrup, that could be taken in one hit, and all of her accumulated wisdom, stupidity, humour, and knowledge could be imparted to the new reader in a single sitting.

When the two trains of thought merged onto one track, the way ahead became clear - The Way of Tank Girl.

I got to work editing, lifting, rearranging, pilfering, touching-up, unearthing, collaging, misappropriating, and re-assessing.

What we're left with is a sampling of Tank Girl through the ages, reflecting her ever-changing style, humour, and attitude.

If you're new to Tank Girl, there are threads to follow, and tastes of deprived pleasures yet to come. If you're a Tank Girl veteran, we hope you'll find plenty that you haven't seen before, and some familiar material, presented in a different light.

My ultimate hope for this book is that anyone picking it up will be able to open it at a random page and find a worthy nugget of wisdom, levity, or stupidity to help them through their day.

Love,

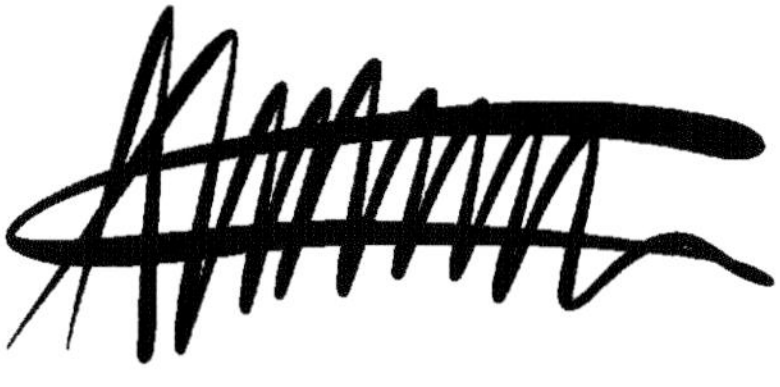

Alan C. Martin

The end of Worthing Pier, October 2017

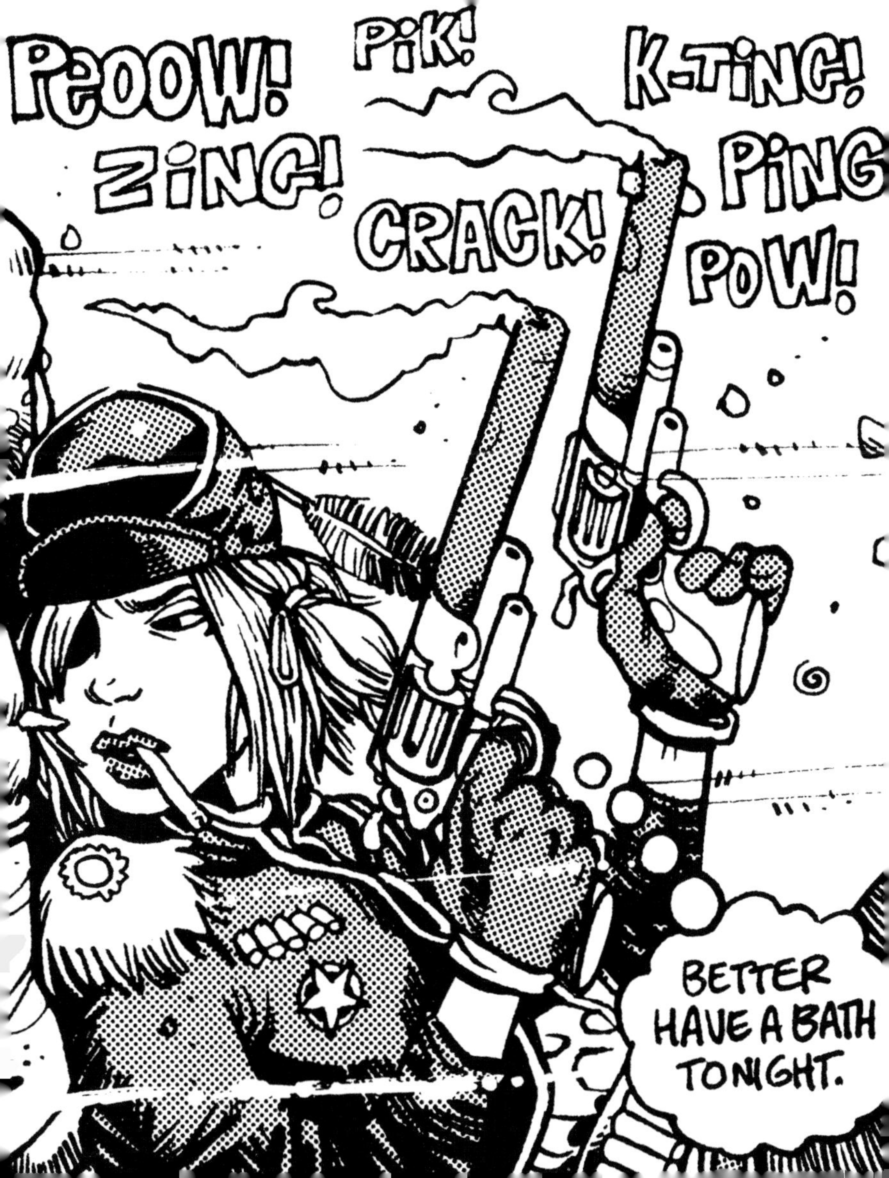
PeOOW!
PiK!
K-TiNG!
ZiNG!
CRACK!
PiNG
POW!
BETTER HAVE A BATH TONIGHT.

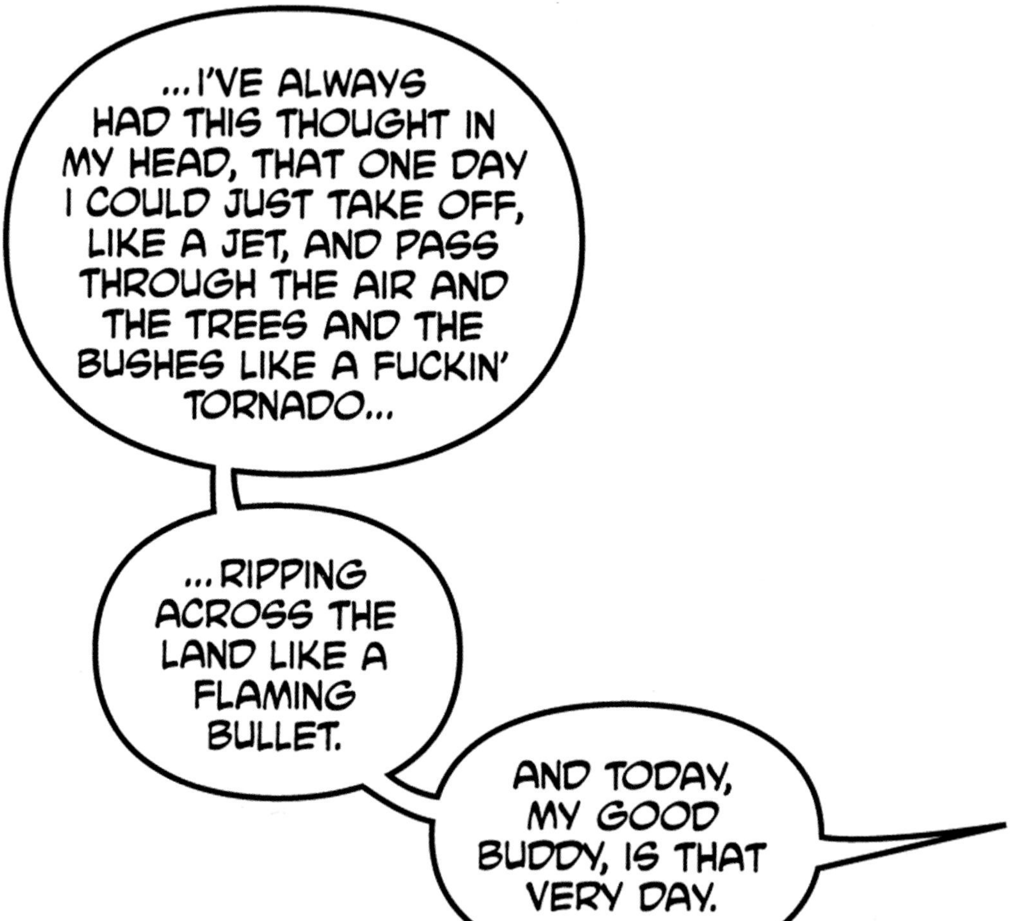
...I'VE ALWAYS HAD THIS THOUGHT IN MY HEAD, THAT ONE DAY I COULD JUST TAKE OFF, LIKE A JET, AND PASS THROUGH THE AIR AND THE TREES AND THE BUSHES LIKE A FUCKIN' TORNADO...
...RIPPING ACROSS THE LAND LIKE A FLAMING BULLET.
AND TODAY, MY GOOD BUDDY, IS THAT VERY DAY.

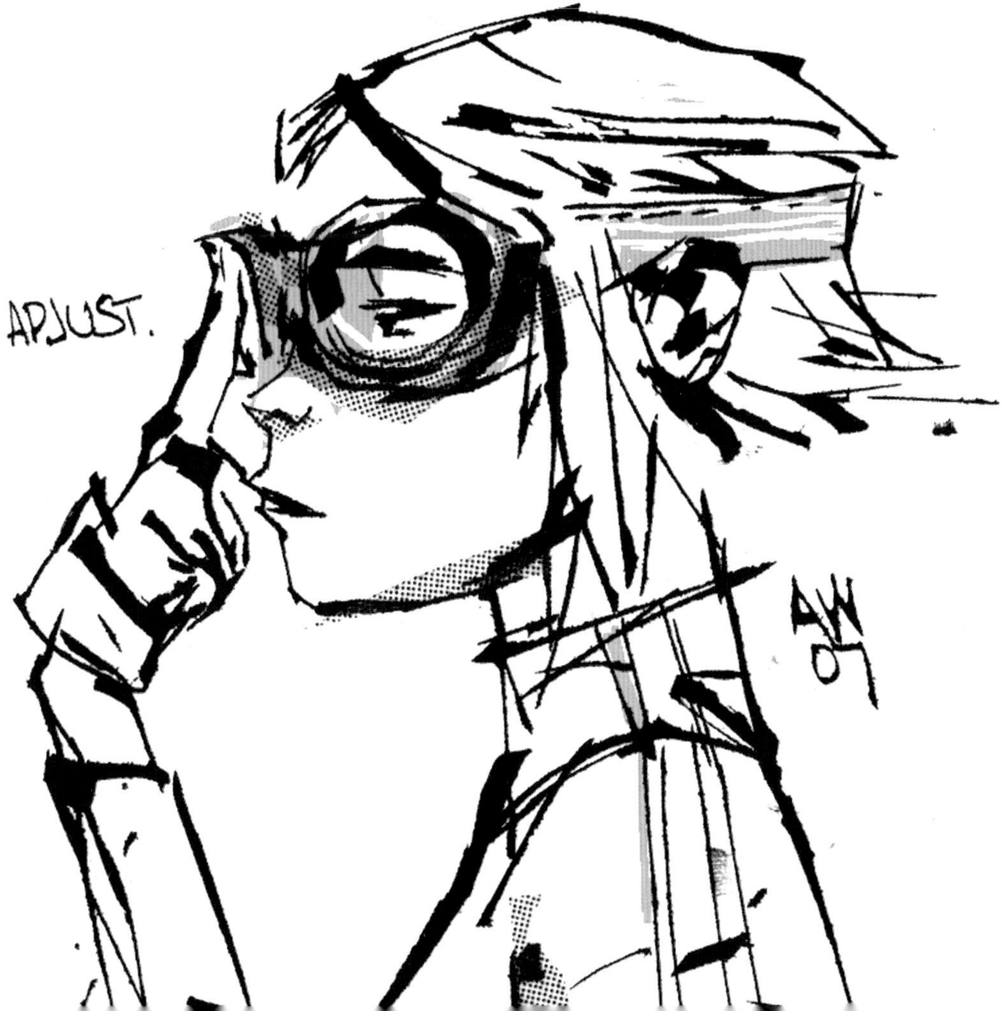
ADJUST.
AW 07

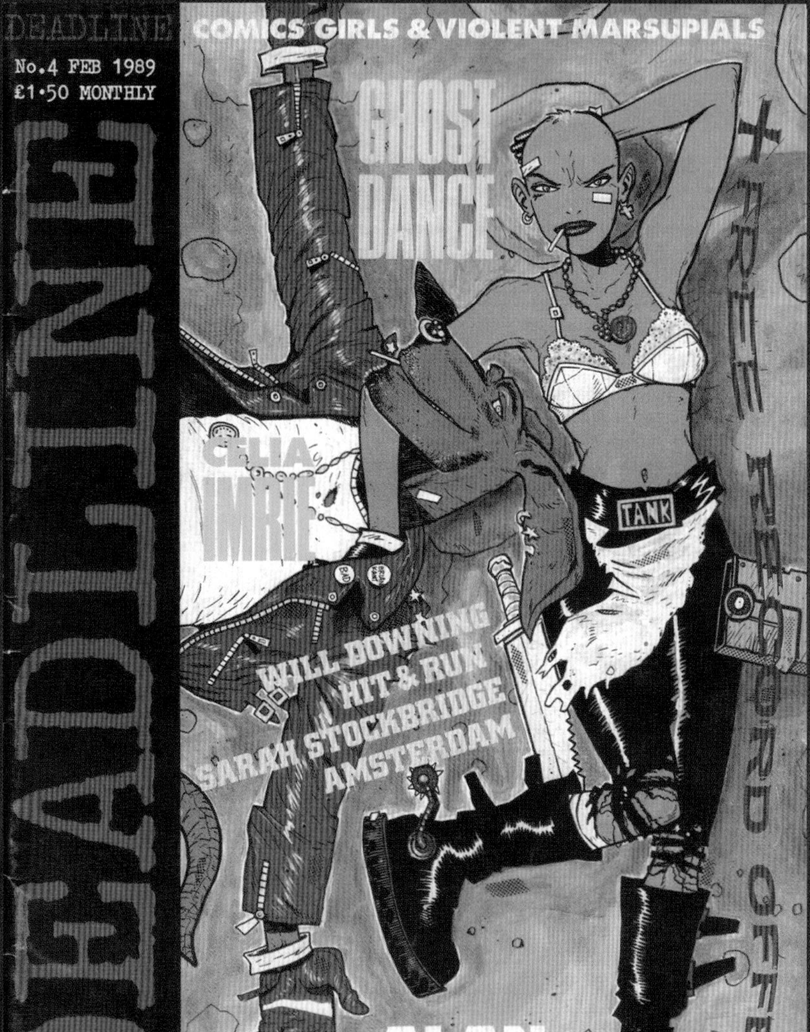
DEADLINE
COMICS GIRLS & VIOLENT MARSUPIALS
No.4 FEB 1989
£1·50 MONTHLY
DEADLINE
GHOST DANCE
CELIA IMRIE
WILL DOWNING
HIT & RUN
SARAH STOCKBRIDGE
AMSTERDAM
ALAN MOORE
FREE RECORD OFFER
TANK

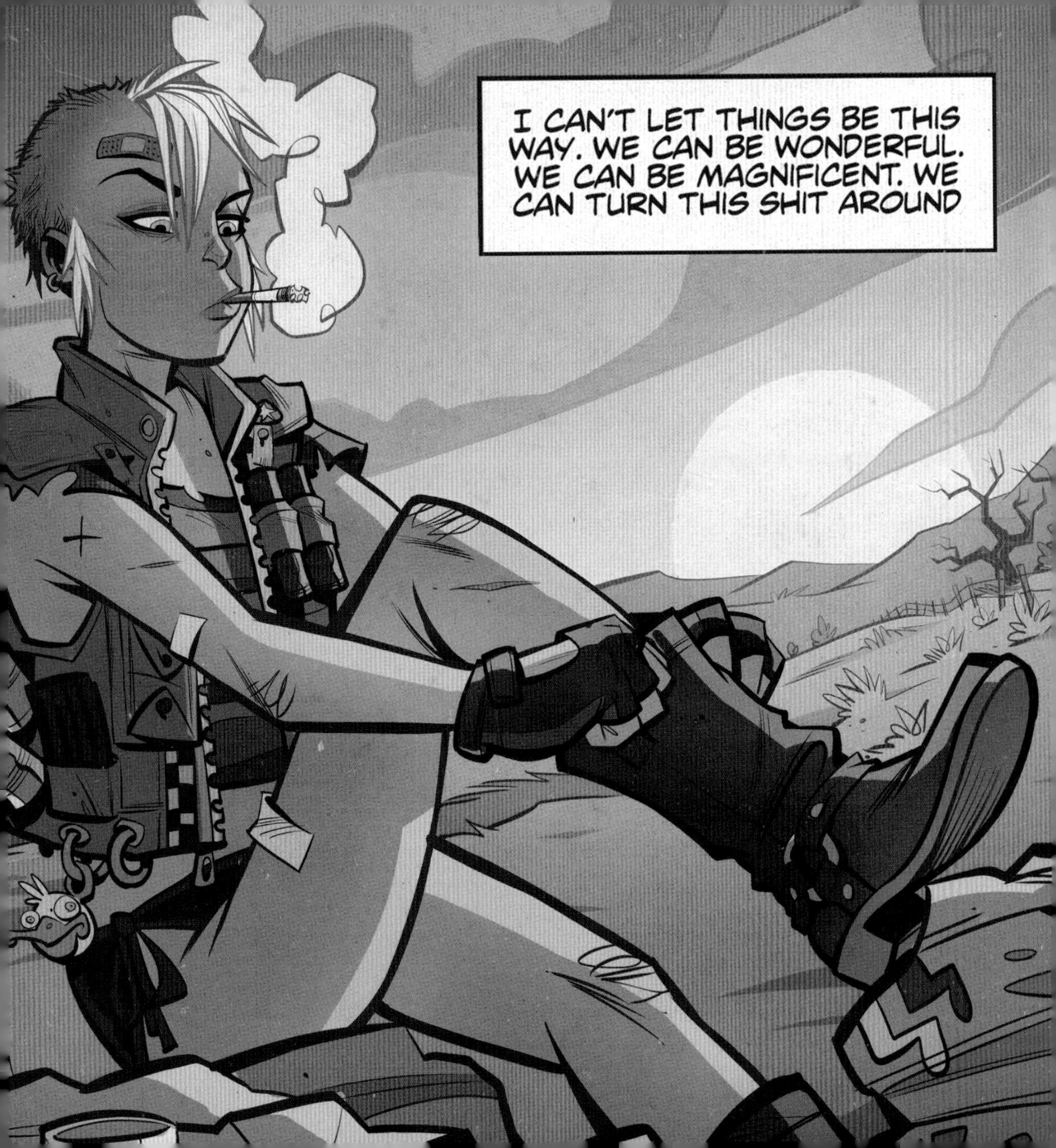
I CAN'T LET THINGS BE THIS WAY. WE CAN BE WONDERFUL. WE CAN BE MAGNIFICENT. WE CAN TURN THIS SHIT AROUND

Fucking kick me, shoot me, burn me, tax me, rob me, dissect me, insult me, scold me, enslave me, brainwash me, drop your fuckin' dirty little bombs on me, send me to bed early, and implant me with your shitty little devices.

But don't you ever touch my tank and don't you ever believe that you own one tiny fucking piece of my life.

Understand?

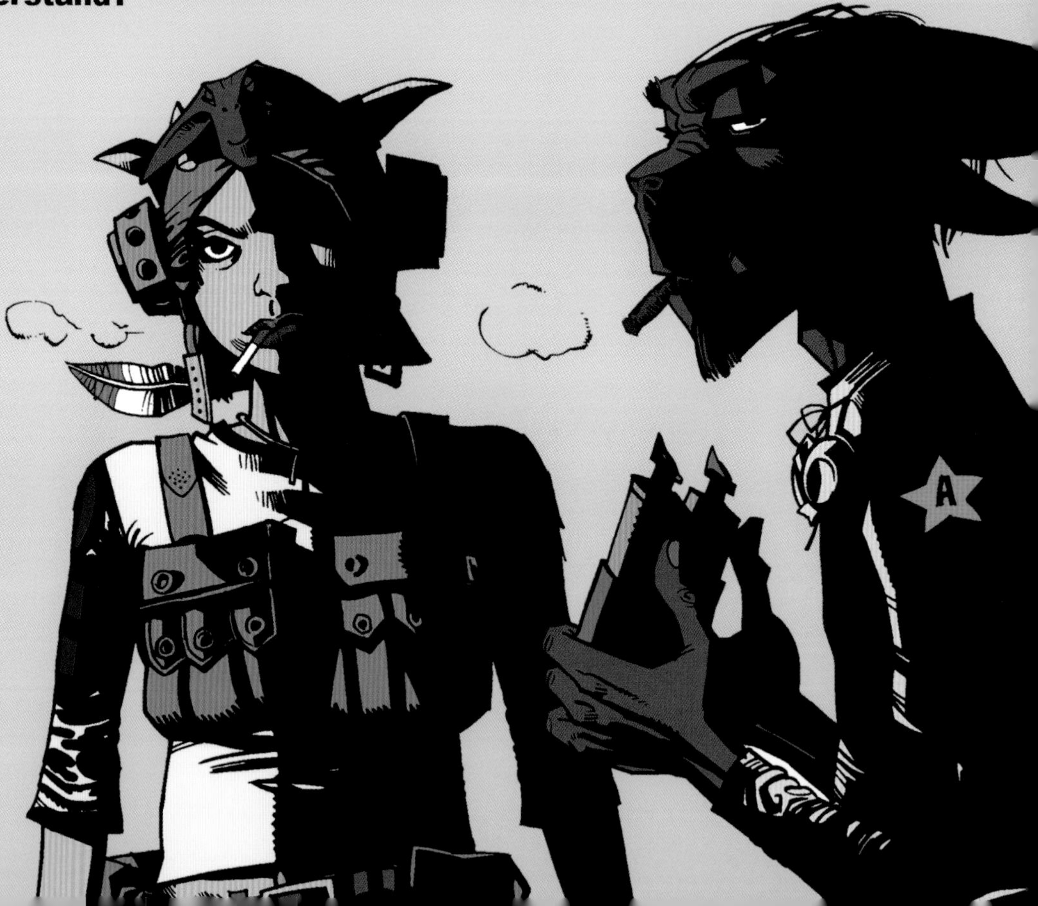

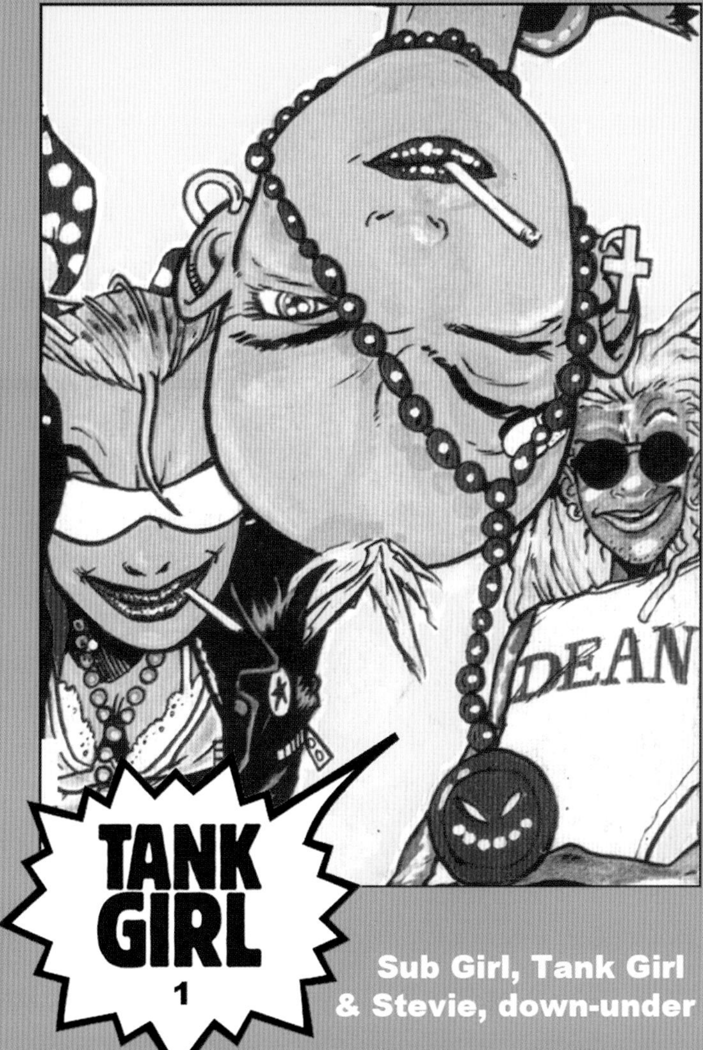
DEAN
TANK GIRL
1

Sub Girl, Tank Girl & Stevie, down-under

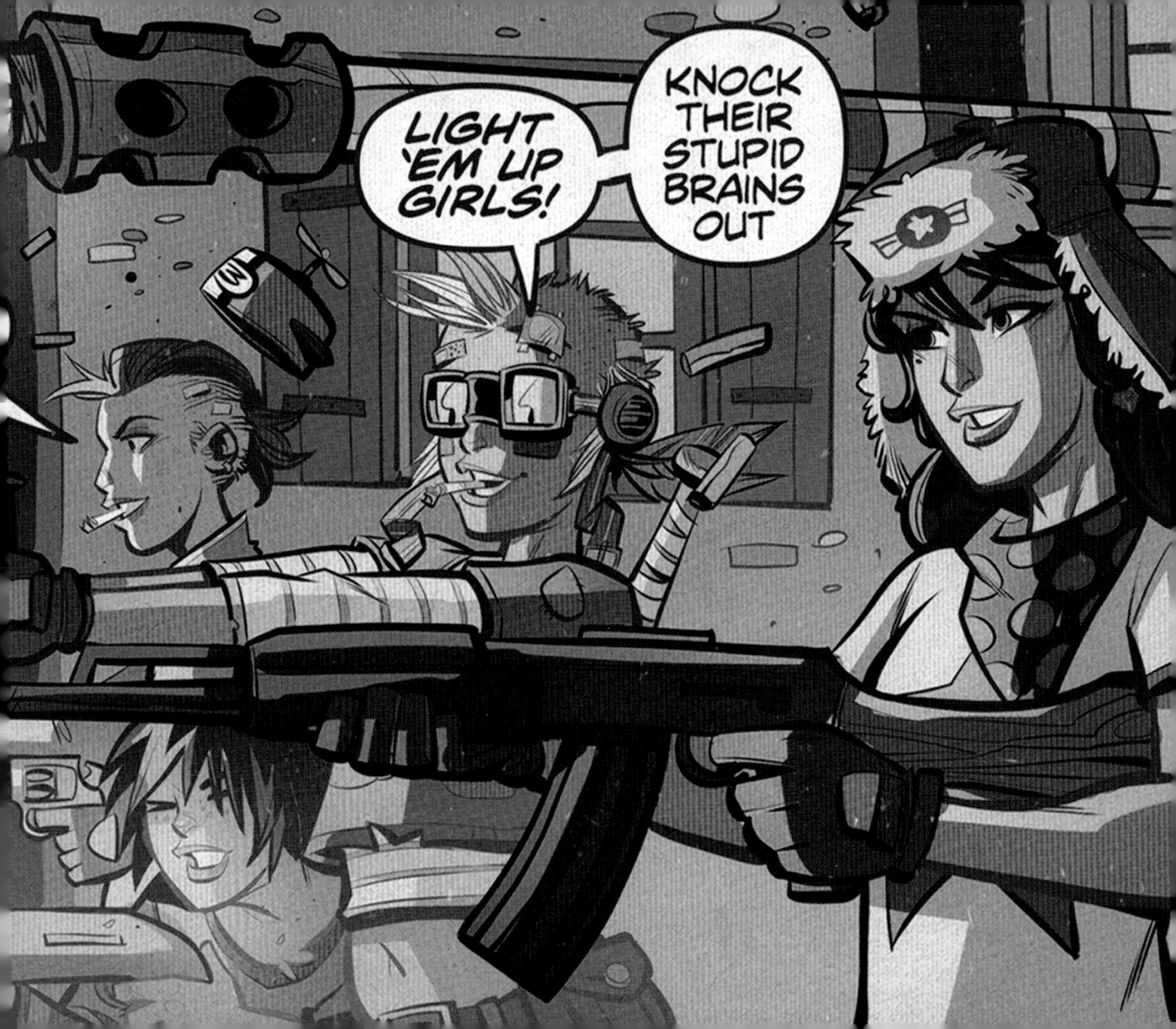
LIGHT 'EM UP GIRLS!
KNOCK THEIR STUPID BRAINS OUT

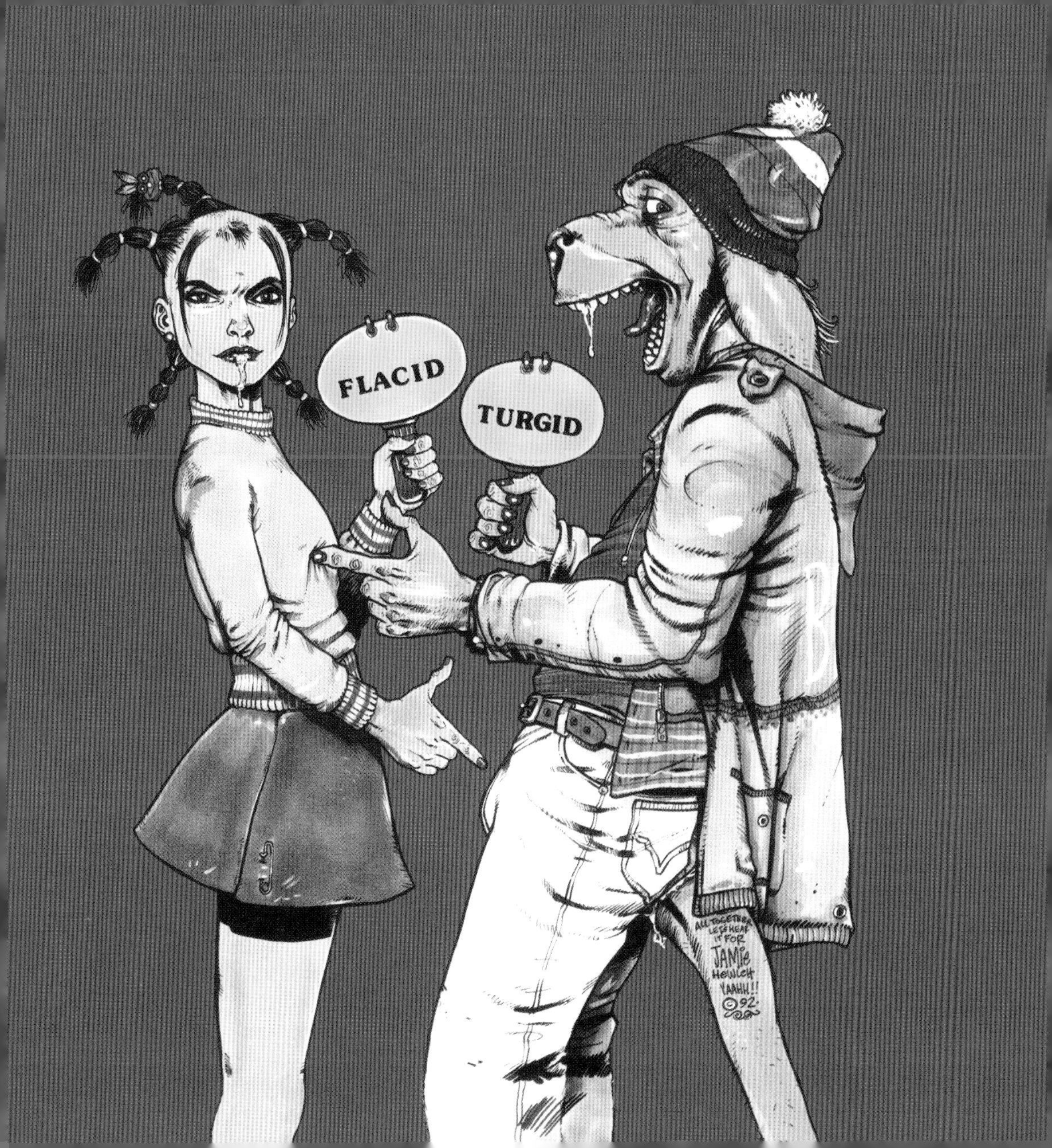
FLACID
TURGID
ALL TOGETHER LETS HEAR IT FOR JAMIE HEWLETT YAAHH!! ©92.

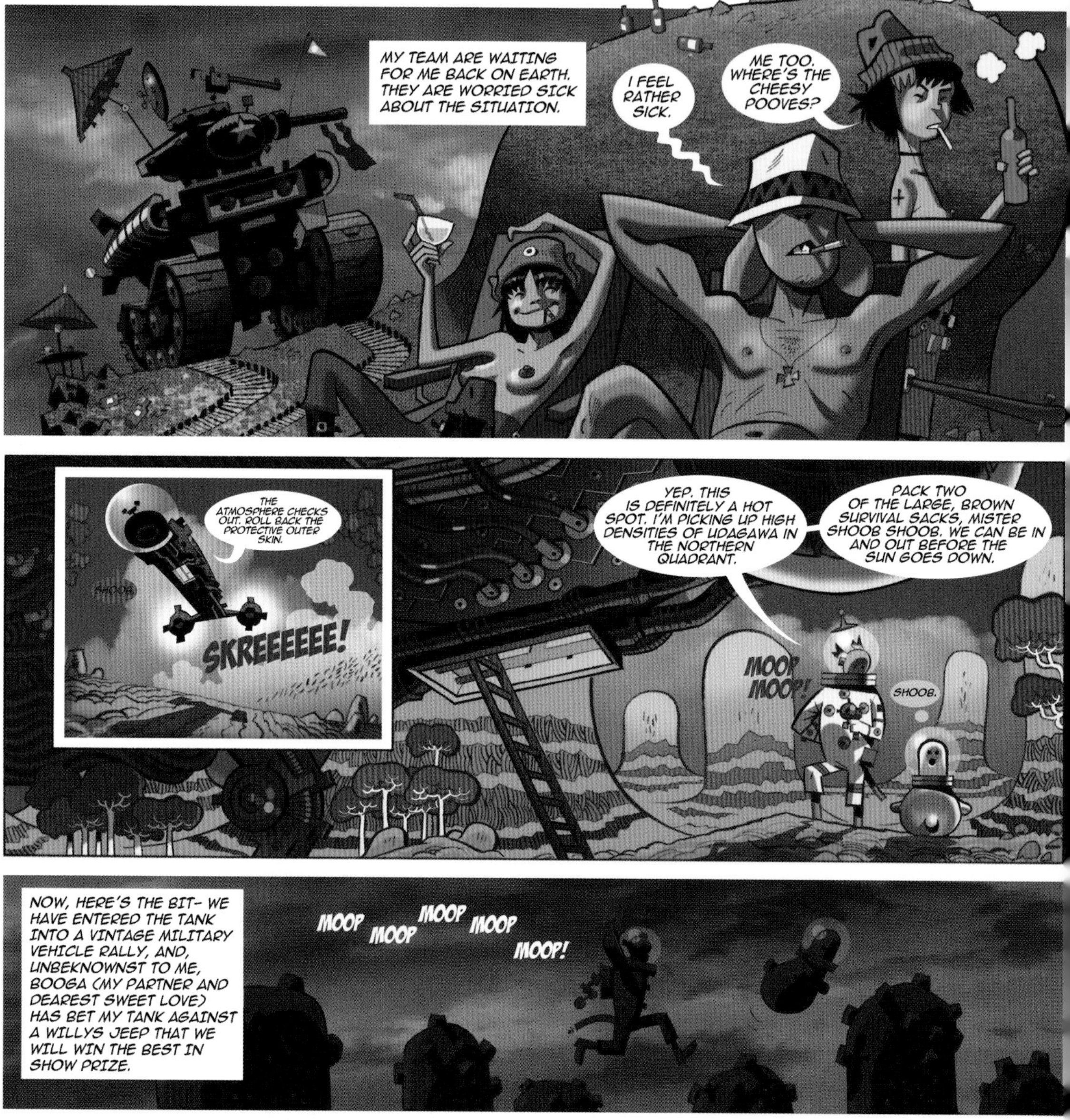
MY TEAM ARE WAITING FOR ME BACK ON EARTH. THEY ARE WORRIED SICK ABOUT THE SITUATION.
I FEEL RATHER SICK.
ME TOO. WHERE'S THE CHEESY POOVES?
THE ATMOSPHERE CHECKS OUT. ROLL BACK THE PROTECTIVE OUTER SKIN.
SHOOB.
SKREEEEEE!
YEP. THIS IS DEFINITELY A HOT SPOT. I'M PICKING UP HIGH DENSITIES OF UDAGAWA IN THE NORTHERN QUADRANT.
PACK TWO OF THE LARGE, BROWN SURVIVAL SACKS, MISTER SHOOB SHOOB. WE CAN BE IN AND OUT BEFORE THE SUN GOES DOWN.
MOOP MOOP!
SHOOB.
NOW, HERE'S THE BIT- WE HAVE ENTERED THE TANK INTO A VINTAGE MILITARY VEHICLE RALLY, AND, UNBEKNOWNST TO ME, BOOGA (MY PARTNER AND DEAREST SWEET LOVE) HAS BET MY TANK AGAINST A WILLYS JEEP THAT WE WILL WIN THE BEST IN SHOW PRIZE.
MOOP MOOP MOOP MOOP MOOP!

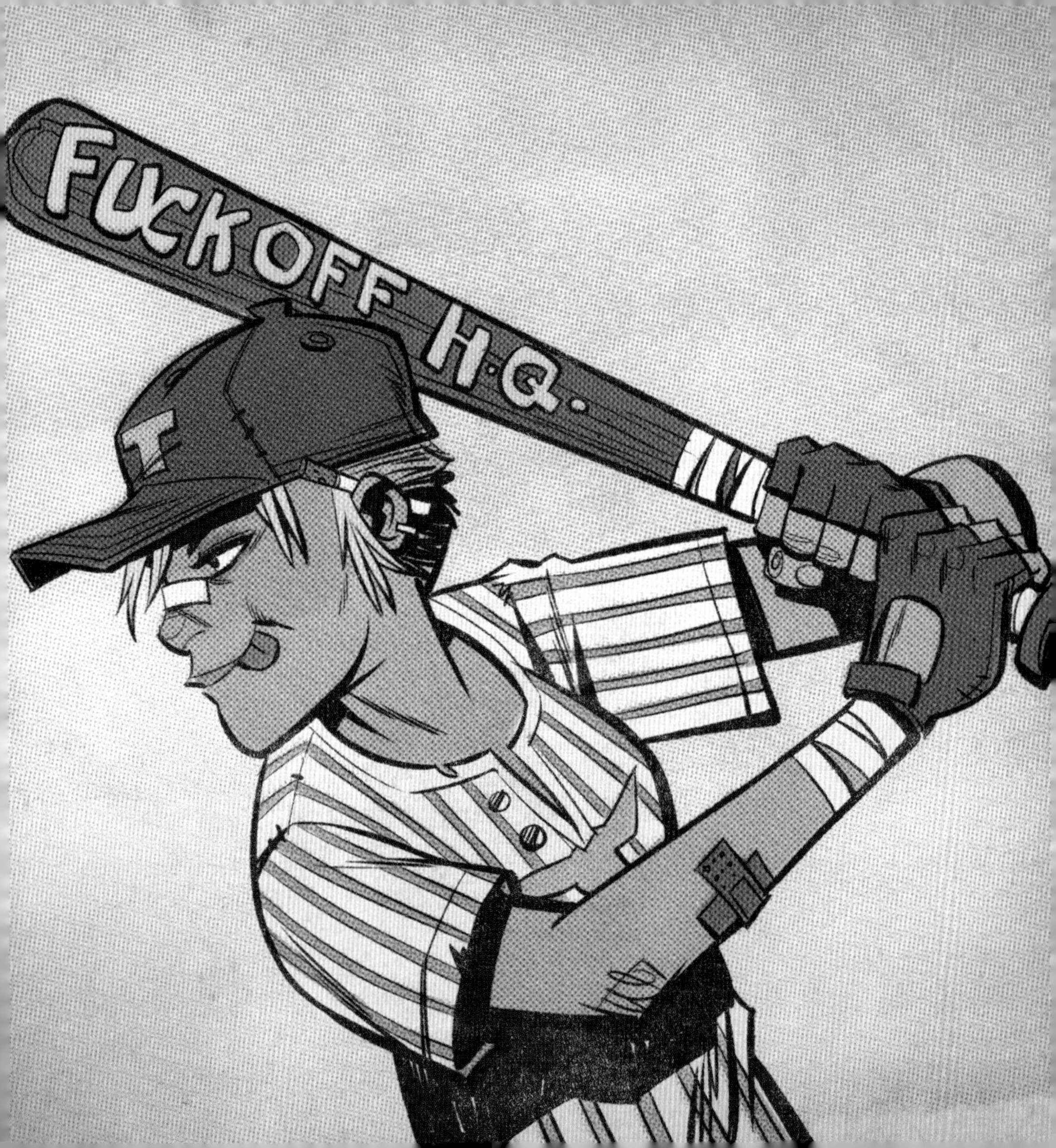
FUCK OFF H.Q.

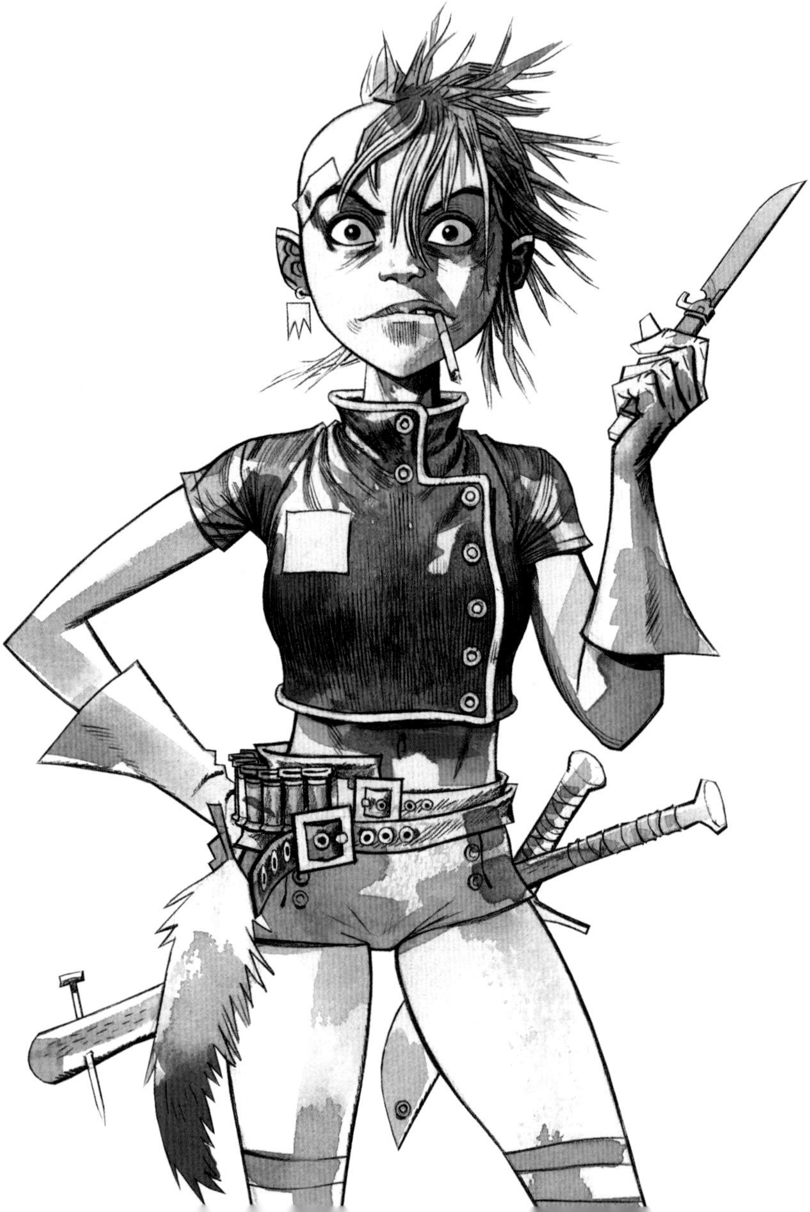

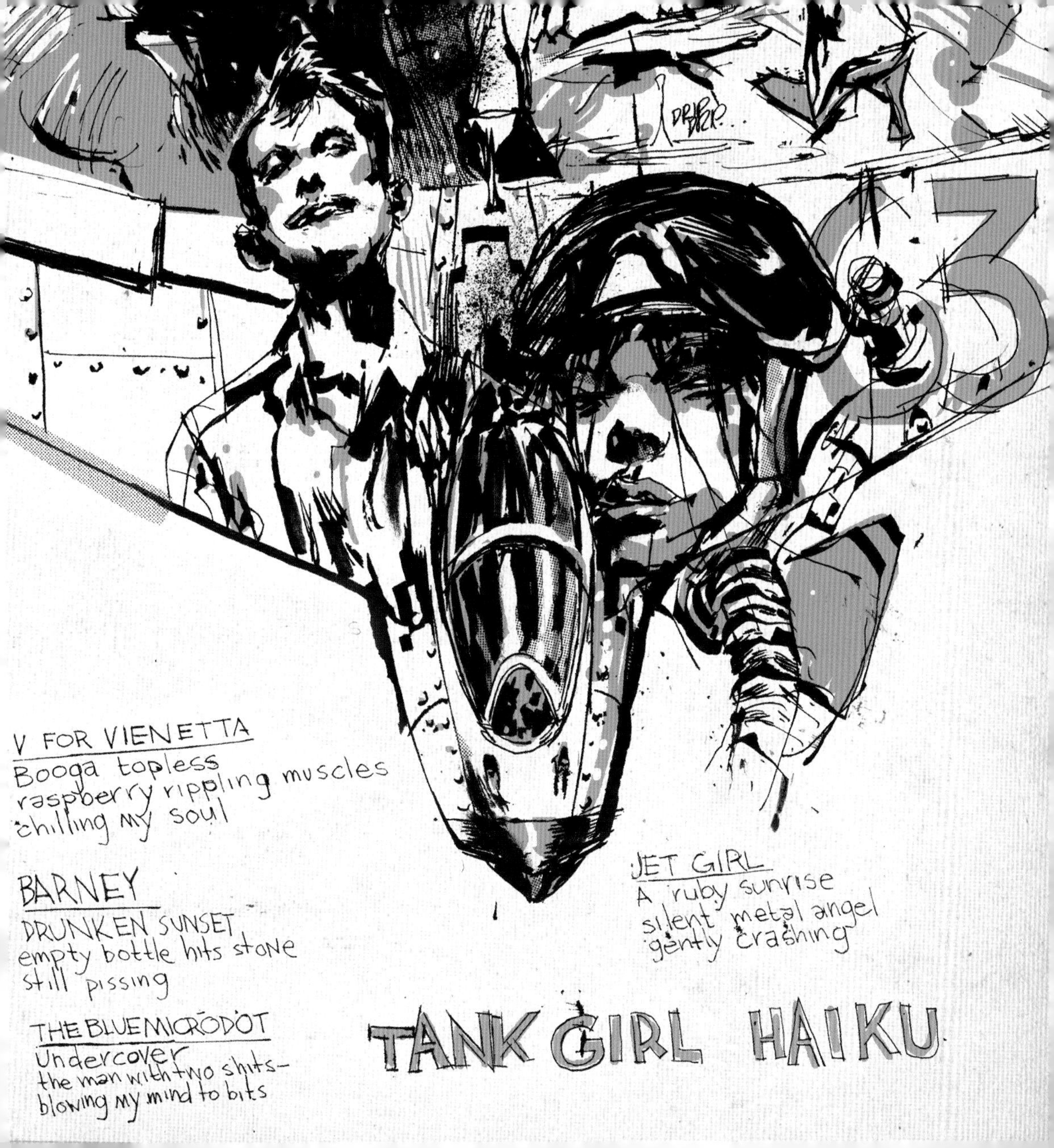
DRIP DRIP
V FOR VIENETTA
Booga topless
raspberry rippling muscles
chilling my soul
BARNEY
DRUNKEN SUNSET
empty bottle hits stone
still pissing
THE BLUE MICRODOT
Undercover
the man with two shits-
blowing my mind to bits
JET GIRL
A ruby sunrise
silent metal angel
gently crashing
TANK GIRL HAIKU

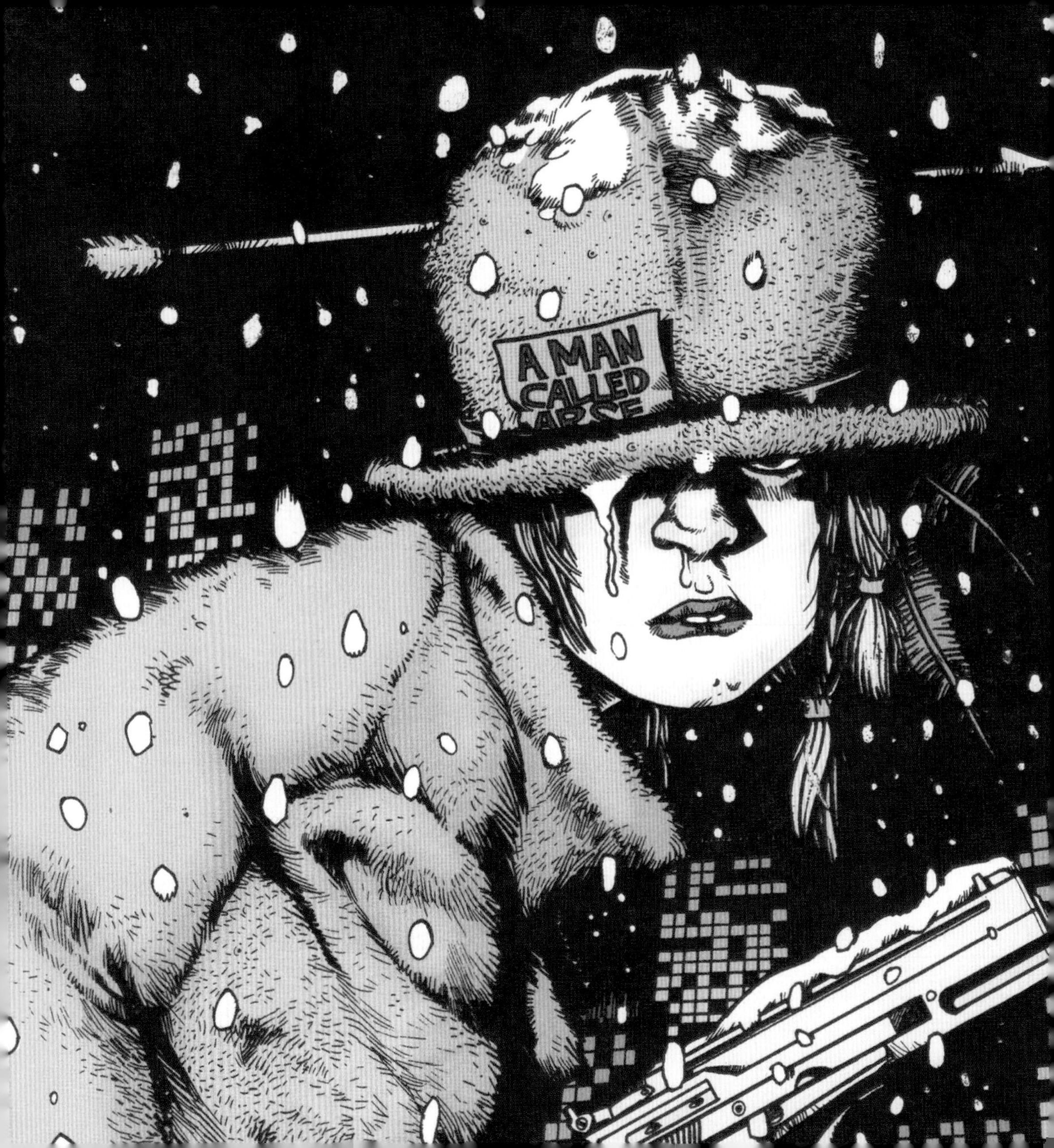
A MAN CALLED ARSE

I WAS A KRAZY KID

When I was young
I had some fun
You should've seen
the things I did
I drank a pint of petrol
Coz I was a Krazy Kid

The Lone Ranger
and Dick Tracy
Casey Jones
and The Flashing Blade
A game of war
The daily chores
A glass of cherryade

Slade were on constant rotation
on a Fidelity record player
I wore six-button loons
and listened to The Goons
and did my hair like Leo Sayer

Now all that stuff means nothing
To the people who were not there
I'm sure you've got some stories
And you may choose to bore me
But, frankly, I don't fucking care

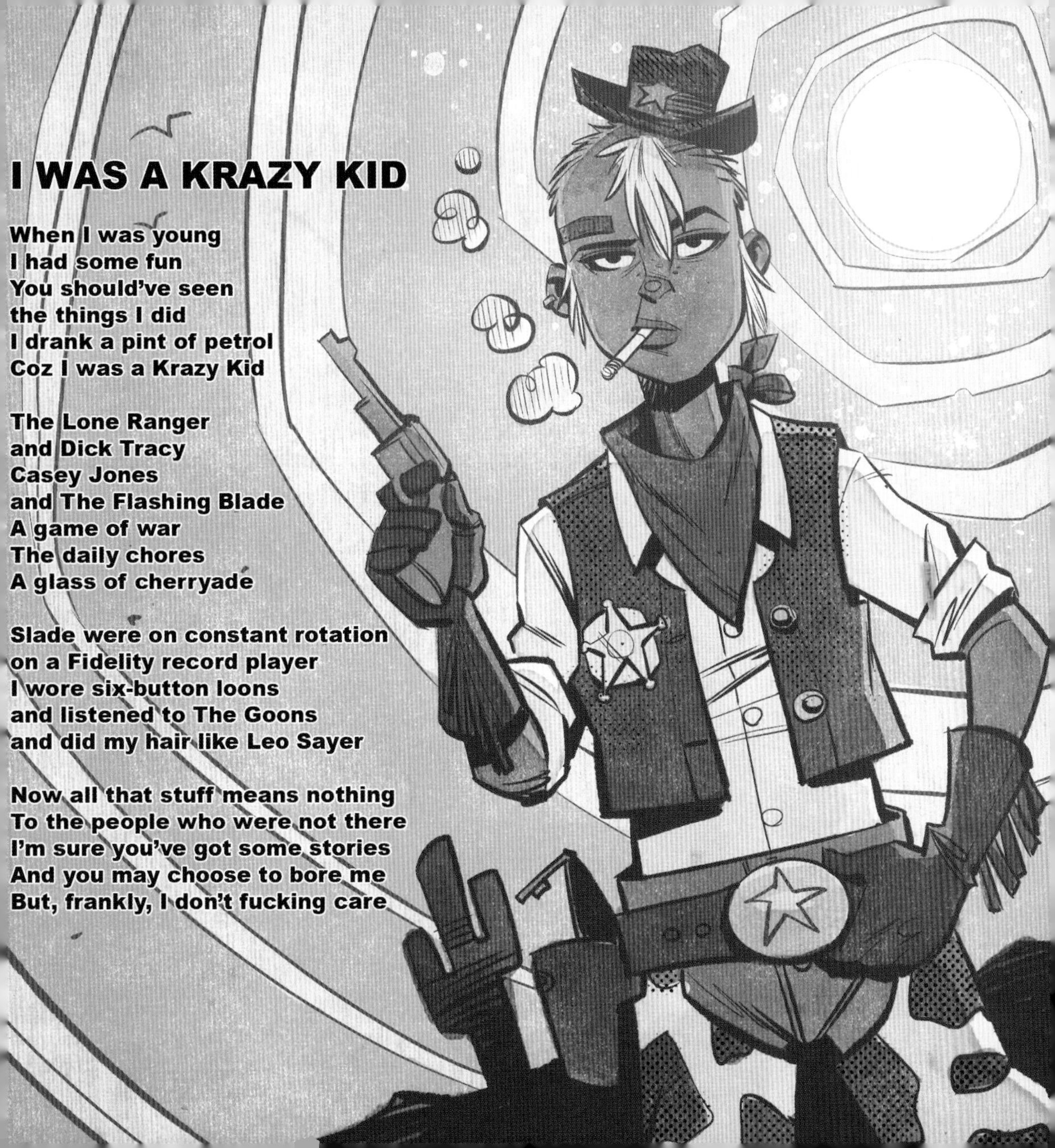

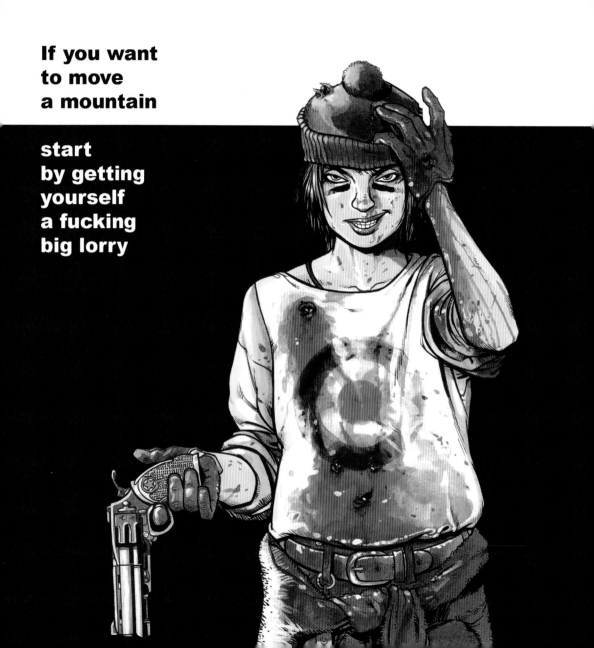

If you want
to move
a mountain

start
by getting
yourself
a fucking
big lorry

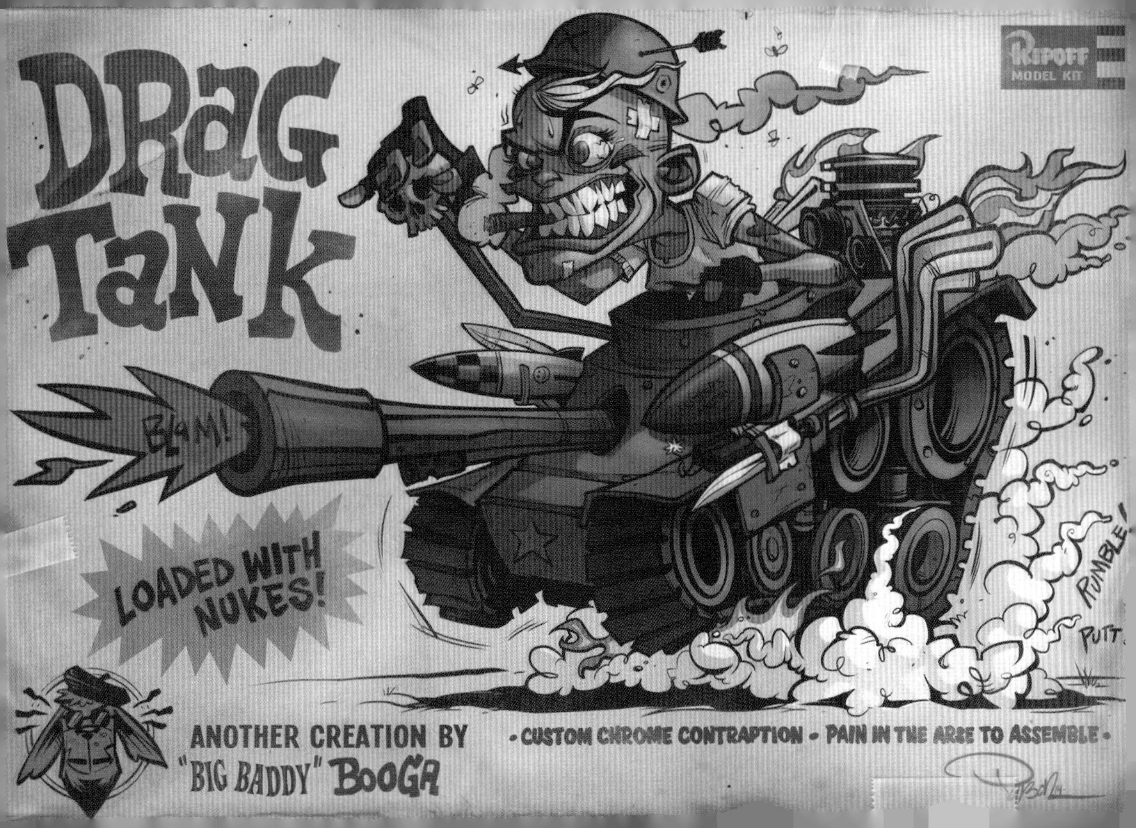
RIPOFF
MODEL KIT
DRAG TANK
BLAM!
LOADED WITH NUKES!
RUMBLE!
PUTT
ANOTHER CREATION BY
"BIG BADDY" BOOGA
• CUSTOM CHROME CONTRAPTION • PAIN IN THE ARSE TO ASSEMBLE •

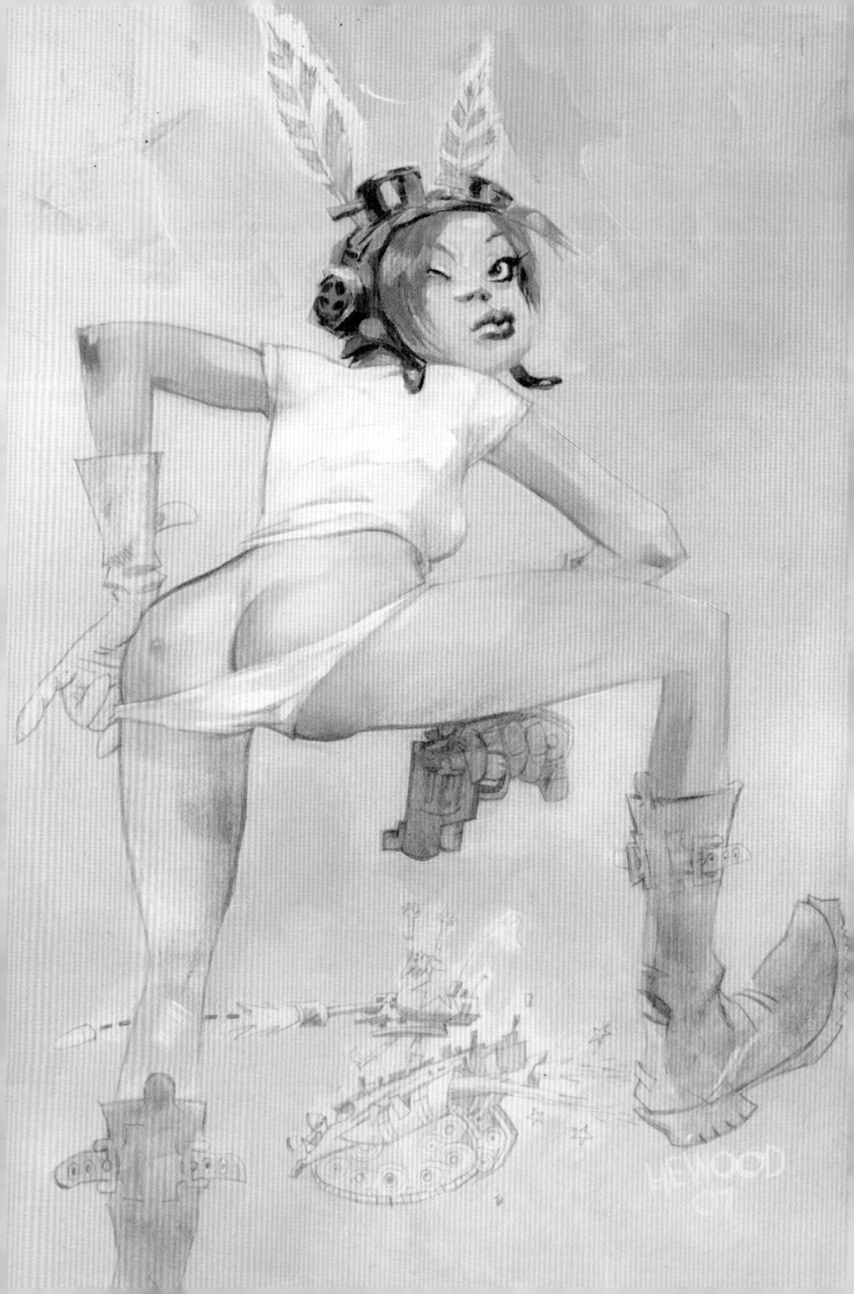

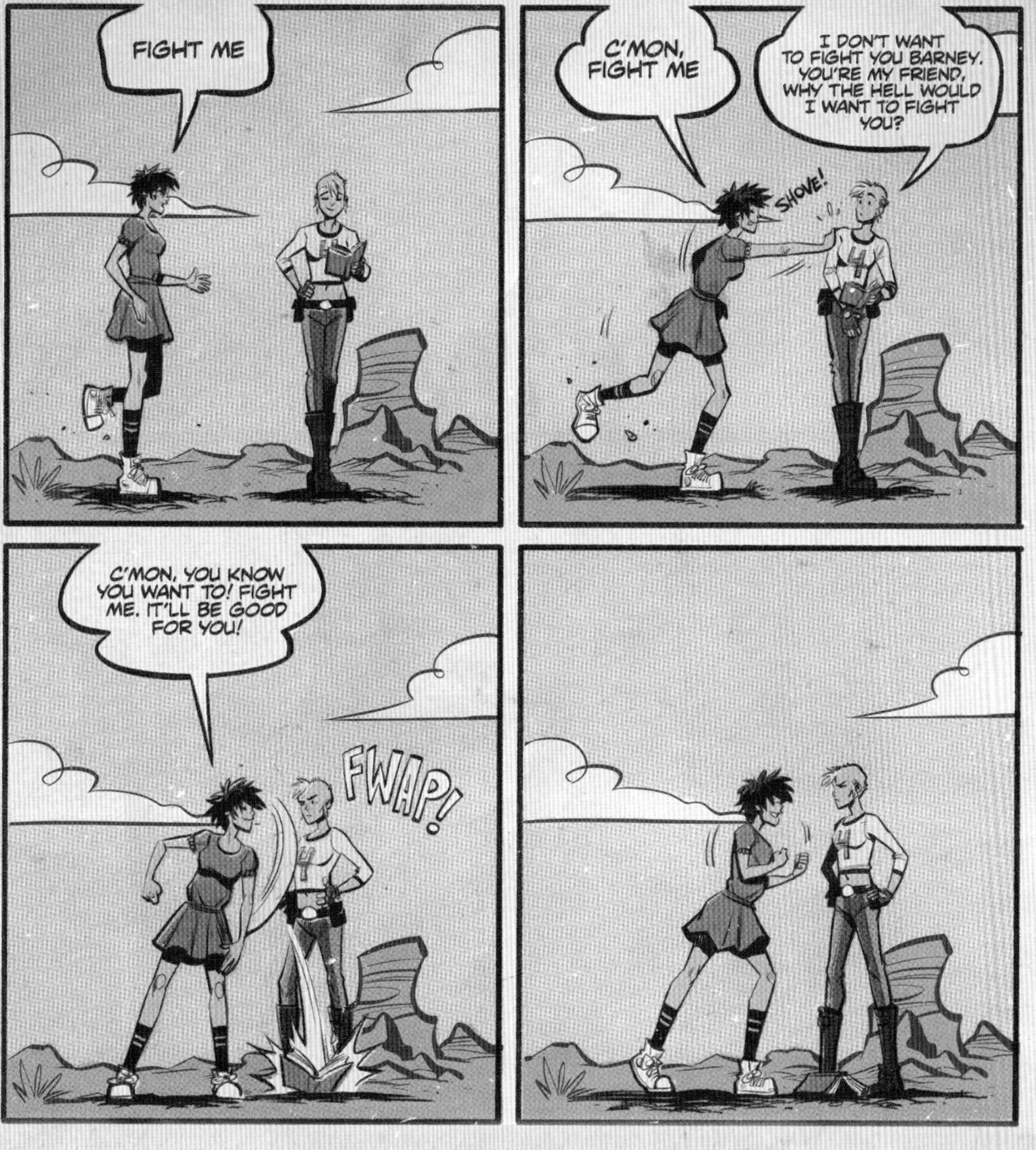

FIGHT ME
C'MON, FIGHT ME
I DON'T WANT TO FIGHT YOU BARNEY. YOU'RE MY FRIEND, WHY THE HELL WOULD I WANT TO FIGHT YOU?
SHOVE!
C'MON, YOU KNOW YOU WANT TO! FIGHT ME. IT'LL BE GOOD FOR YOU!
FWAP!

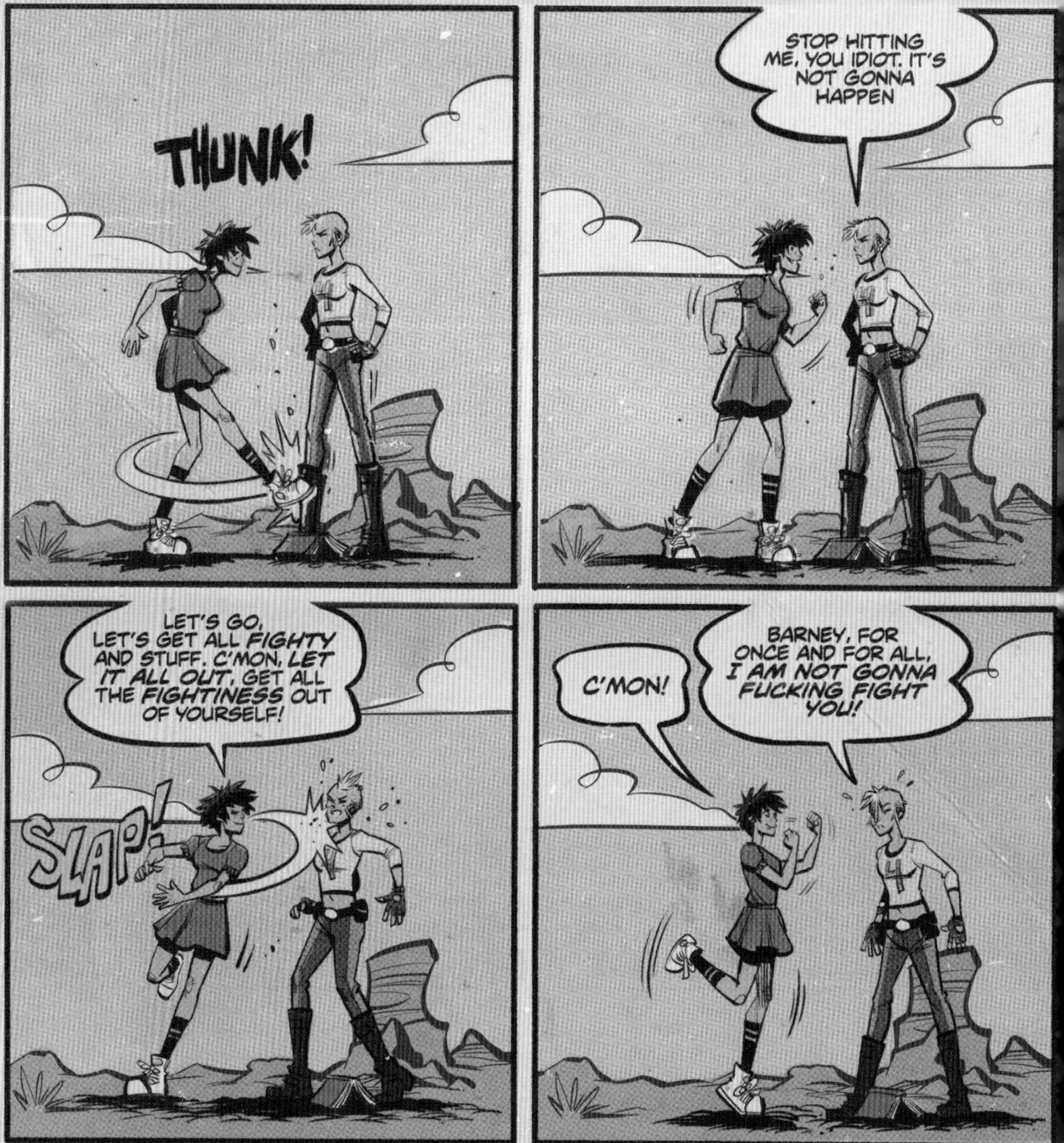
THUNK!
STOP HITTING ME, YOU IDIOT. IT'S NOT GONNA HAPPEN
LET'S GO, LET'S GET ALL FIGHTY AND STUFF. C'MON, LET IT ALL OUT, GET ALL THE FIGHTINESS OUT OF YOURSELF!
SLAP!
C'MON!
BARNEY, FOR ONCE AND FOR ALL, I AM NOT GONNA FUCKING FIGHT YOU!

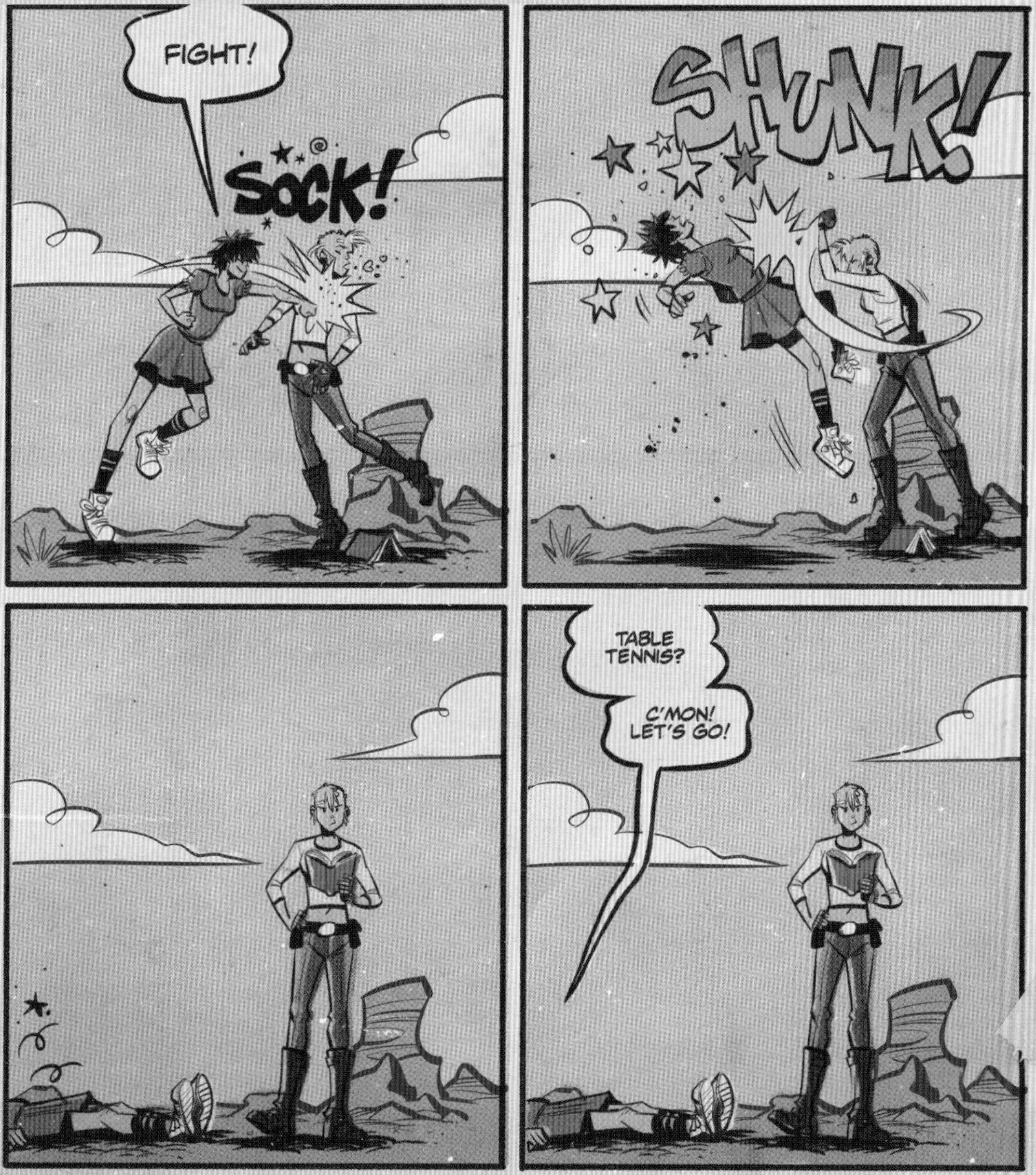
FIGHT!
SOCK!
SHUNK!
TABLE TENNIS?
C'MON! LET'S GO!

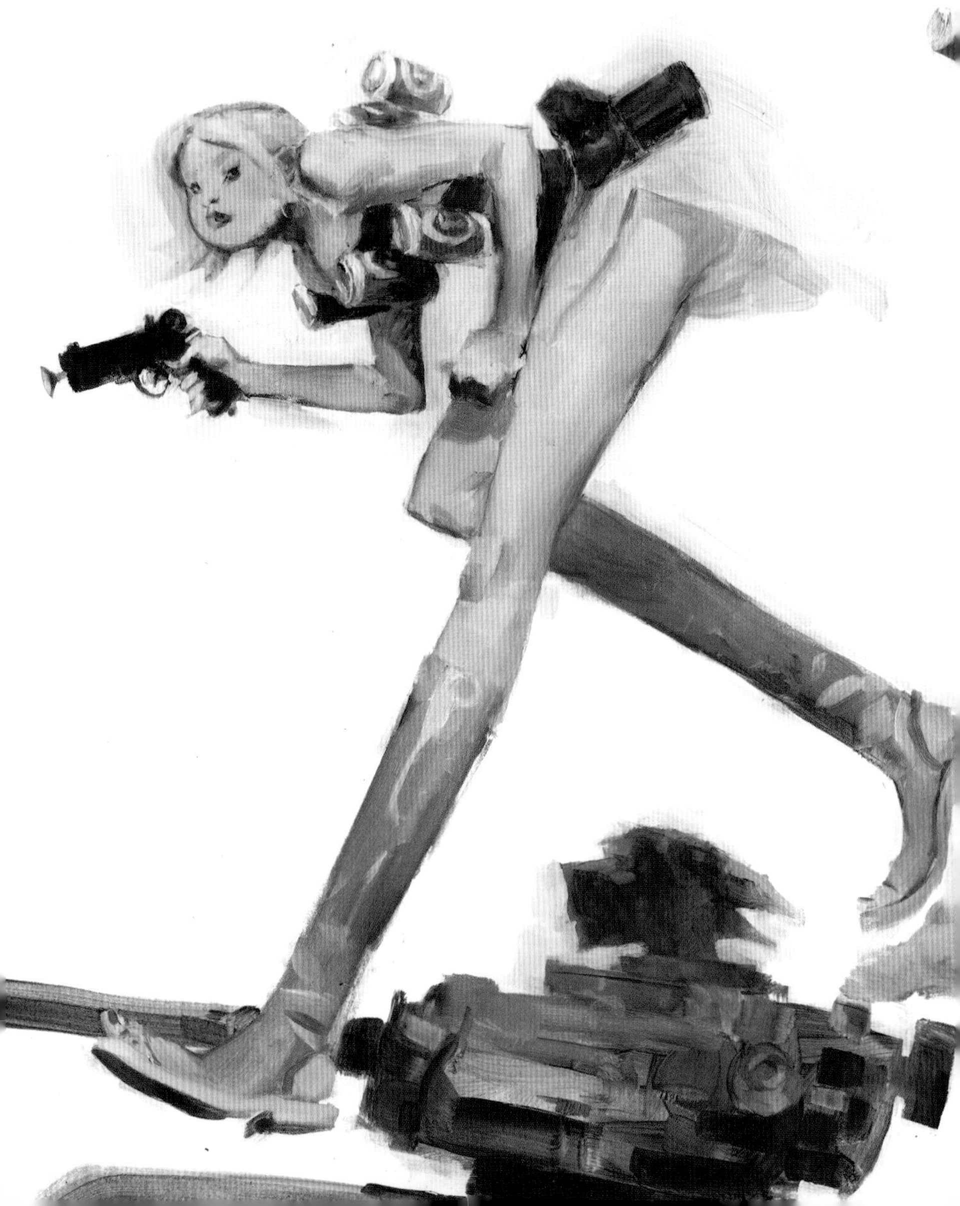

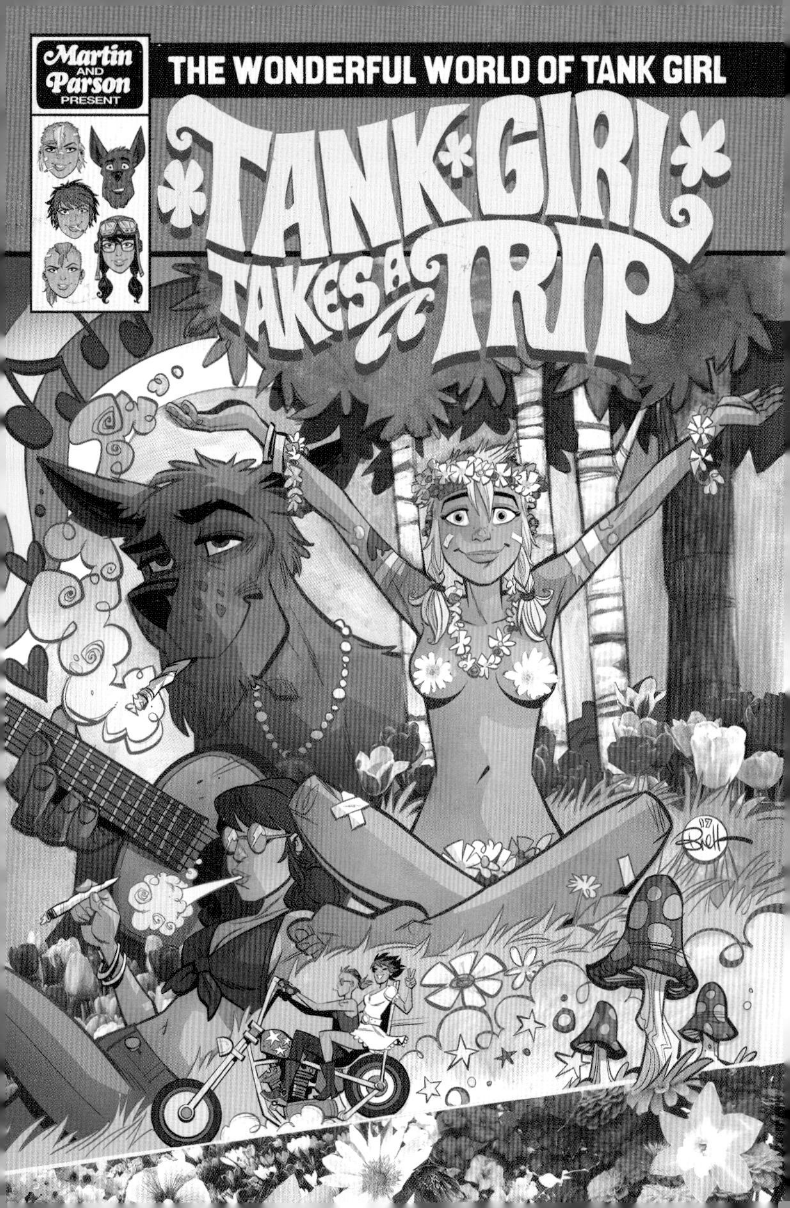

Martin AND Parson PRESENT
THE WONDERFUL WORLD OF TANK GIRL
TANK GIRL TAKES A TRIP

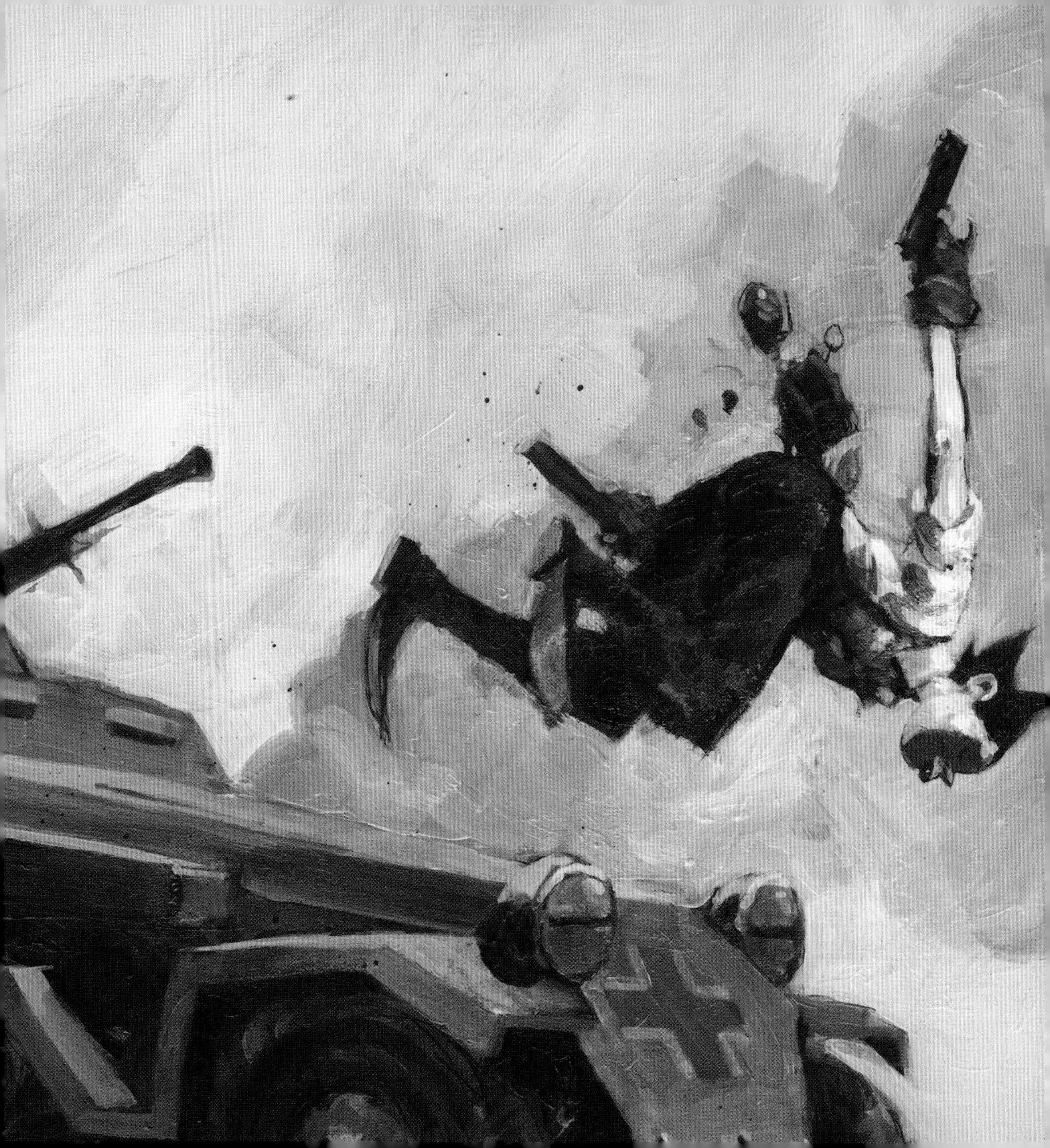

TANK GIRL tattoo

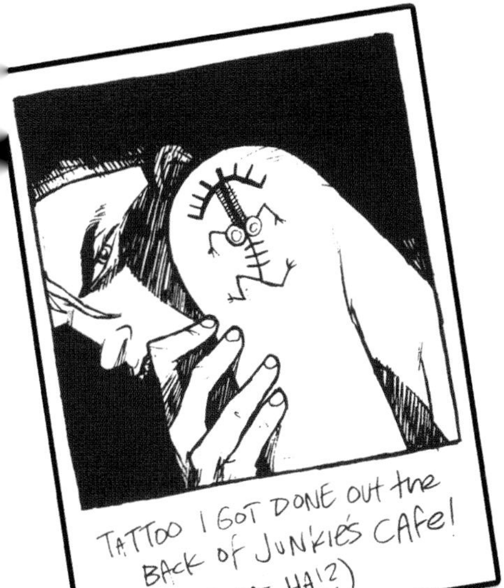
TATTOO I GOT DONE OUT the
BACK OF JUNKIE'S CAFE!
(NEAT HA!?)

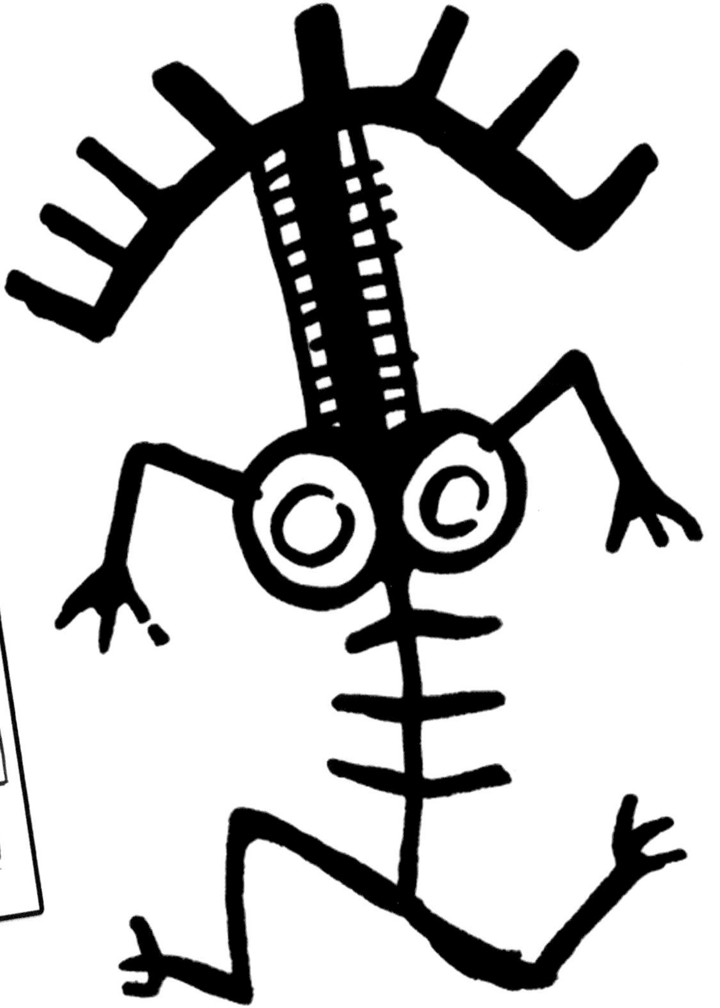

you are beaten
you're berated
you are tortured
and isolated

you are caught
you're dissected
you are tested
you're infected

you are bought
you are sold
you're too young
you're too old

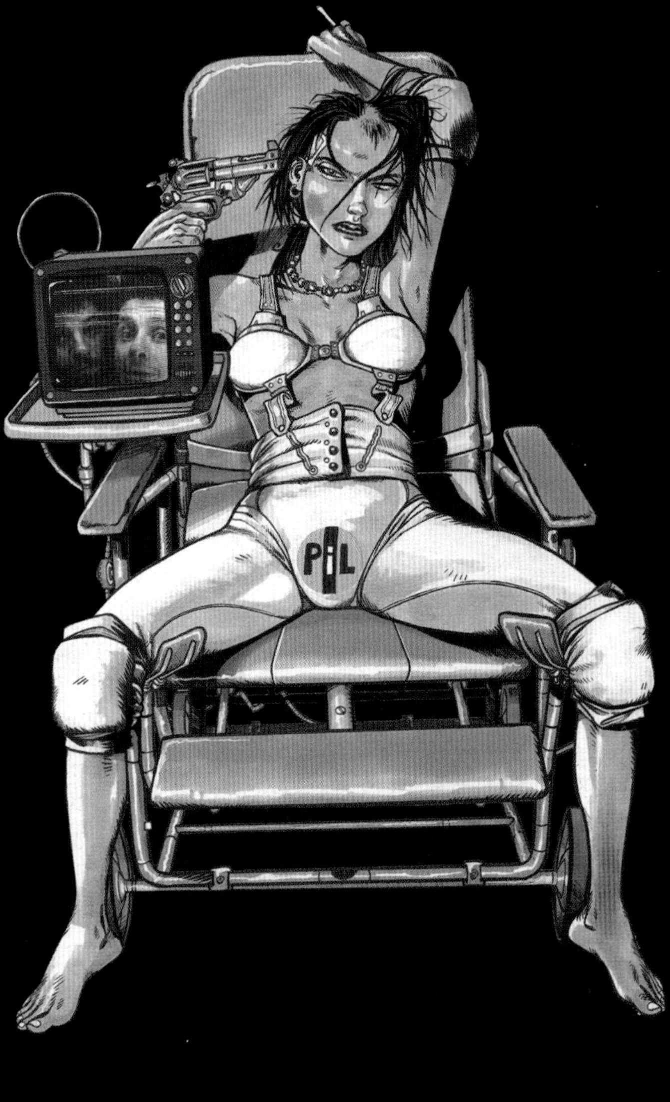
PiL

but you are loved
by me and Booga
we both think
you are super

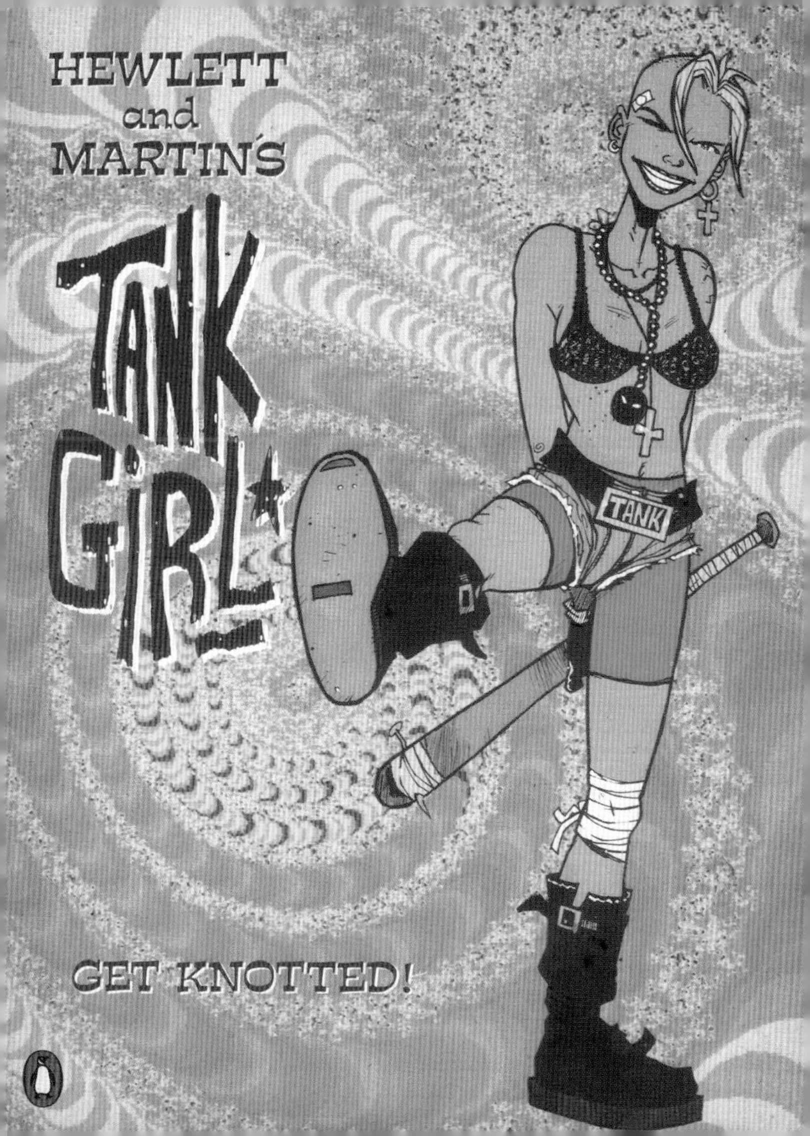
HEWLETT
and
MARTIN'S
TANK GIRL
TANK
GET KNOTTED!

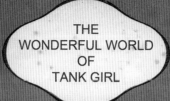

THE WONDERFUL WORLD OF TANK GIRL

THE IMPORTANCE OF BEING TANK GIRL

MARTIN PARSON

COMPLETE 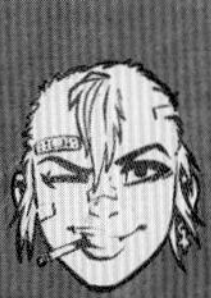 UNABRIDGED

2/6

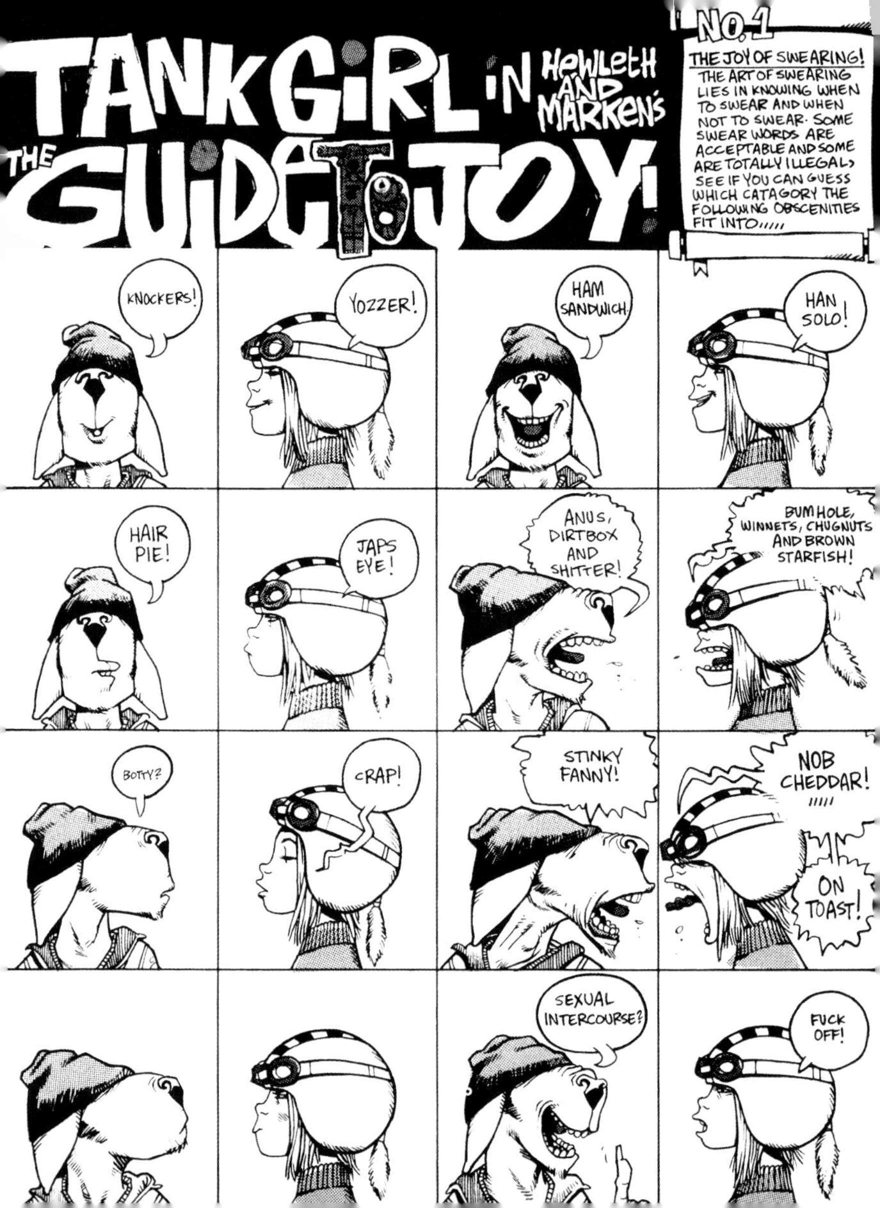
TANK GIRL 'N THE GUIDE TO JOY!
HEWLETT AND MARTIN'S
NO. 1
THE JOY OF SWEARING!
THE ART OF SWEARING LIES IN KNOWING WHEN TO SWEAR AND WHEN NOT TO SWEAR. SOME SWEAR WORDS ARE ACCEPTABLE AND SOME ARE TOTALLY ILLEGAL, SEE IF YOU CAN GUESS WHICH CATAGORY THE FOLLOWING OBSCENITIES FIT INTO......
KNOCKERS!
YOZZER!
HAM SANDWICH.
HAN SOLO!
HAIR PIE!
JAPS EYE!
ANUS, DIRTBOX AND SHITTER!
BUM HOLE, WINNETS, CHUGNUTS AND BROWN STARFISH!
BOTTY?
CRAP!
STINKY FANNY!
NOB CHEDDAR!!!!!
ON TOAST!
SEXUAL INTERCOURSE?
FUCK OFF!

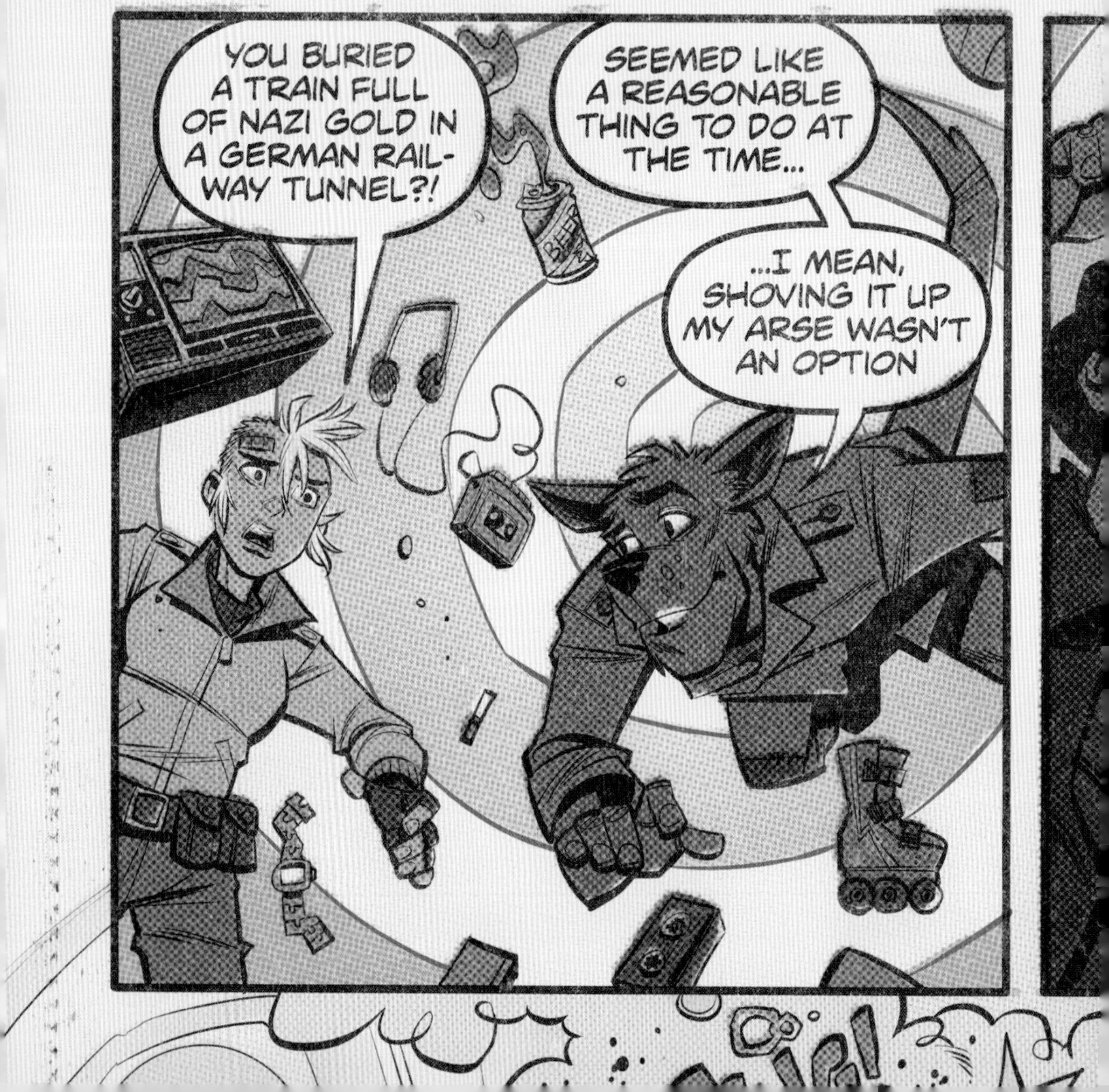
YOU BURIED A TRAIN FULL OF NAZI GOLD IN A GERMAN RAILWAY TUNNEL?!
SEEMED LIKE A REASONABLE THING TO DO AT THE TIME...
...I MEAN, SHOVING IT UP MY ARSE WASN'T AN OPTION

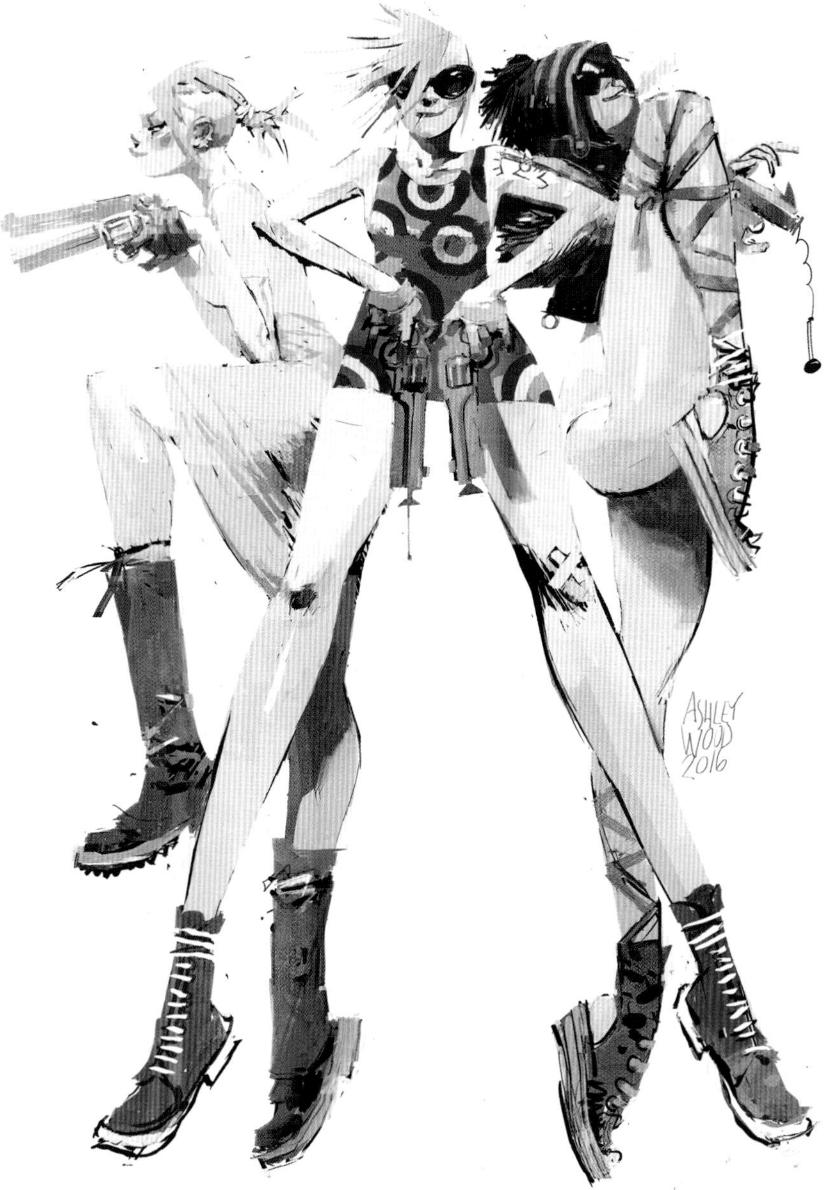
ASHLEY
WOOD
2016

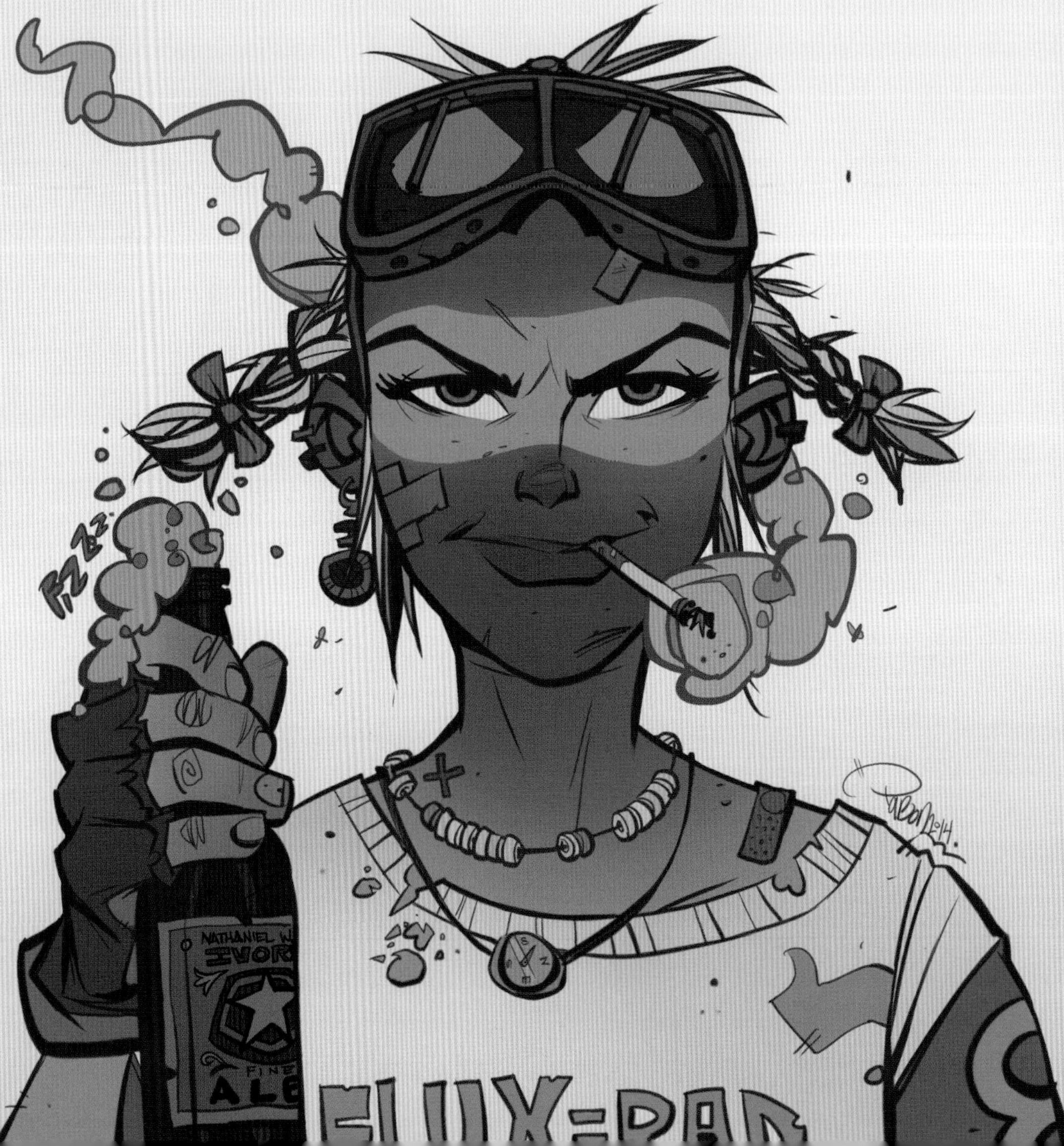
FIZZZ
NATHANIEL

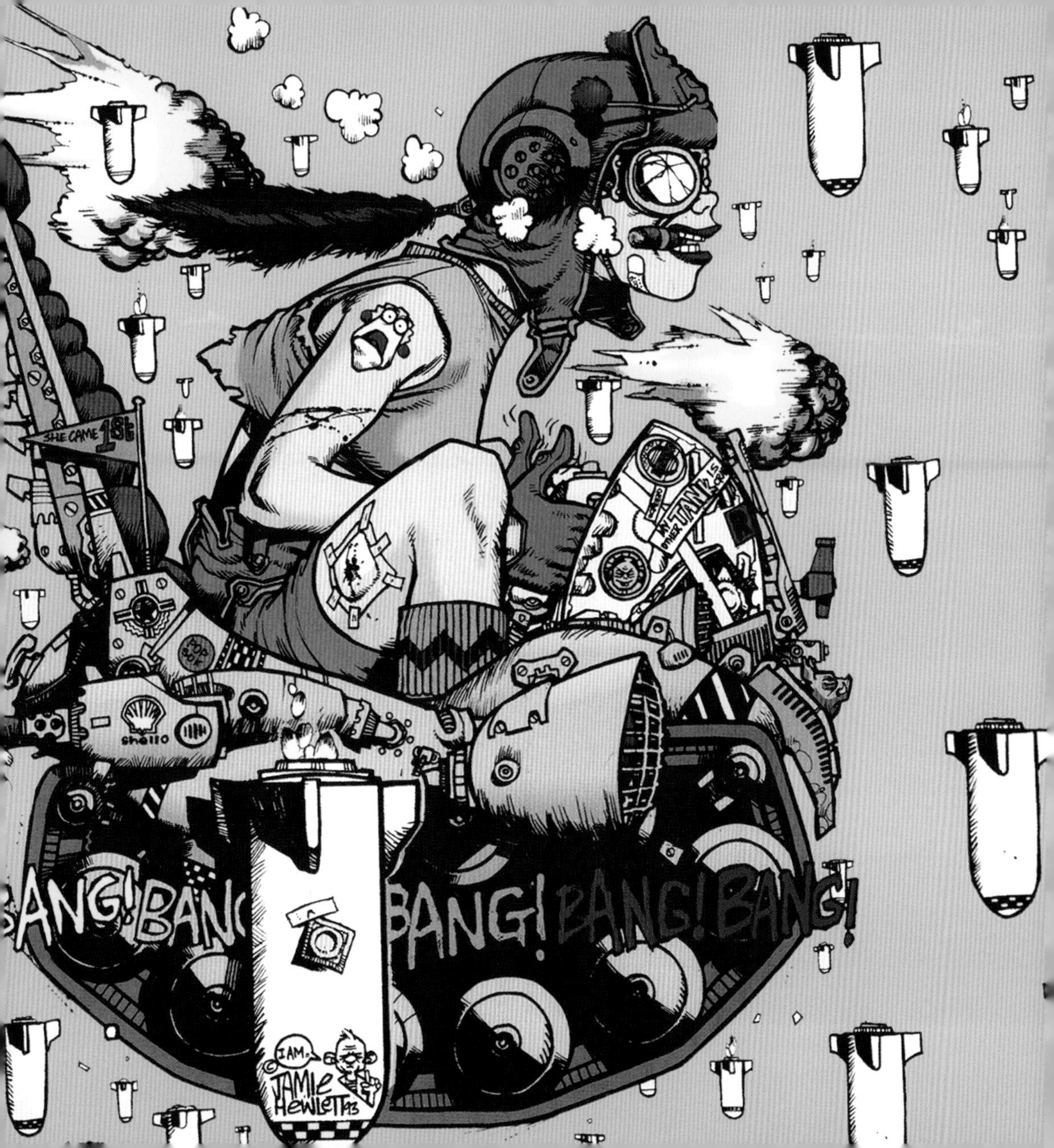
SHE CAME 1st
shell
MY OTHER TANK IS
BANG! BANG BANG! BANG! BANG!
I AM.
© JAMIE HEWLETT 93

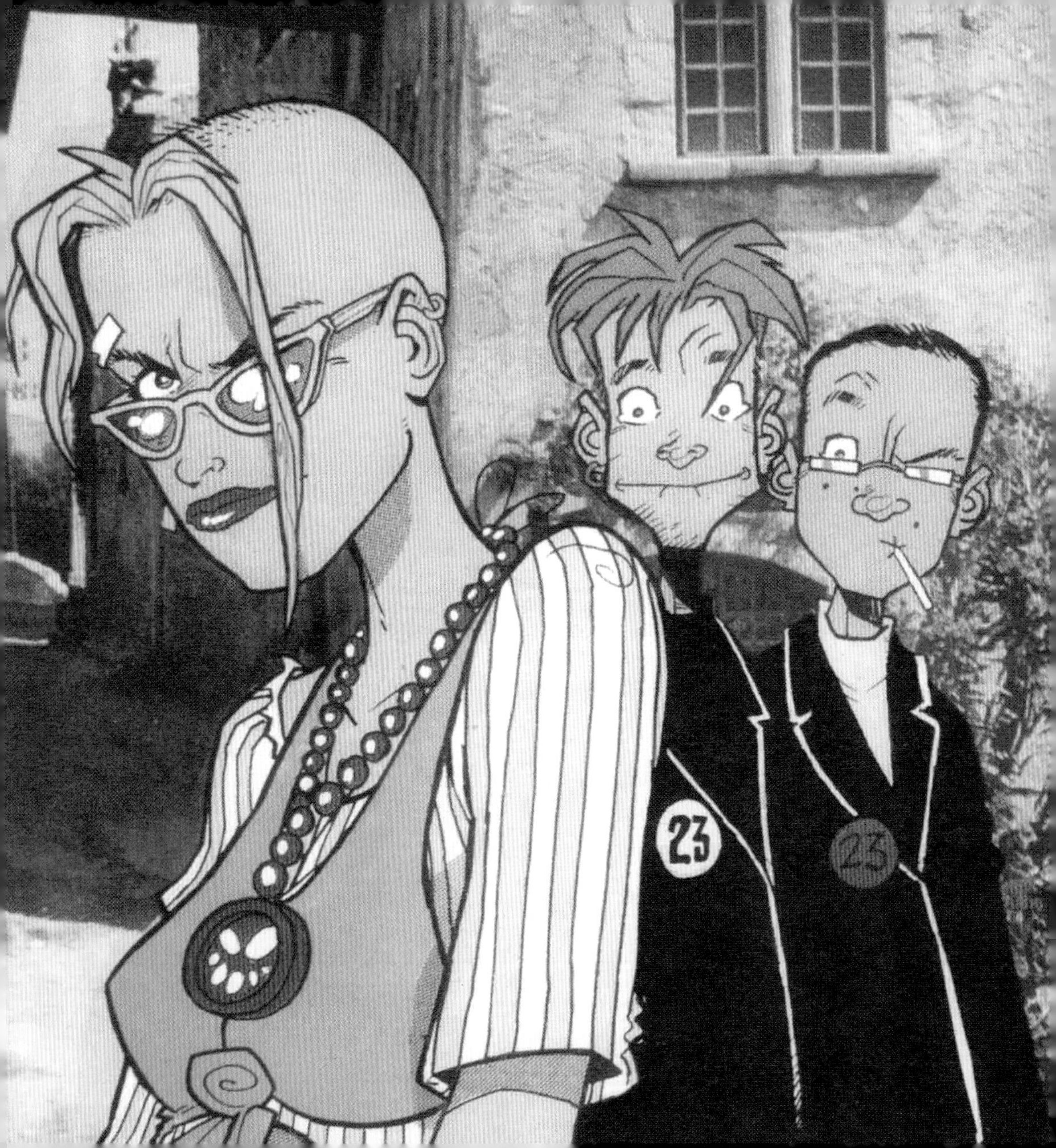
23
23

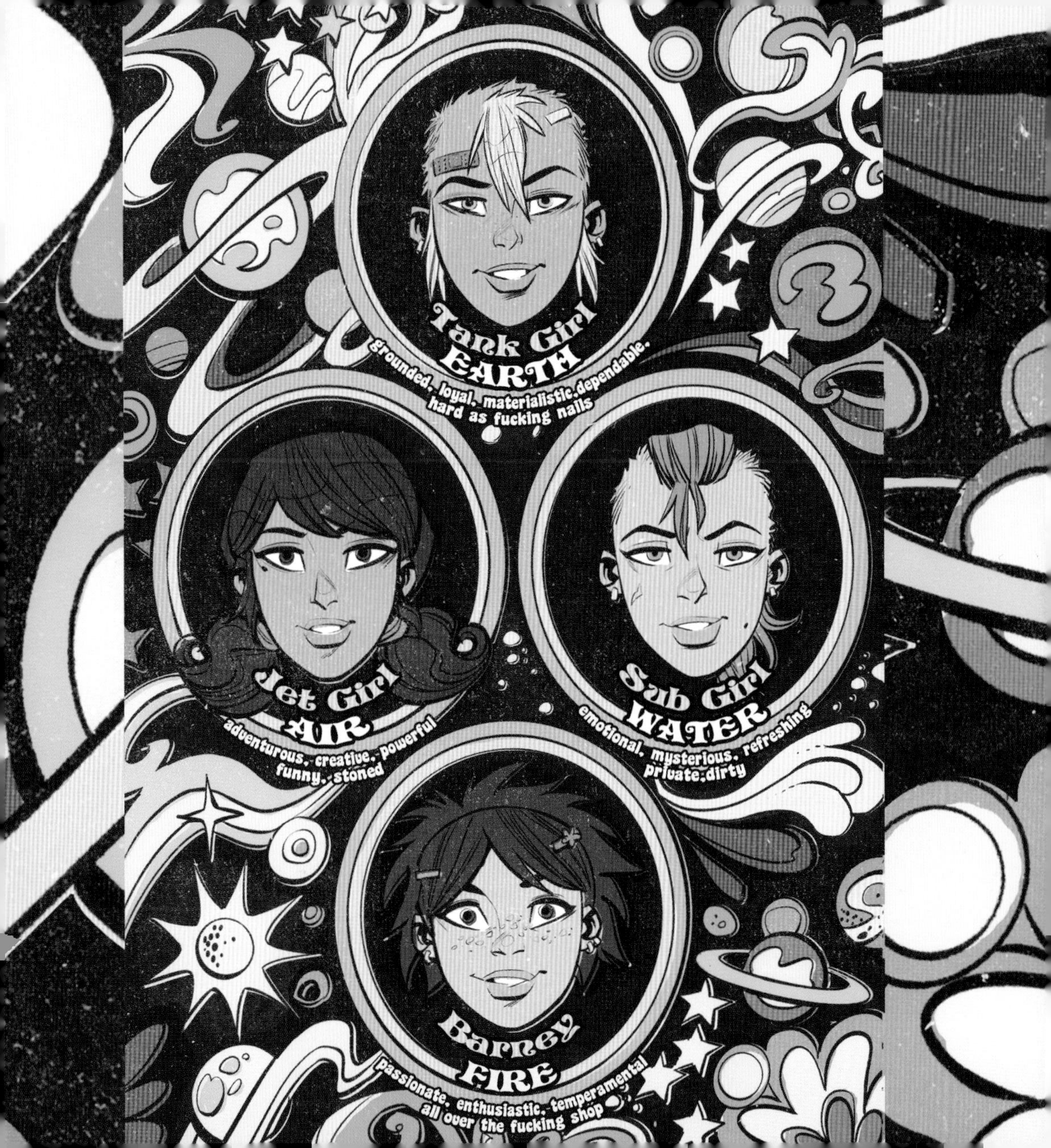

Tank Girl
EARTH
grounded, loyal, materialistic, dependable, hard as fucking nails
Jet Girl
AIR
adventurous, creative, powerful funny, stoned
Sub Girl
WATER
emotional, mysterious, refreshing private, dirty
Barney
FIRE
passionate, enthusiastic, temperamental all over the fucking shop

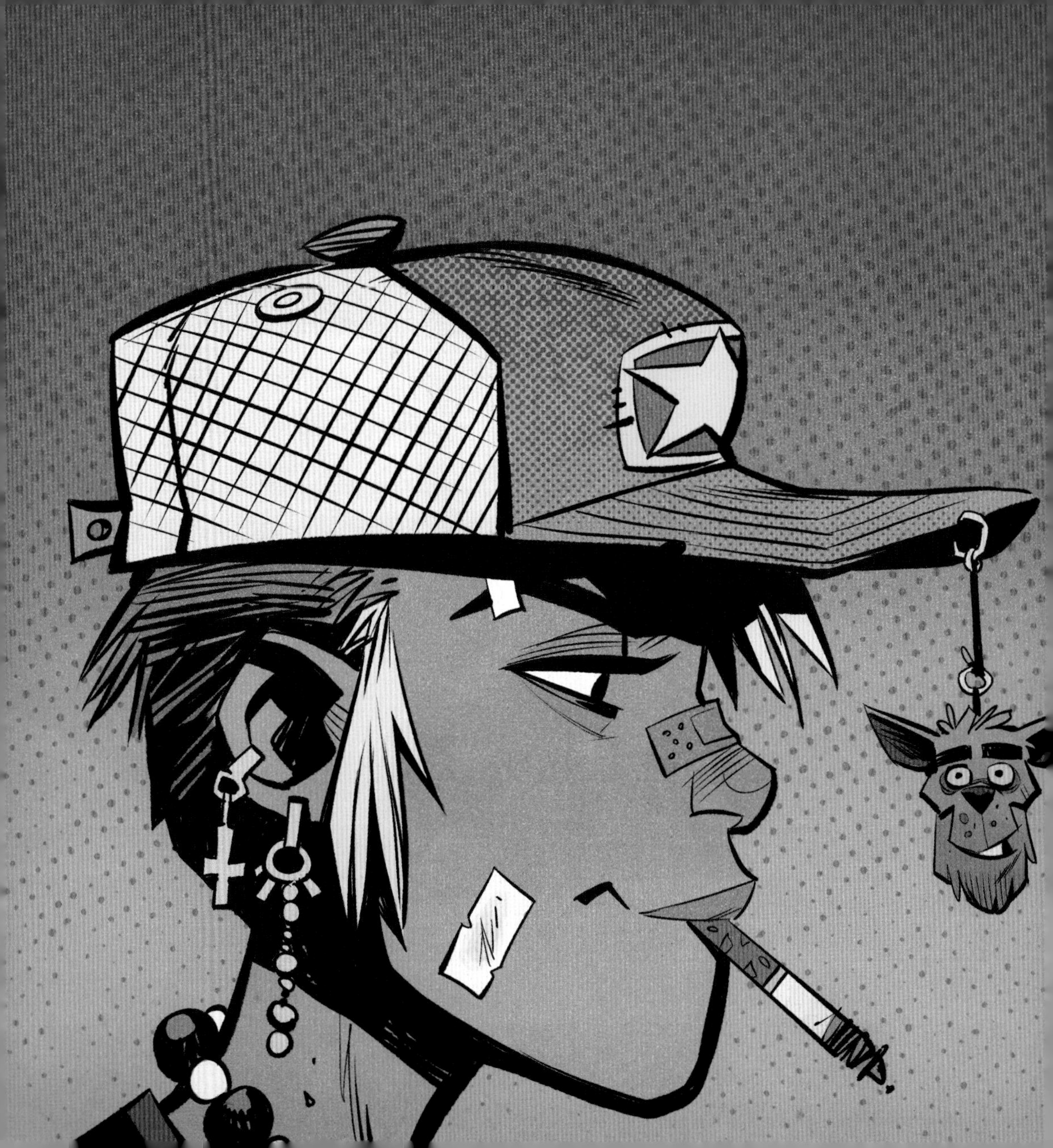

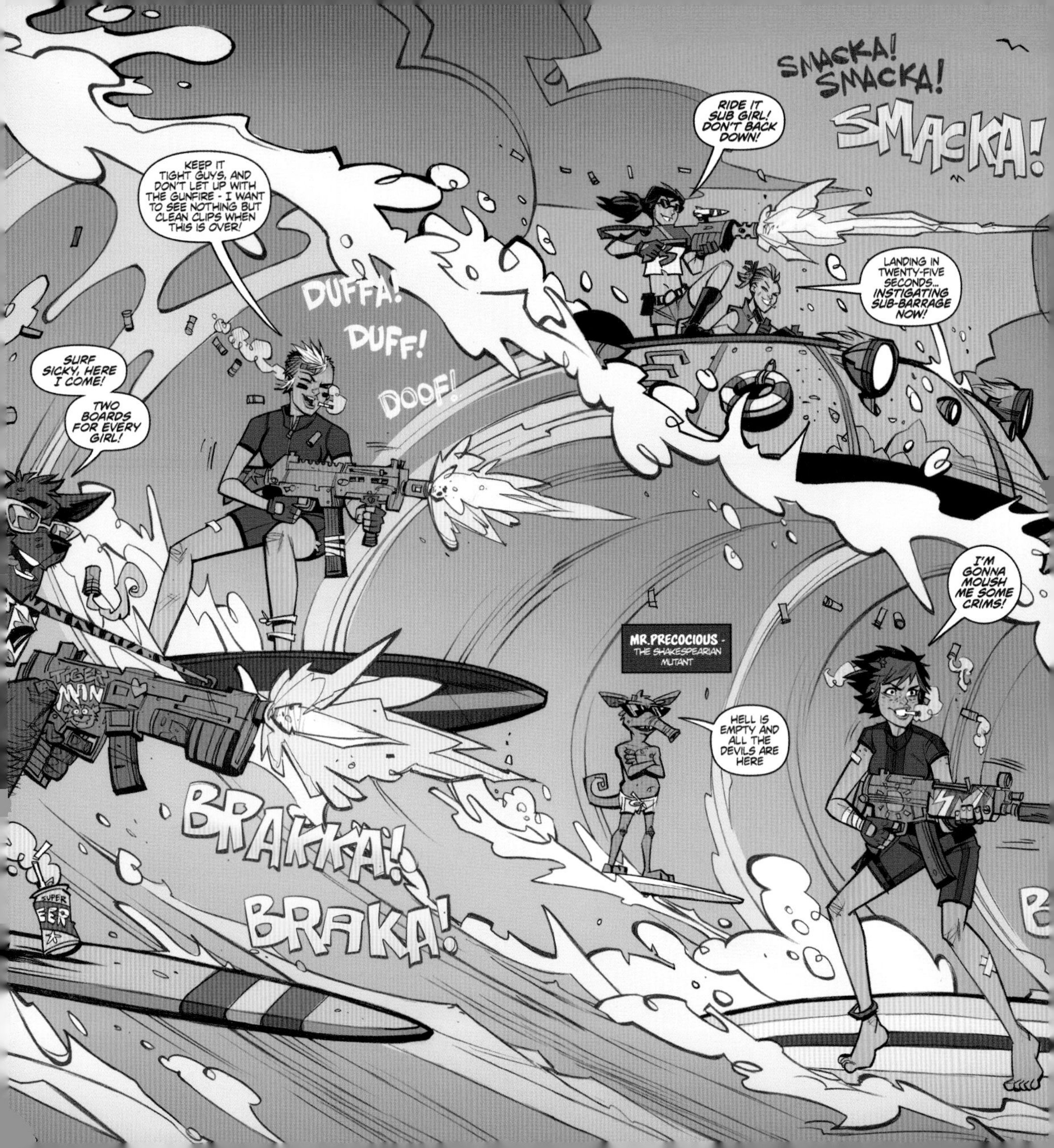
KEEP IT TIGHT GUYS, AND DON'T LET UP WITH THE GUNFIRE - I WANT TO SEE NOTHING BUT CLEAN CLIPS WHEN THIS IS OVER!
RIDE IT SUB GIRL! DON'T BACK DOWN!
SMACKA! SMACKA!
SMACKA!
LANDING IN TWENTY-FIVE SECONDS... INSTIGATING SUB-BARRAGE NOW!
DUFFA! DUFF! DOOF!
SURF SICKY, HERE I COME!
TWO BOARDS FOR EVERY GIRL!
I'M GONNA MOUSH ME SOME CRIMS!
MR. PRECOCIOUS - THE SHAKESPEARIAN MUTANT
HELL IS EMPTY AND ALL THE DEVILS ARE HERE
BRAKKA! BRAKA!

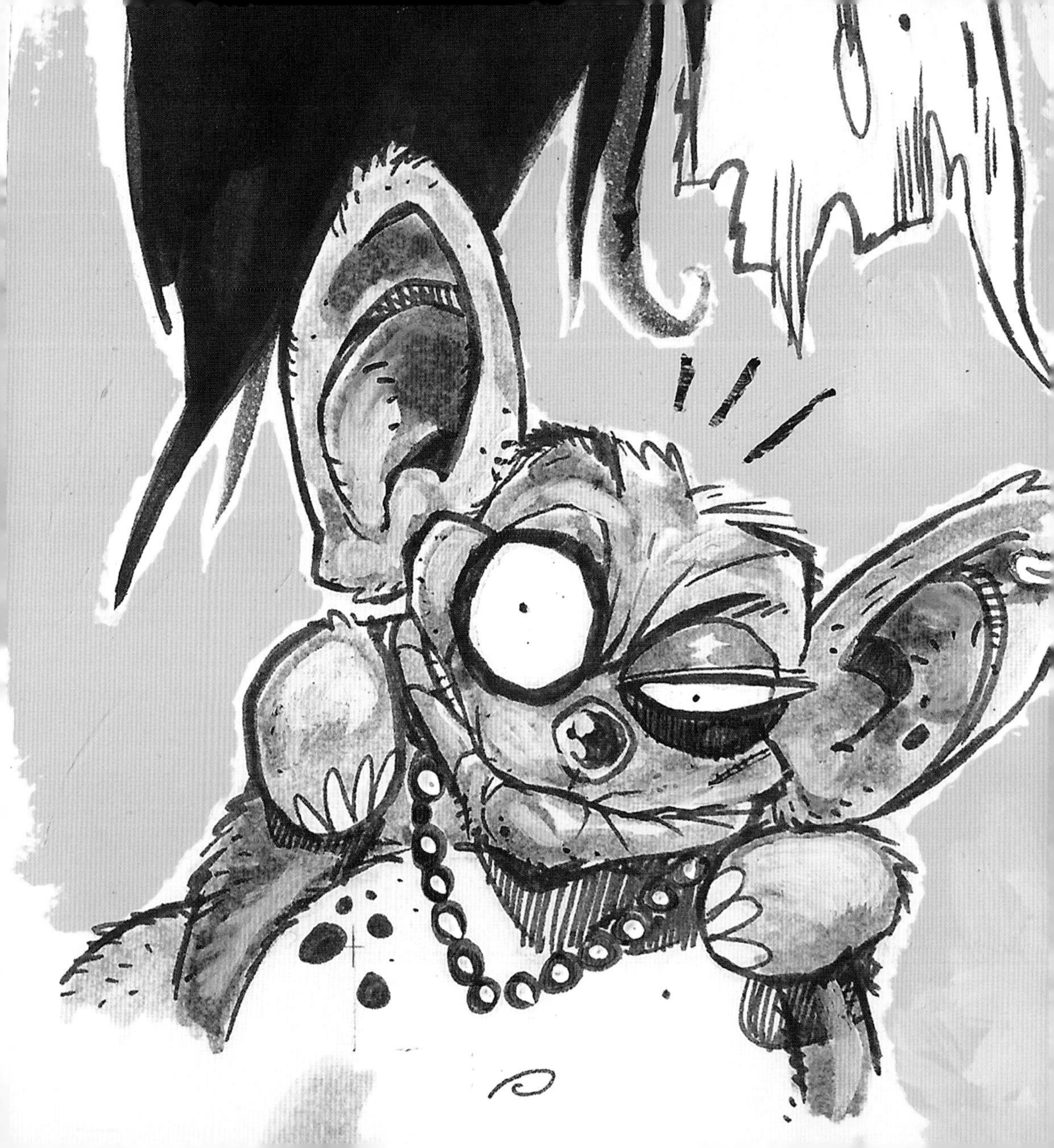

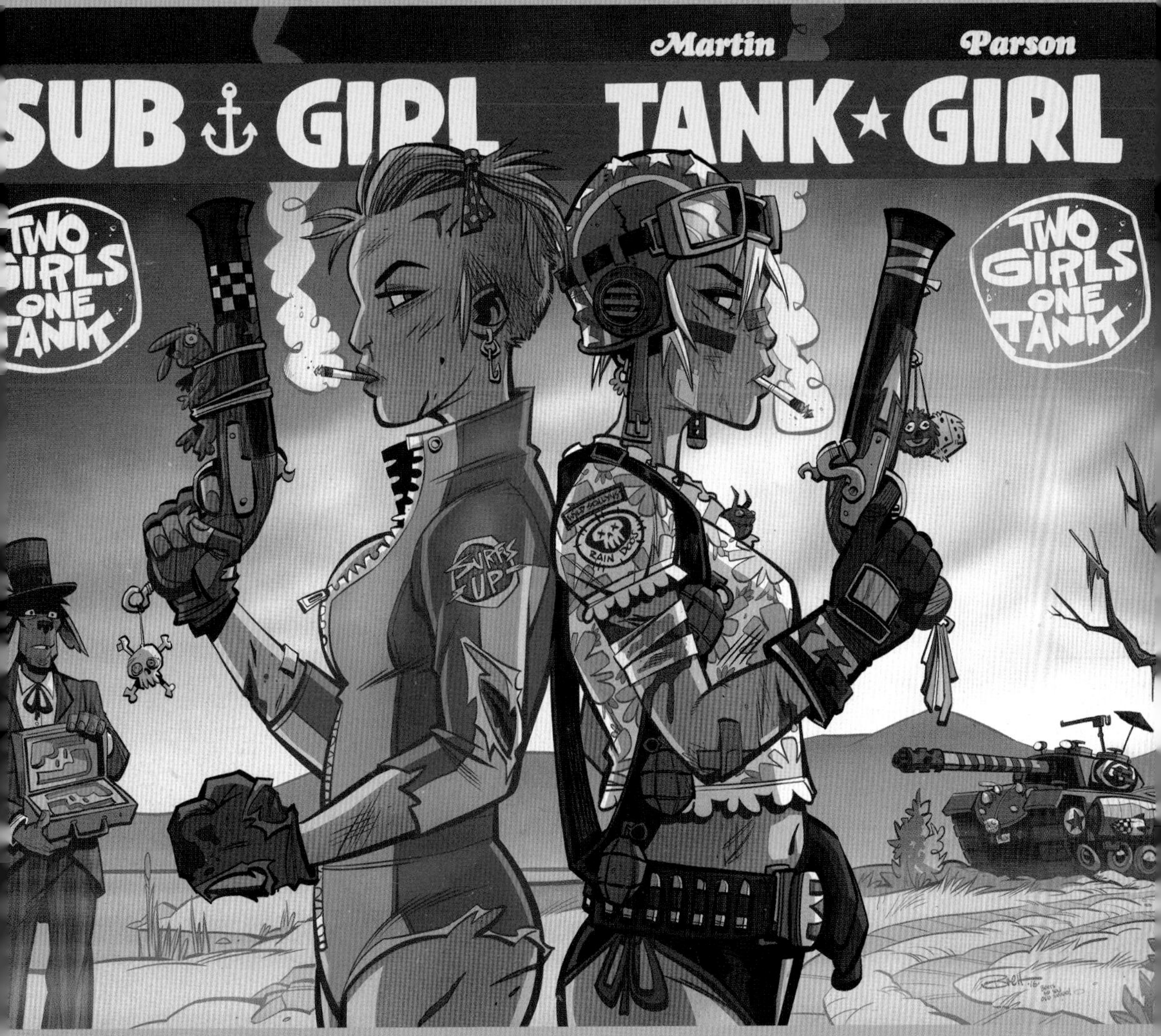
Martin
Parson
SUB GIRL
TANK GIRL
TWO GIRLS ONE TANK
TWO GIRLS ONE TANK

GLYN.

THIS IS MY FRIEND GLYN, WE WENT TO SCHOOL TOGETHER, WE LIKED THE JAM AND THE WHO AND WE BOTH HAD SCOOTERS. WE BEAT UP ON SQUARES AND SMOKED VANGUARD CIGARETTES. I HADN'T SEEN HIM IN 10 YEARS, BUT I COULD TELL BY HIS TRANSLUCENT COMPLEXION, HIS DARK EYELIDS AND HIS SHIT CLOTHES, THAT WE STILL HAD A LOT IN COMMON. HE LIKES TOM WAITS, AL PACINO AND DRUGS. WE BOTH AGREE THAT SUEDE ARE SHIT AND PORNOGRAPHY IS HOT. IT'S BEEN 10 MONTHS SINCE OUR LAST MEETING BUT I KNOW WHEN I SEE HIM NEXT HE'LL KNOW.

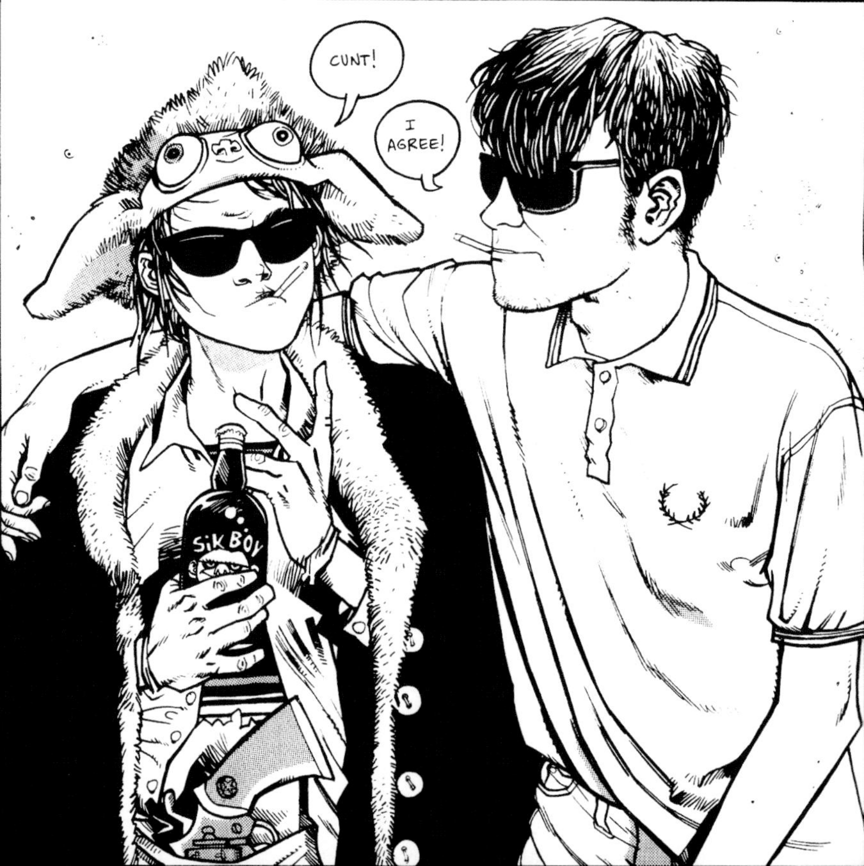
CUNT!
I AGREE!
SIK BOY

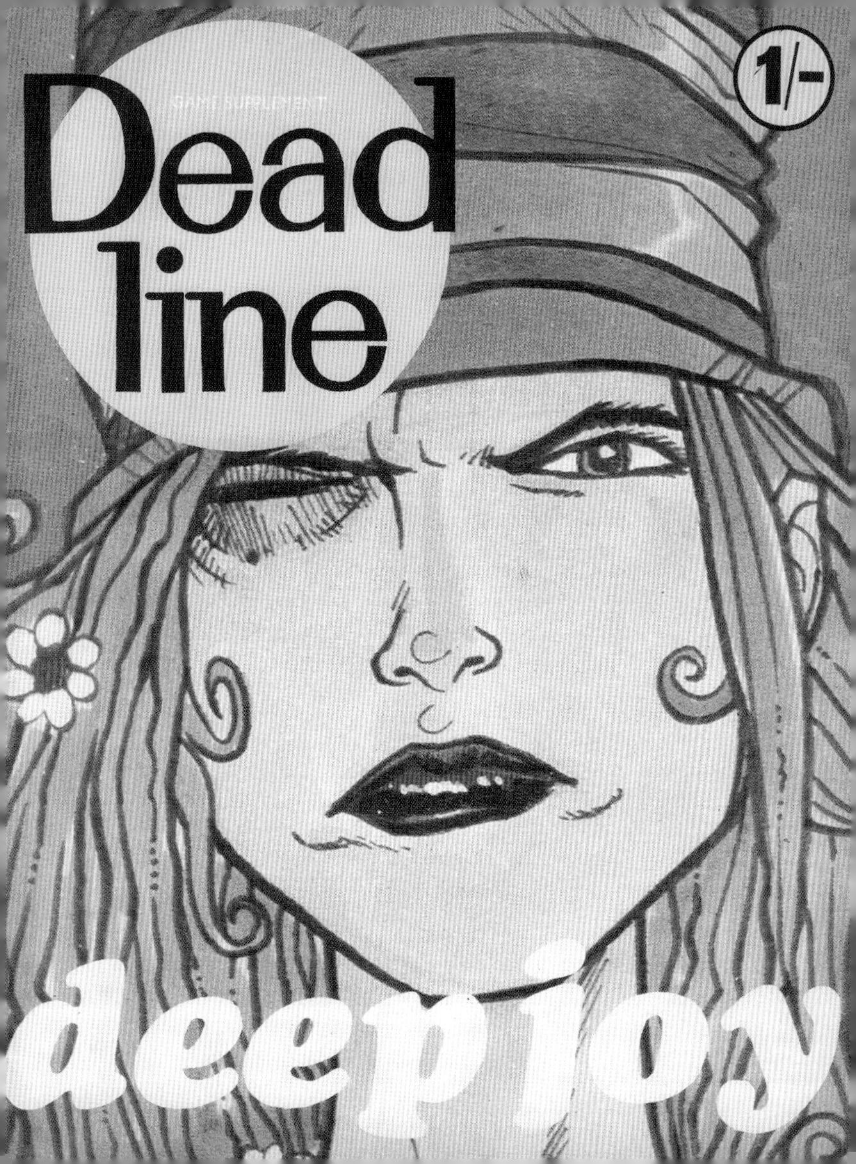
GAME SUPPLEMENT
Dead
line
1/-
deep joy

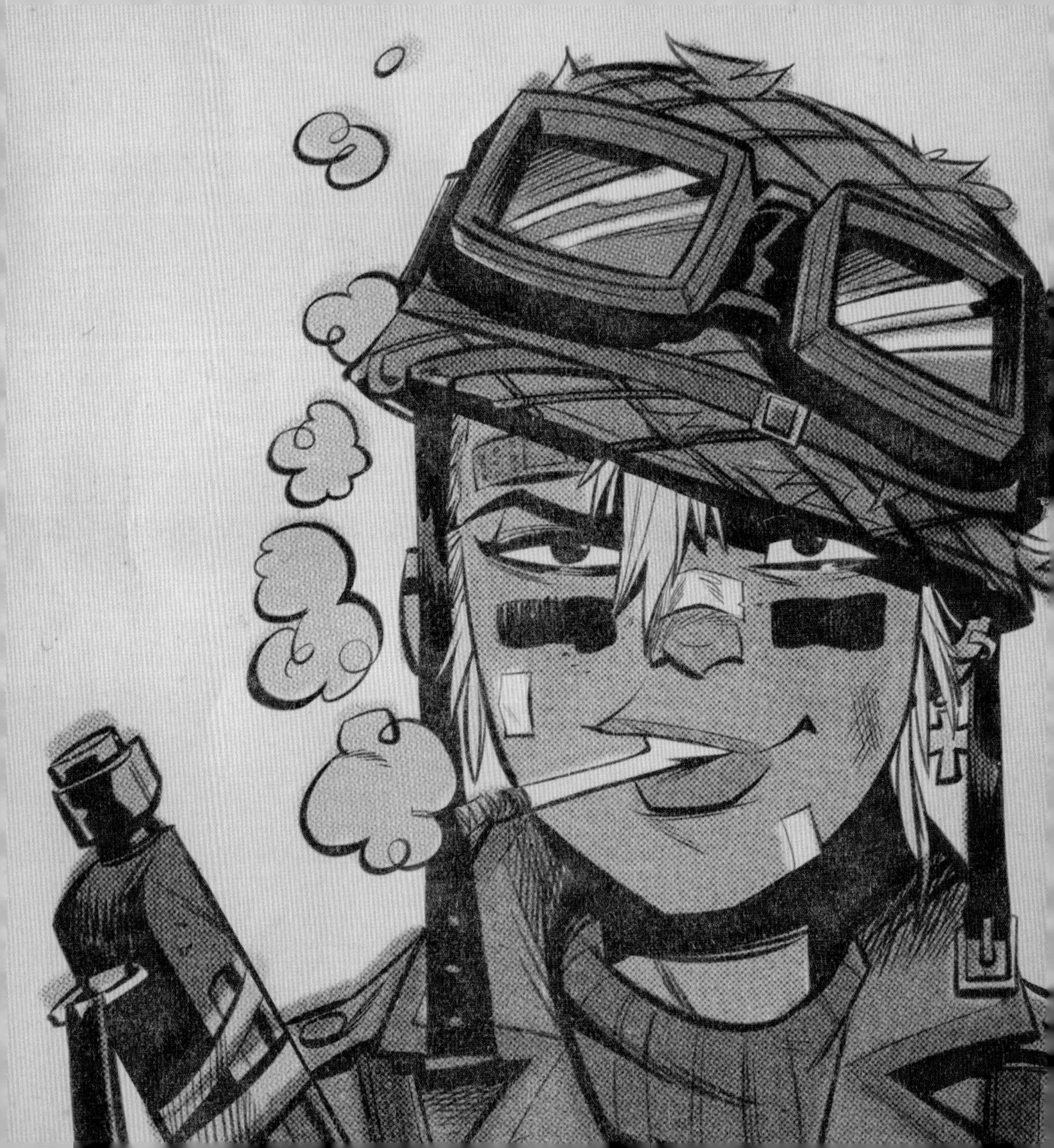

M.I.A.

Where were you?
Did I leave you behind?
Back there
Back in the jungle
On those telepathic beaches
Amongst those broken ruins
of history yet to come?

Did I leave you there?

I never meant to

Were you lost
or were you found?
Did you watch for me?
Did I slip from memory
like a forgotten soldier
Missing In Action
never to come back
until the day
the knock on the door
the touch
of a hand on a wrist
the eyes of tears

and
an
electrical
connection
through
magical
cups
of
tea

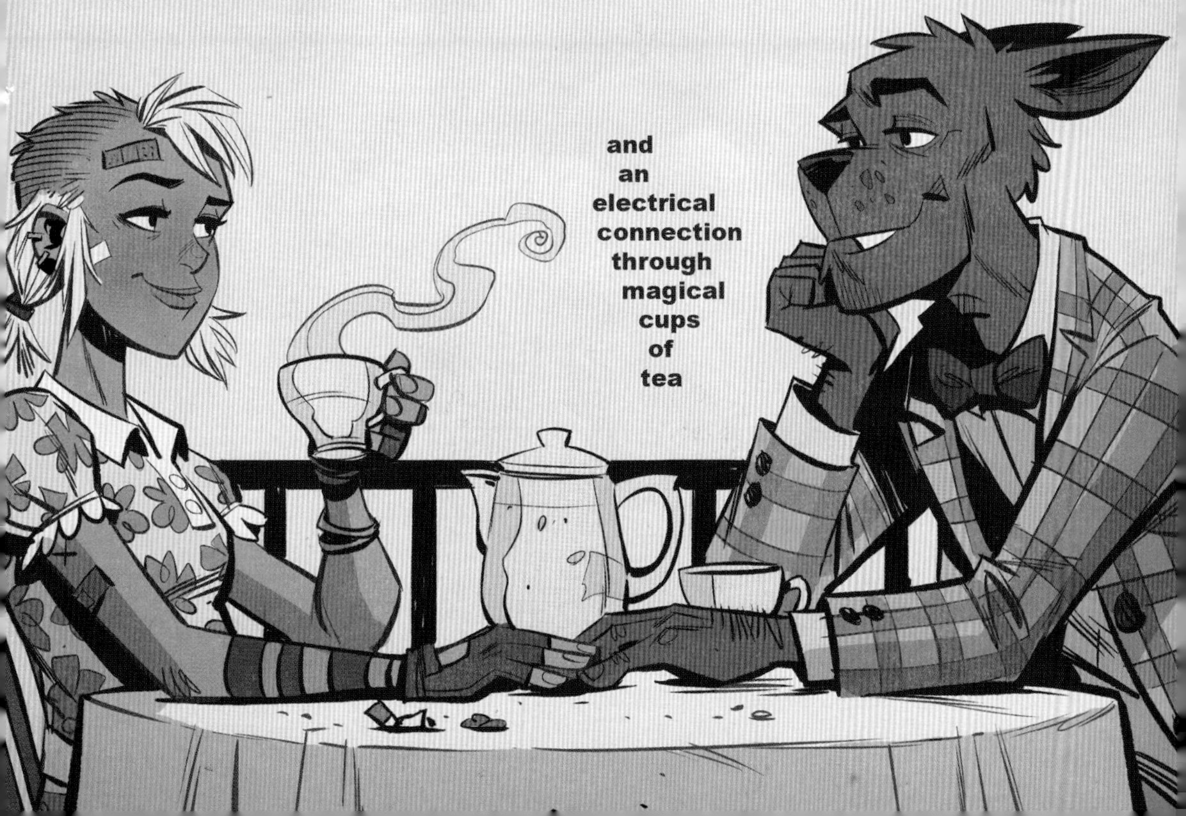

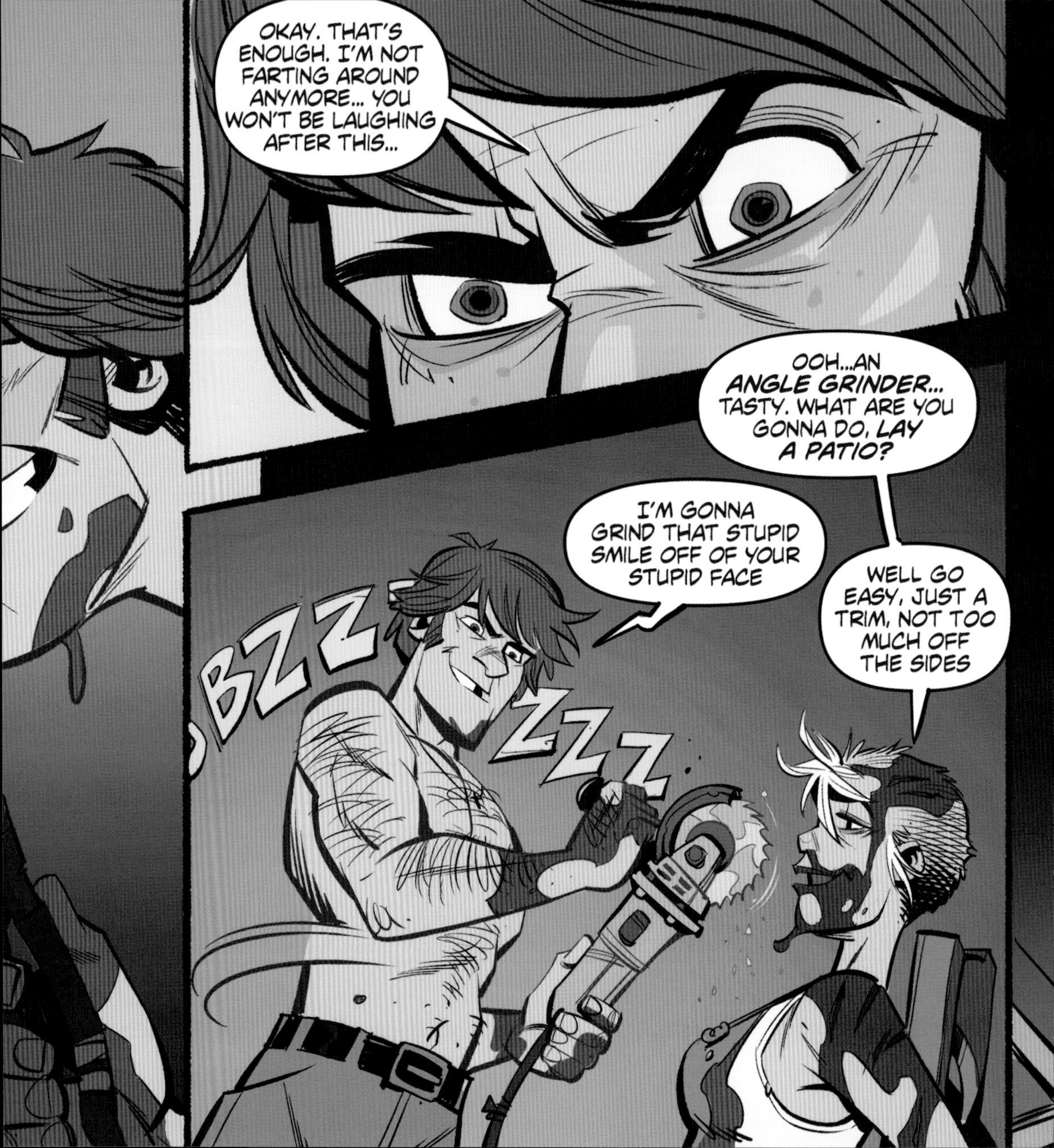

OKAY. THAT'S ENOUGH. I'M NOT FARTING AROUND ANYMORE... YOU WON'T BE LAUGHING AFTER THIS...
OOH...AN *ANGLE GRINDER*... TASTY. WHAT ARE YOU GONNA DO, *LAY A PATIO?*
I'M GONNA GRIND THAT STUPID SMILE OFF OF YOUR STUPID FACE
WELL GO EASY, JUST A TRIM, NOT TOO MUCH OFF THE SIDES
BZZZZZZ

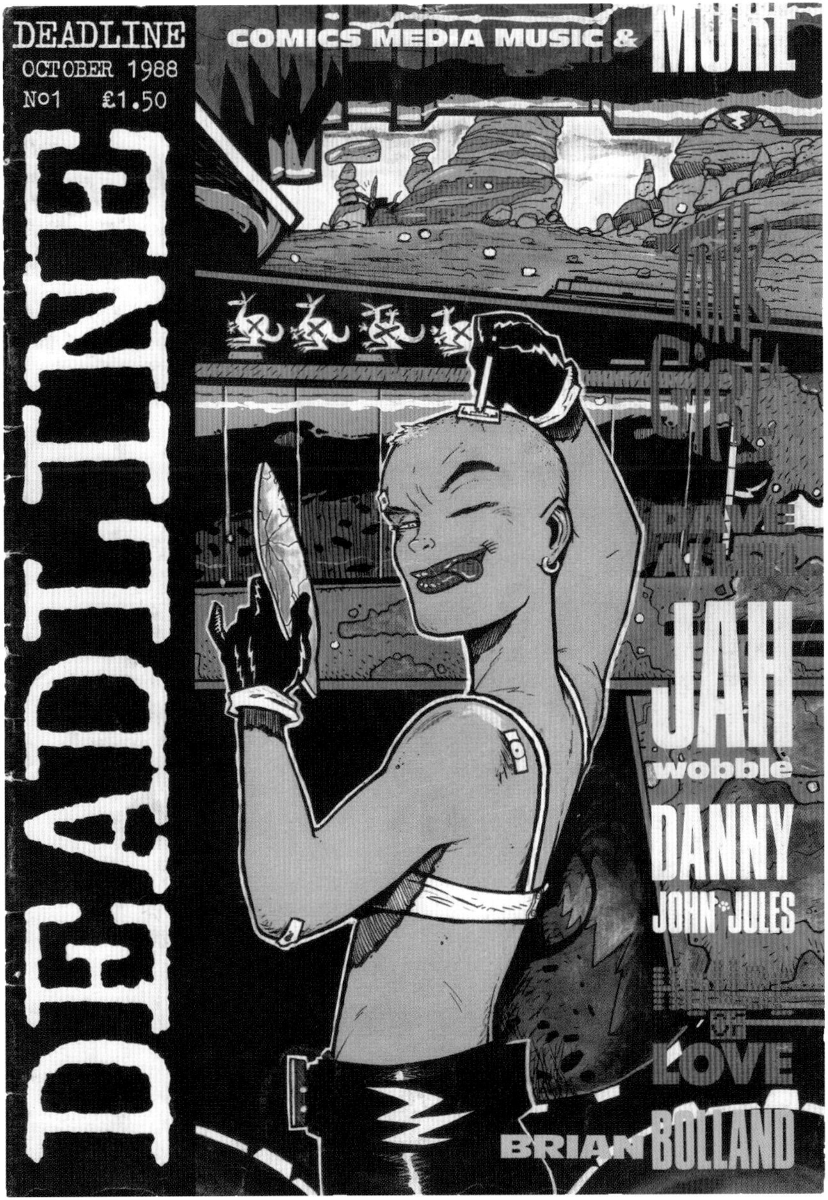
DEADLINE
OCTOBER 1988
No1 £1.50
DEADLINE
COMICS MEDIA MUSIC & MORE
JAH
wobble
DANNY
JOHN JULES
LOVE
BRIAN BOLLAND

"Oh why oh why oh why did this have to happen today?" moaned Tank Girl, as she pulled back the net curtain and looked out of the first floor bedroom window. It was the morning of Jet Girl's birthday and everyone had gathered together at her country house. A great celebration had been planned in the garden, which included the erection of a marquee and a small stage, on which local band Total Skill had been hired to play.

Fate, however, had once again intervened, and the garden was full of something much more sinister than a bunch of spotty, teenage, would-be pop stars.

Booga, Tank Girl's kangaroo boyfriend, looked over her shoulder, resting his hairy chin on the side of her face, "What is it, my dove?" he enquired in his best, deep, Barry White, come-back-to-bed voice.

"Zombies. Hundreds of the bastards." Tank Girl tugged the curtain back across the window and started to pull her boots on. "You know, I've waited my whole life to have a crack at some of those bastards, and now they're here. Couldn't they have picked tomorrow instead, when I've got some time to spare, and I'm guaranteed to have a bad hangover and be really pissed off? I always kill best when I'm hung over."

Booga buttoned up his shirt, pulled his braces over his shoulders, and fastened his belt and holster around his waist. He smiled reassuringly at Tank Girl, "If we're smart about it, there'll still be time to clear them out of the area before the caterers turn up."

"That's if the zombies haven't already eaten the caterers by now. They may already be here, with half their brains hanging out and excrement all over their trousers. That's not the kind of buffet I had in mind."

They made their way downstairs to Jet Girl's ample and bountiful kitchen. Jet Girl was sitting at the big oak kitchen table with Barney (Tank Girl's psycho-secret-weapon-girlfriend), drinking grapefruit juice and eating individual Cheerios like they were peanuts.

"It's okay, I've bolted the doors shut," said Jet Girl, beckoning them over to the table whilst simultaneously nodding towards the window.

Dozens of zombies were cramming their faces into the window frame, squashing their rotten, bleeding faces against the glass and trying to head-butt their way into the kitchen. The sight of the two girls, absent-mindedly chatting away over their easy breakfast was driving the zombies insane.

"How comes they haven't made it through the windows yet?" asked Tank Girl, getting herself a cereal bowl from the cupboard and helping herself to some Honey Nut Clusterfucks.

"Plexiglass," mumbled Jet Girl through her Cheerios, "I had it fitted last year, after that twat Unreasonable Nigel tried to have me assassinated."

"So, we were discussing the party," chipped in Barney, "and we were thinking that maybe we should hold it indoors instead, what with all the zombies and all. What do you think?"

Tank Girl didn't look too impressed, "But it's such a beautiful day out there. It would be a terrible shame to waste it, just because of a few troublemakers."

The sound of broken fists hammering on the doors and windows was almost deafening and the girls were struggling to hear one another.

Booga decided that prompt and immediate action should be taken, "It would be most inconvenient to change plans now. It would throw our guests into utter confusion. No, what must be done is a quick and thorough clean-up operation. Agreed?"

They all agreed in a hearty chorus.

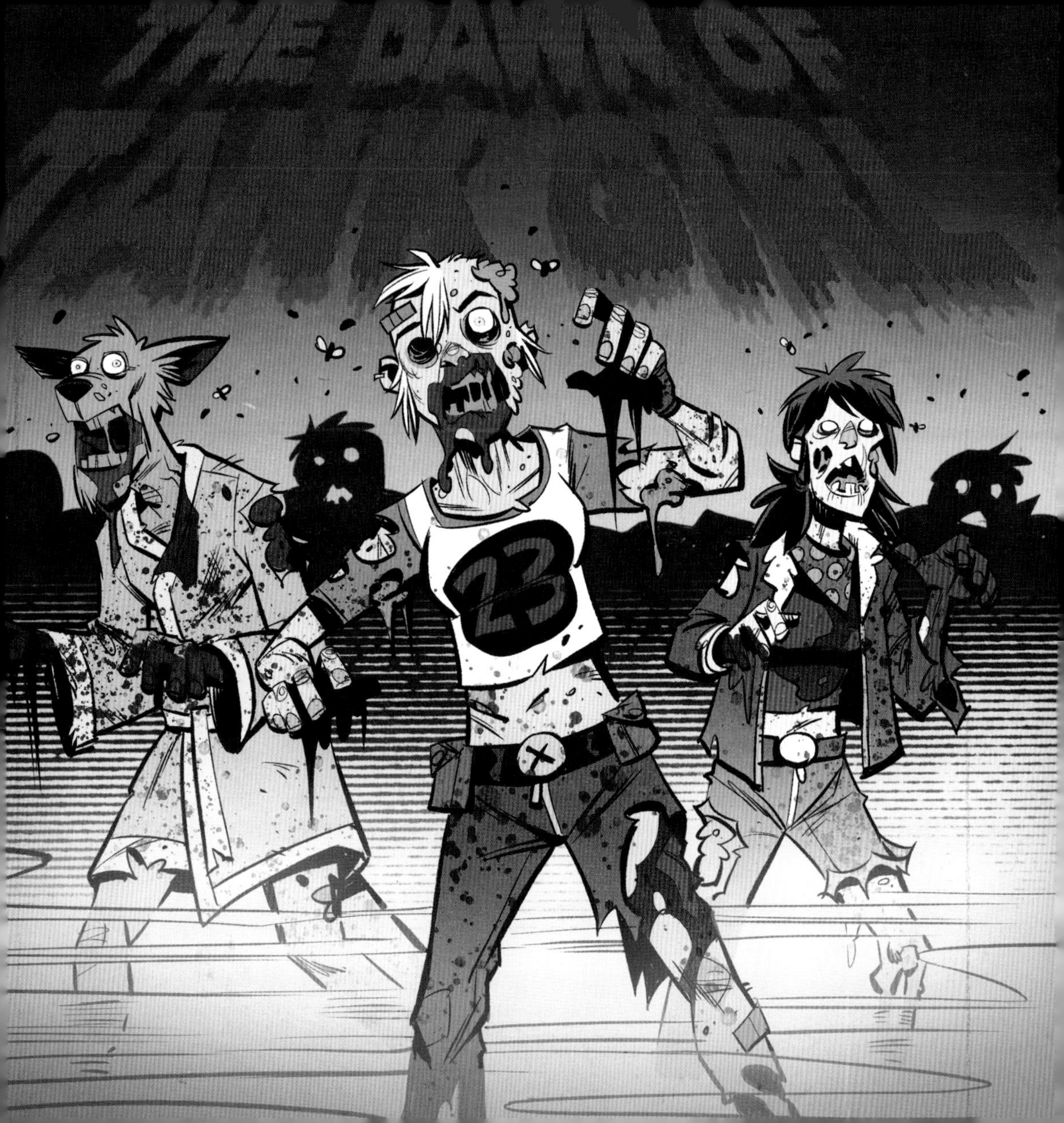

"Now then, first things first," continued Booga, pushing up his sleeves and striding across the kitchen like a well-hung cowboy, "does anyone else want a full English breakfast?"

One hour later, after they had all showered, shaved, shampooed, shat, shined shoes, and slipped into their best suits, the crew reconvened in the kitchen. Barney was already there, flicking through the TV stations, most of which had disappeared, save one emergency channel, broadcasting sporadic reports on the zombie invasion. They all sat in Jet Girl's over-stuffed armchairs, watching the emergency broadcast until the television station itself was overrun by zombies and all of the presenters turned into zombies too.

The picture finally went dead and Barney turned slowly to the others. "Wow. That's pretty good TV, I haven't seen anything that exciting since Terry Nation's "Survivors". Looks like there's nothing worth watching now, maybe we'd better pull our fingers out of our arses and get on with it."

Tank Girl sighed and heaved herself out of her chair. "So Jet Girl, what have you got in the house that we can use?"

"Nothing state-of-the-art, I'm afraid. The best I can offer is my Granddad's collection of World War Two weapons of the Pacific. Come on, I'll show you."

Jet Girl led them down several long corridors, down a flight of steps that must've taken them into part of the basement, through two locked doors, and into a windowless strong-room. The walls of the room were lined with every possible weapon you can imagine that existed in 1944. They were all presented as if in a museum, and every gun had cases of corresponding ammunition on the floor beneath it. A small adjoining room was filled with uniforms and accessories.

"Well, this I did not expect," smiled Tank Girl, taking a Tommy Gun down from the wall and checking the chamber.

Within minutes the whole team were decked-out in combat gear, and all had as many weapons and as much ammo as they could carry. They trooped upstairs and had a quick briefing in the grand hallway.

"Okay, me and Jet Girl will take the front garden. Booga and Barney, you can take the back," ordered Tank Girl, "the first one to the gazebo is the winner."

Opening the doors was gong to be the trickiest part, as the sheer pressure of the zombies against them meant that they would be sent sprawling into the hall and kitchen before the crew could get a round off. Booga and Barney spread chairs and objects across the kitchen floor to stumble them, and Tank Girl and Jet Girl did similar in the hall.

Cautiously, poised ready to run, Booga slowly turned the key in the lock of the kitchen door. It sprang open immediately and Booga dived back behind the upturned kitchen table in a flash, popping back up with his helmet on and his gun at the ready. But the zombies had become so compacted against the doorframe that none of them could move. One started to worm himself free, so Barney walked straight up to him and blew the side of his head off with a pistol. A hand reached out of the mass of decaying bodies and tried to make a grab for her, but Booga was right there with a machete, taking the arm off at the elbow like a trained butcher.

"I'm glad they're not the really fast type of zombie that you get in movies nowadays," joked Booga, as he rattled away at the doorway with his machine gun.

"Wait until we get outside," grunted Barney, stabbing away with a rifle-mounted bayonette, "these fuckers couldn't move fast if their lives depended on it."

She carried on scrunching into the bodies with her blade. It was clear that they weren't going to make much progress until the doorway was cleared of corpses.

"Step to one side if you please," came a shout from behind them. Surprised to hear another voice in the same room, Booga and Barney stepped back from the door and turned in unison.

Right behind them was Tank Girl, sat on a tiny four-wheeled truck, on which was mounted a large calibre canon. The front of the truck was boxed off with a riveted metal shield, and a small motor chugged brown smoke out across the kitchen floor.

"What. The. Fuck. Is. That?" asked Barney, her eyes wide and her jaw dropped.

Tank Girl cranked the little vehicle forward and lined up the cannon with the kitchen door, "There was no way out of the front door, so we had a little scout around and found this in the maid's room. We think it might be very, very old."

"No shit," frowned Barney, as she and Booga got behind it and trained their weapons at the zombies.

"Okay kids," shouted Tank Girl, over the noise of her engine and the zombies outside, "I'll lead the charge, you guys form an orderly queue and follow through, cleaning up any stragglers."

"Let's form a box, like they used to do in the Napoleonic wars, and give them what-for," suggested Booga enthusiastically.

"I'll give your Napoleonic box what-for in a minute, if you don't shut your big, fat gob and do what I say," thundered Tank Girl, as she put her foot down and let rip with her first shell, "follow me men! Let's rid the planet of this shit!"

Nine hours later Tank Girl was resting on a deckchair in the gazebo, soaking up the afternoon sun and sipping an icy-fresh Mojito. An old portable television on the decking next to her was blurting the news that half of the population of Australia had been wiped out in the zombie outbreak, but things were now back under control.

Total Skill were still on stage in the marquee, finishing their latest song "I.M.A. Carfax" before launching into a gloriously messy rendition of Julian Cope's "All the blowing-themselves-up-motherfuckers". Booga was still removing zombie corpses from the lawn, and Barney was filling in the last bomb crater with a hefty shovel. Party guests were happily strewn around the place like tinsel on a badly decorated christmas tree.

Jet Girl staggered up to the gazebo with a ropey looking girl, dressed in a suede tassel jacket and cowboy boots, hanging onto her arm. They were both very wobbly with the booze and crashed down onto the deck in a writhing, leggy mess.

"Hey Tank Girl, this is my old college buddy Craig Nancy!" squealed Jet Girl, pulling her friend up.

Craig Nancy stooped forward, placing her face right in front of Tank Girl's. Her mouth opened, almost involuntarily and she said, "This is...this is...this the fucking best time...this is it. I...fucking know everything now. Can we live like this forever? Can I be like this from now on? Can we be free of all that shit that's been dragging us down for so long? I mean...I mean...I've got this feeling building inside of me and it's good, y'know? It's really good. And no one's ever gonna get close to it with all that fake shit and bogus garbage. I want to reach into my skull and pull out my brain and squeeze the ancient truth out of it. All over the fucking carpet, y'know? I mean...humans...humans are human too, right?"

Tank Girl took a long, slow draw on her drink and stared off to the horizon. After a moment she looked up at Craig Nancy and smiled subtly. "Yeah," she said, "that is so fucking damned right."

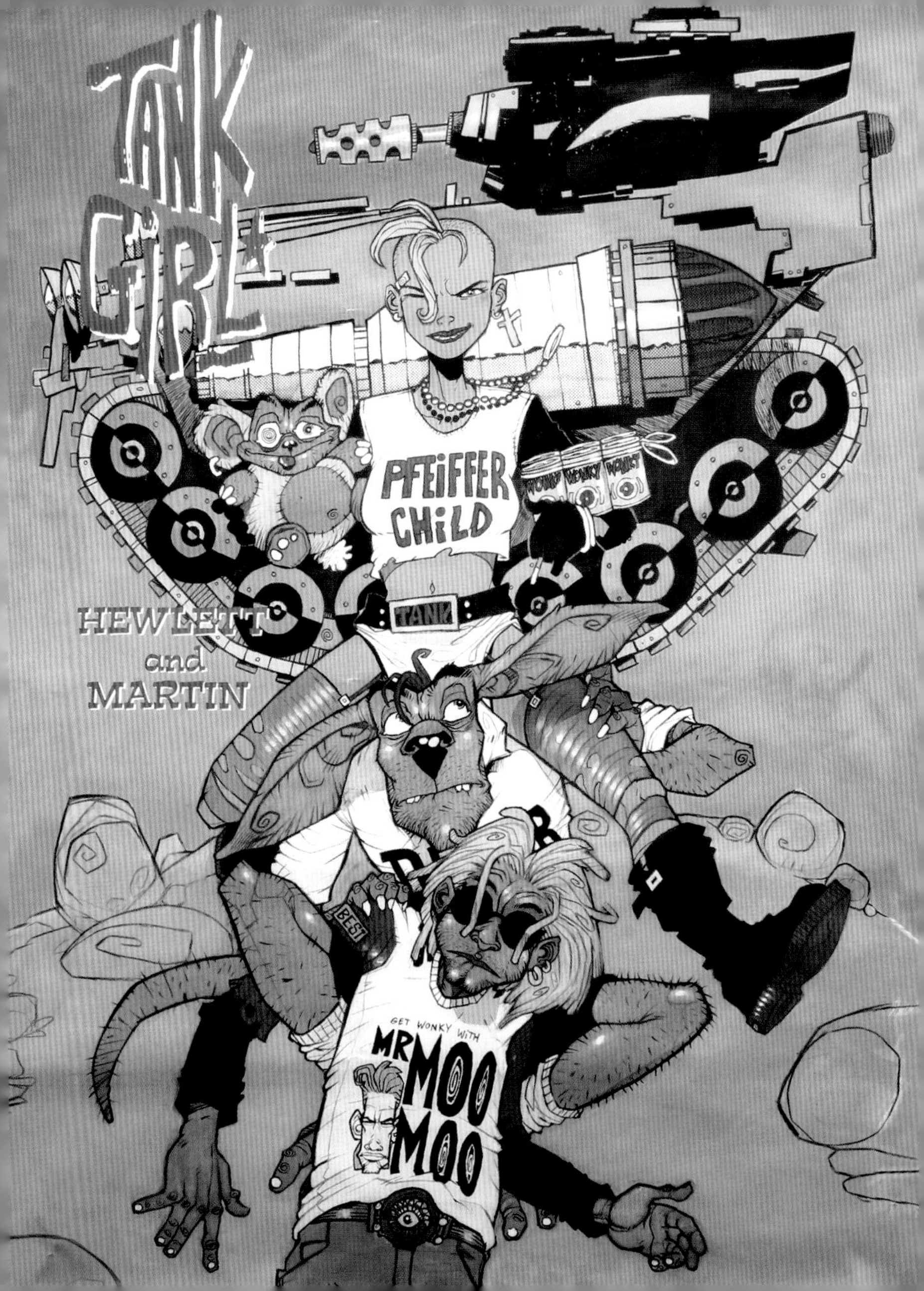
TANK GIRL
HEWLETT and MARTIN
PFEIFFER CHILD
TANK
GET WONKY WITH
MR MOO MOO

TANKGIRL★

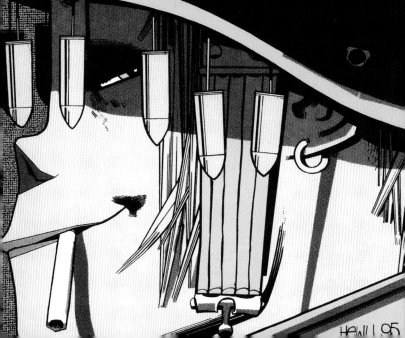

HEWLLI 95

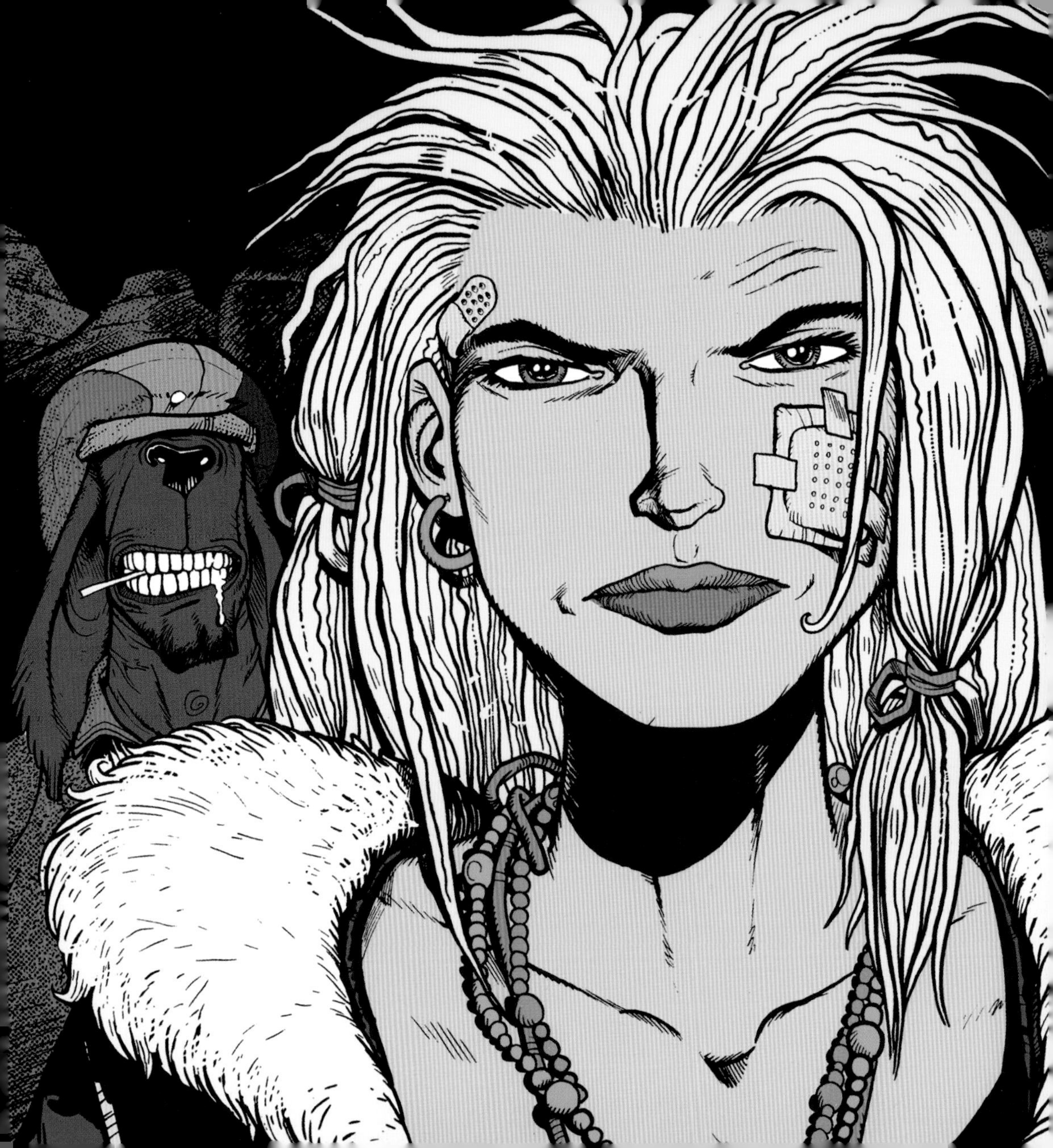

THEY TRY TO MAKE YOU THINK THAT IT'S ALL NORMAL, ALL BORING. BUT IT ISN'T. IT'S MAGIC. IT'S ALL MAGIC. EVERYTHING IS MAGIC

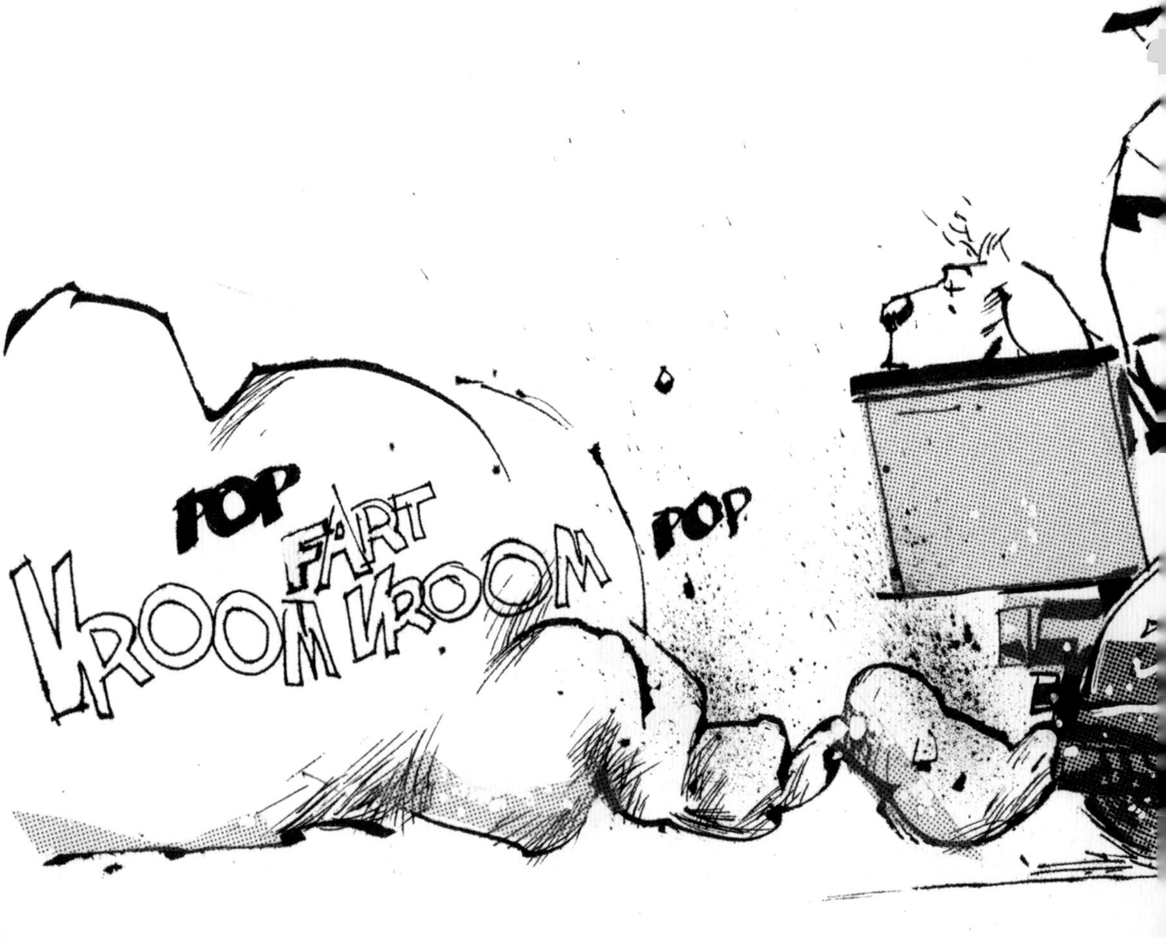
POP
FART
POP
VROOM VROOM

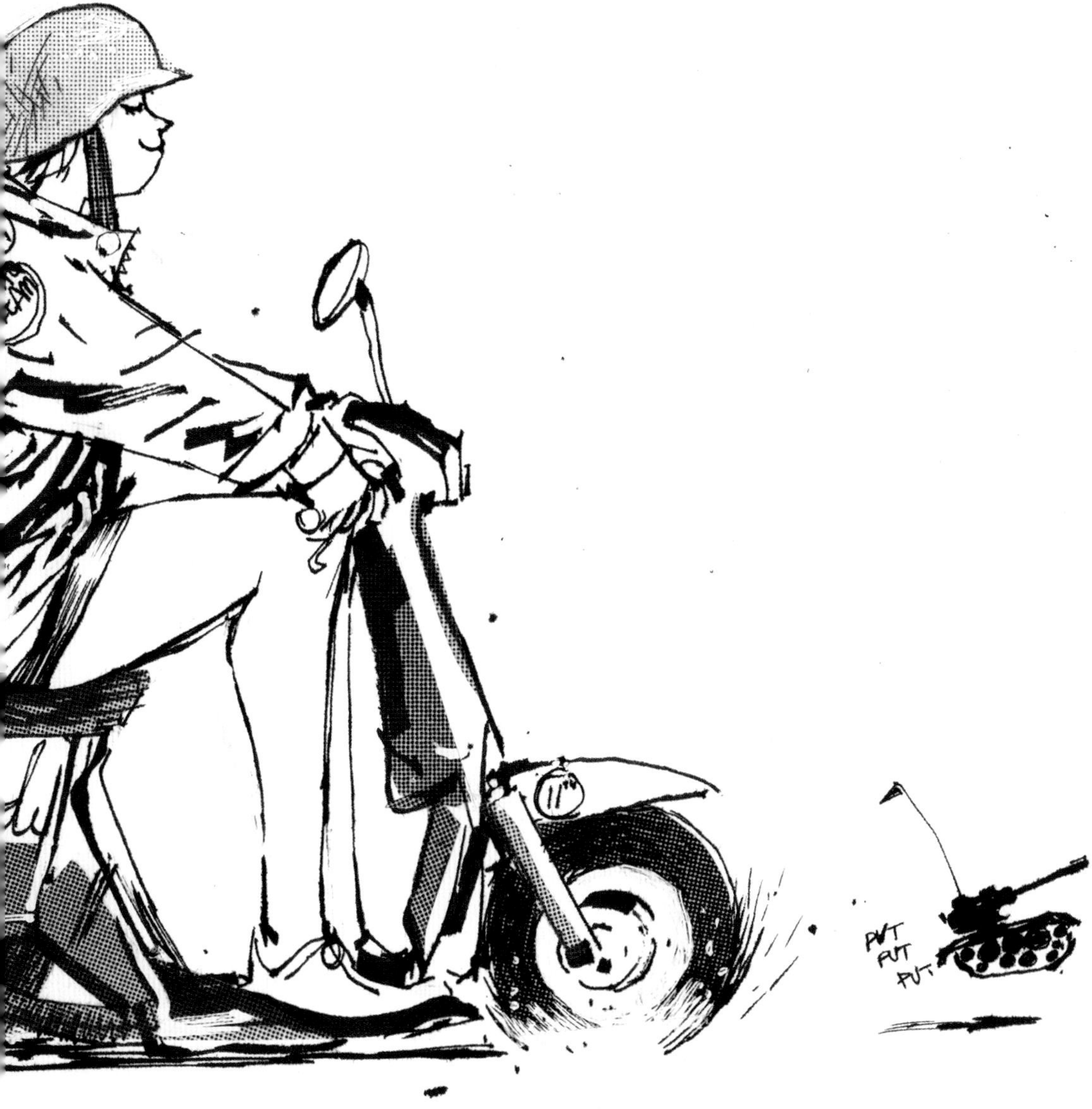
PUT
PUT
PUT

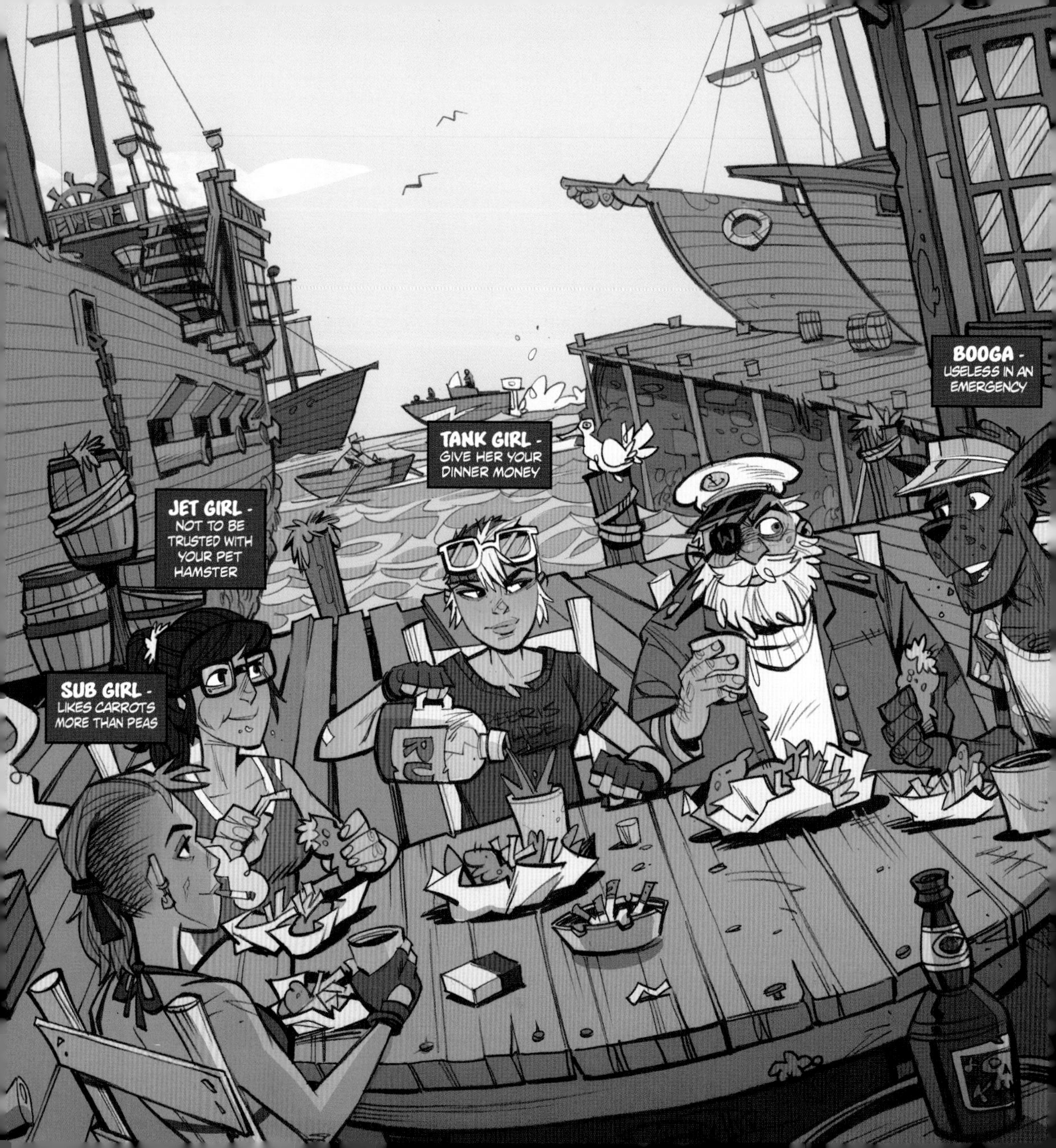
BOOGA - USELESS IN AN EMERGENCY
TANK GIRL - GIVE HER YOUR DINNER MONEY
JET GIRL - NOT TO BE TRUSTED WITH YOUR PET HAMSTER
SUB GIRL - LIKES CARROTS MORE THAN PEAS

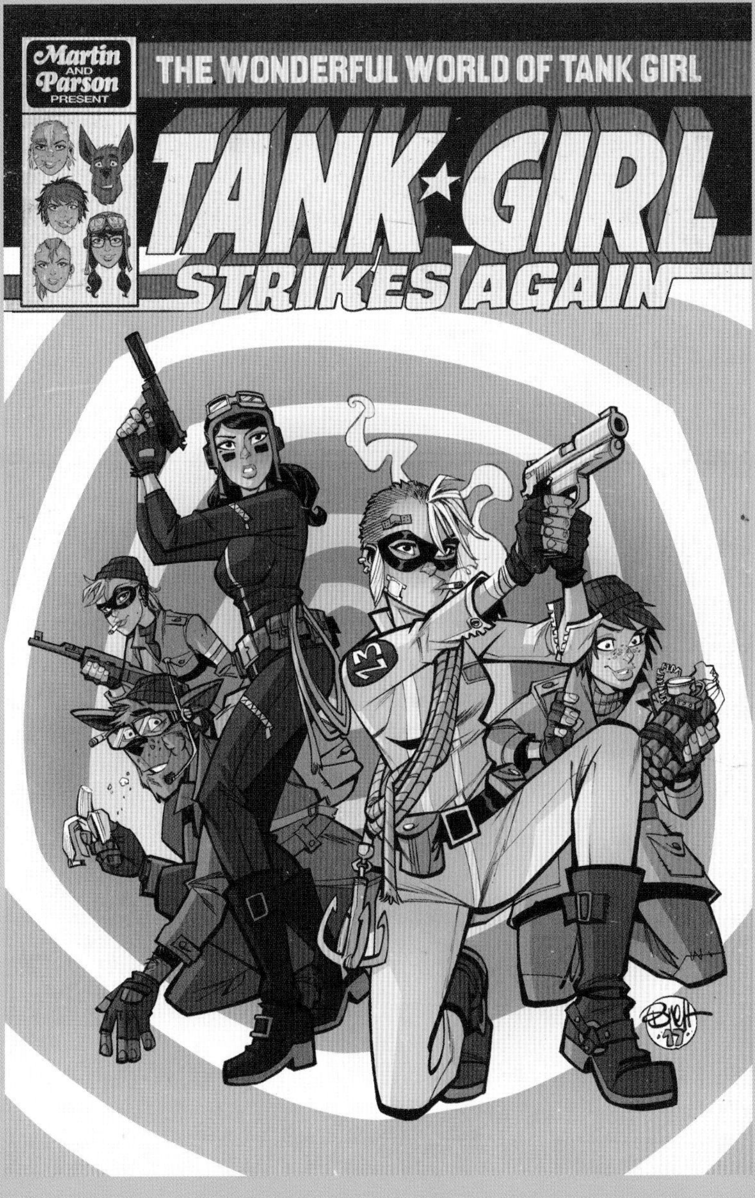
Martin AND Parson PRESENT
THE WONDERFUL WORLD OF TANK GIRL
TANK GIRL
STRIKES AGAIN

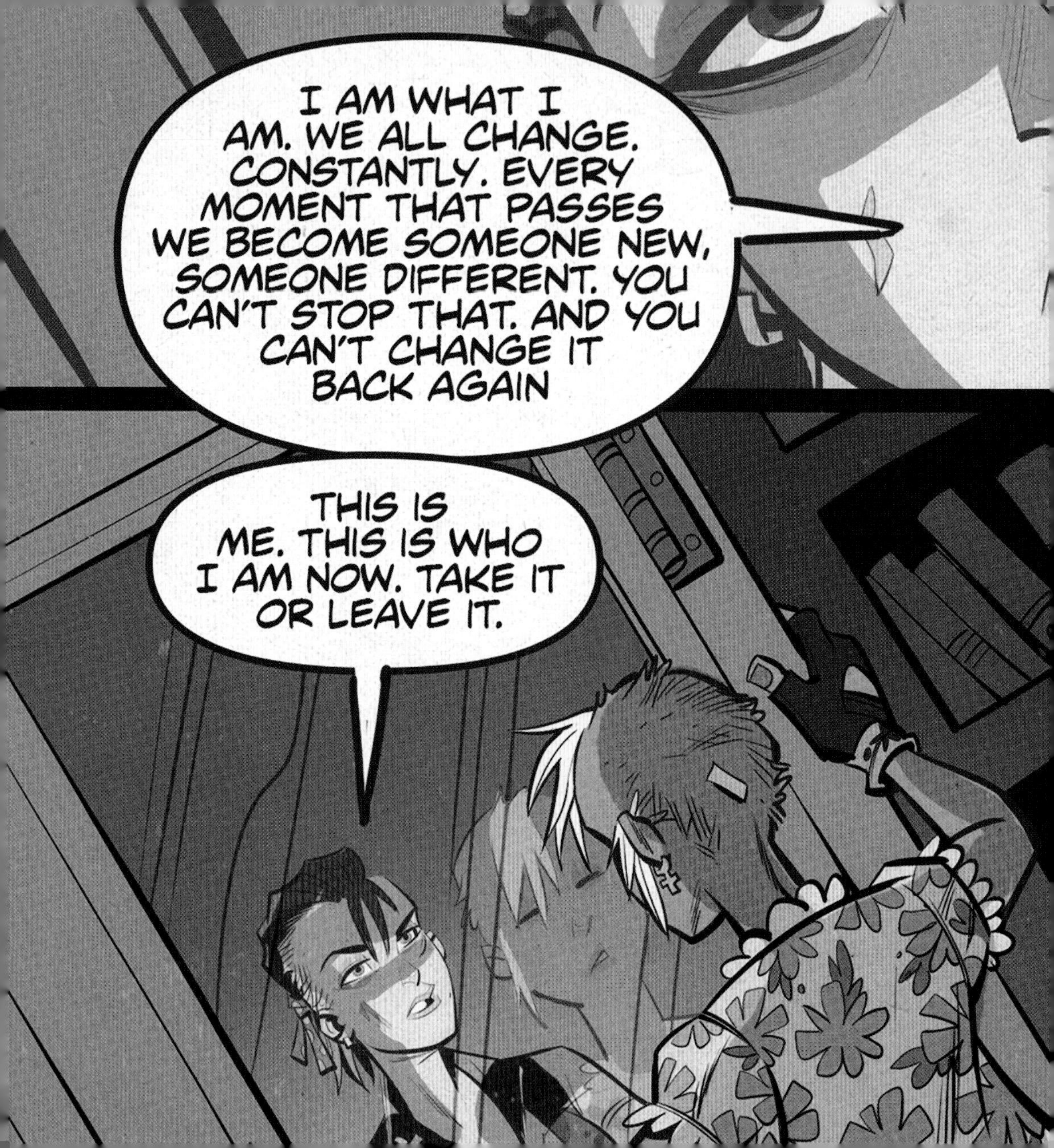
I AM WHAT I AM. WE ALL CHANGE. CONSTANTLY. EVERY MOMENT THAT PASSES WE BECOME SOMEONE NEW, SOMEONE DIFFERENT. YOU CAN'T STOP THAT. AND YOU CAN'T CHANGE IT BACK AGAIN
THIS IS ME. THIS IS WHO I AM NOW. TAKE IT OR LEAVE IT.

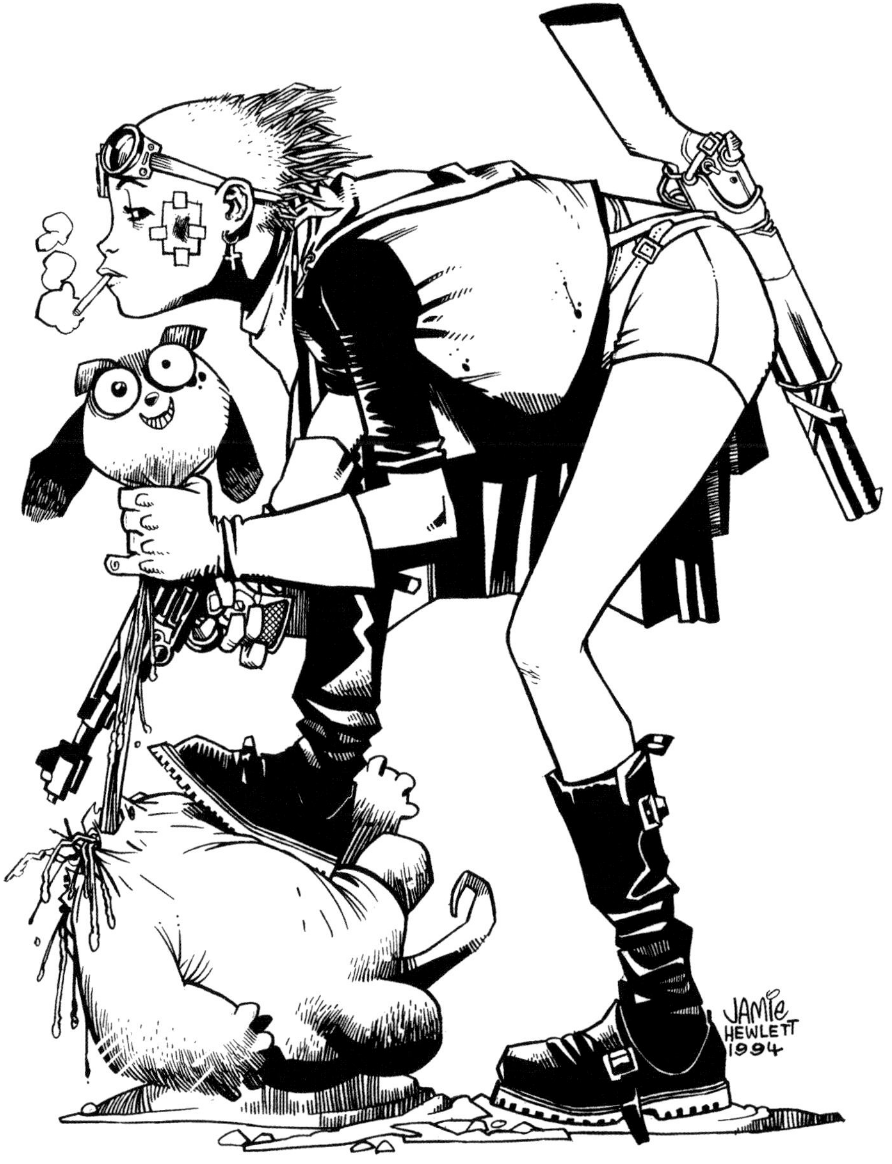
JAMIE
HEWLETT
1994

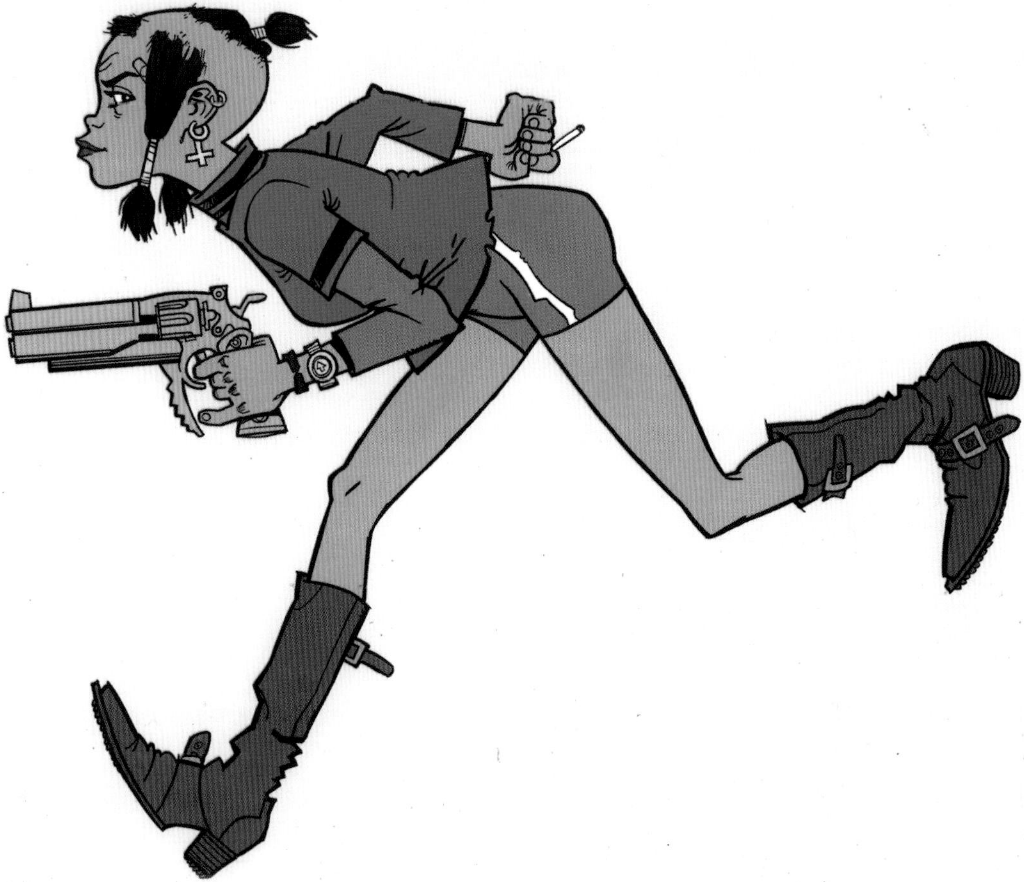

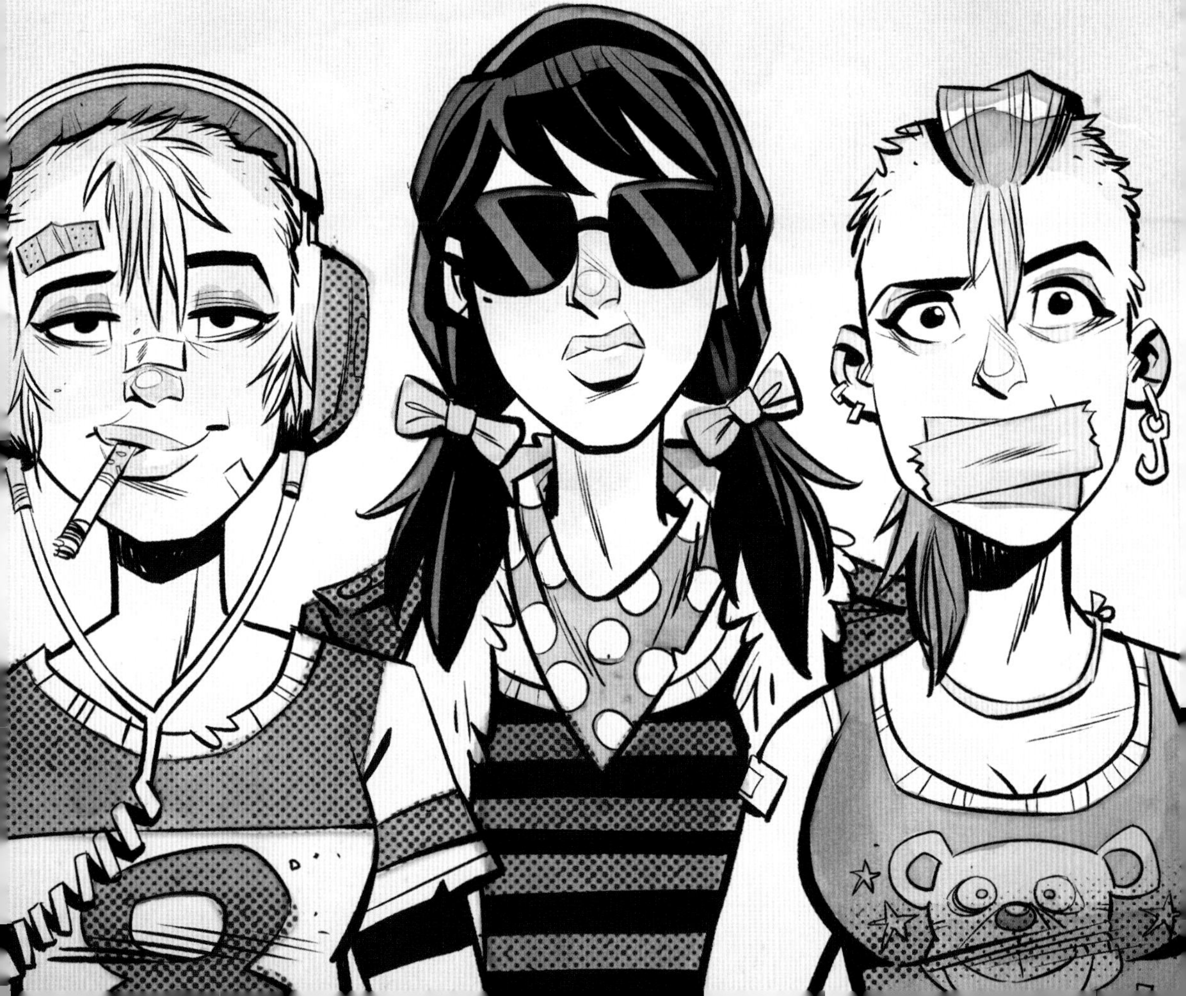

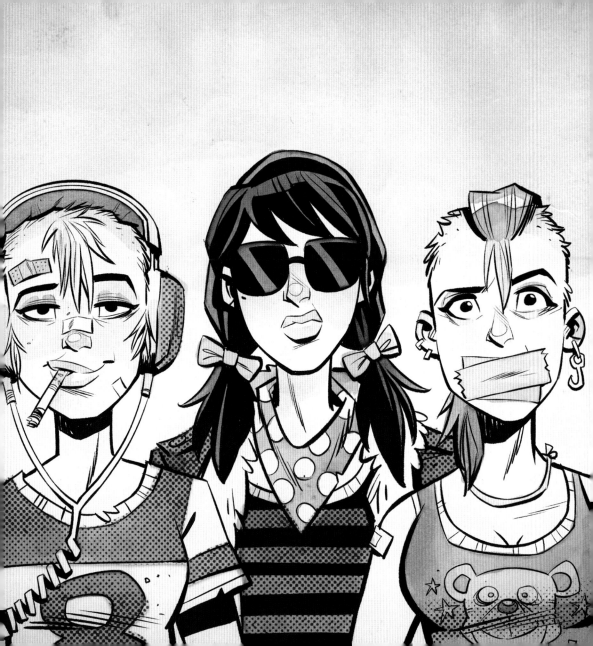

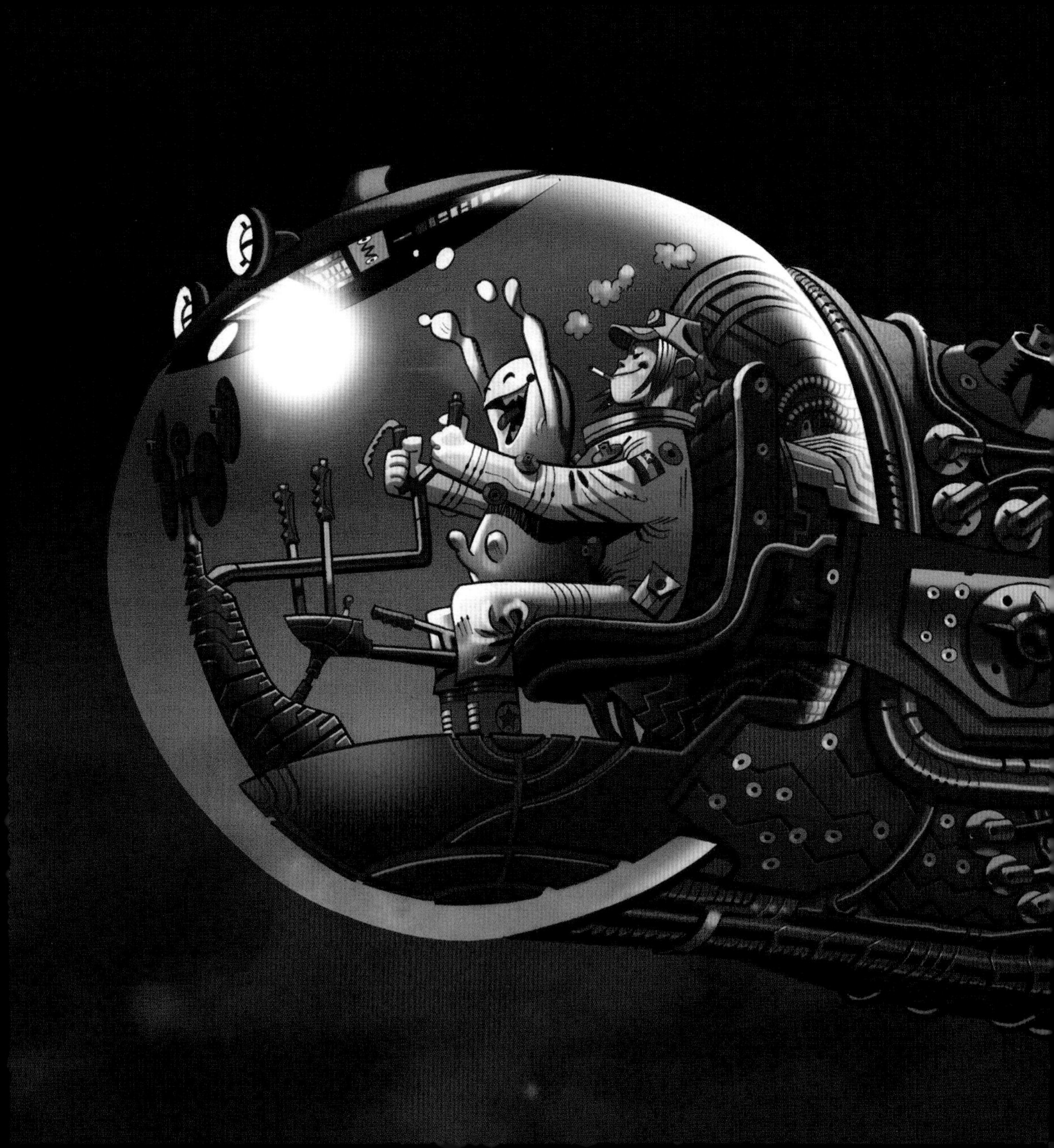

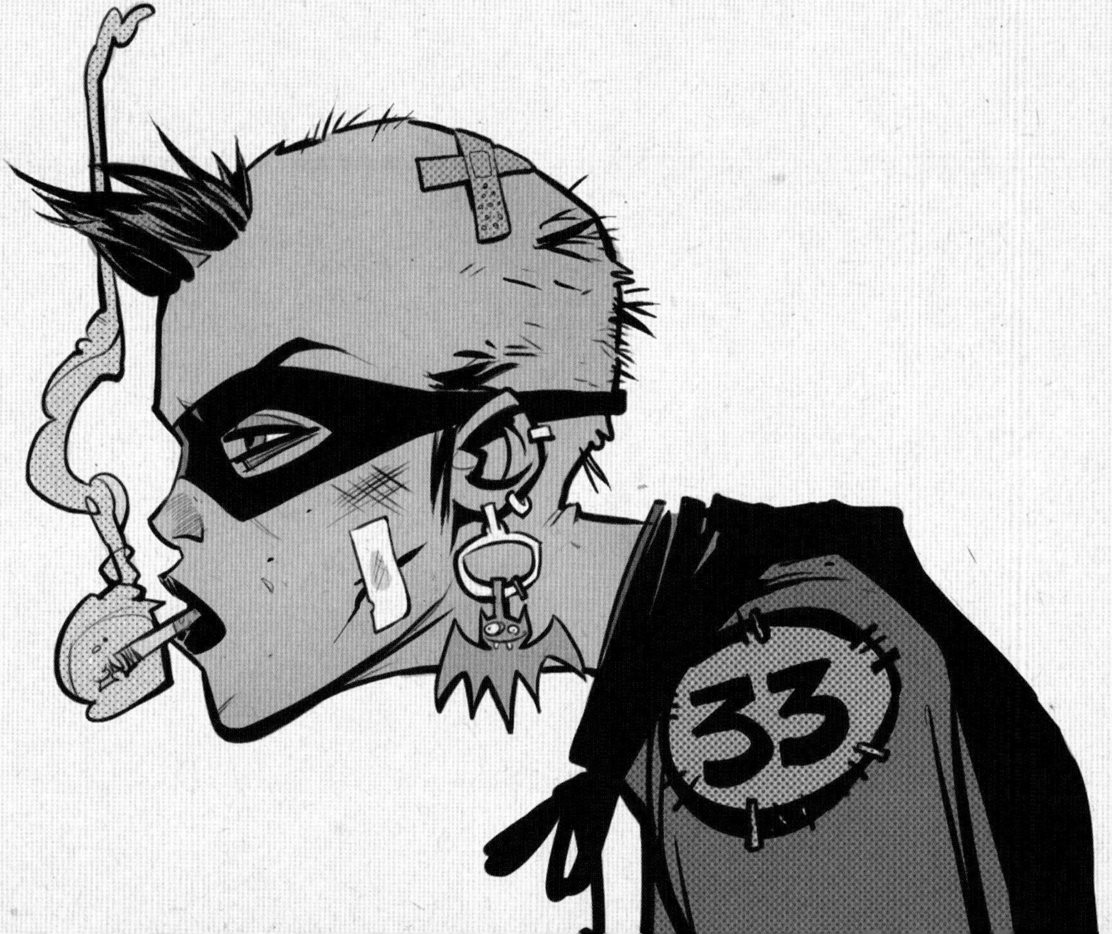
33

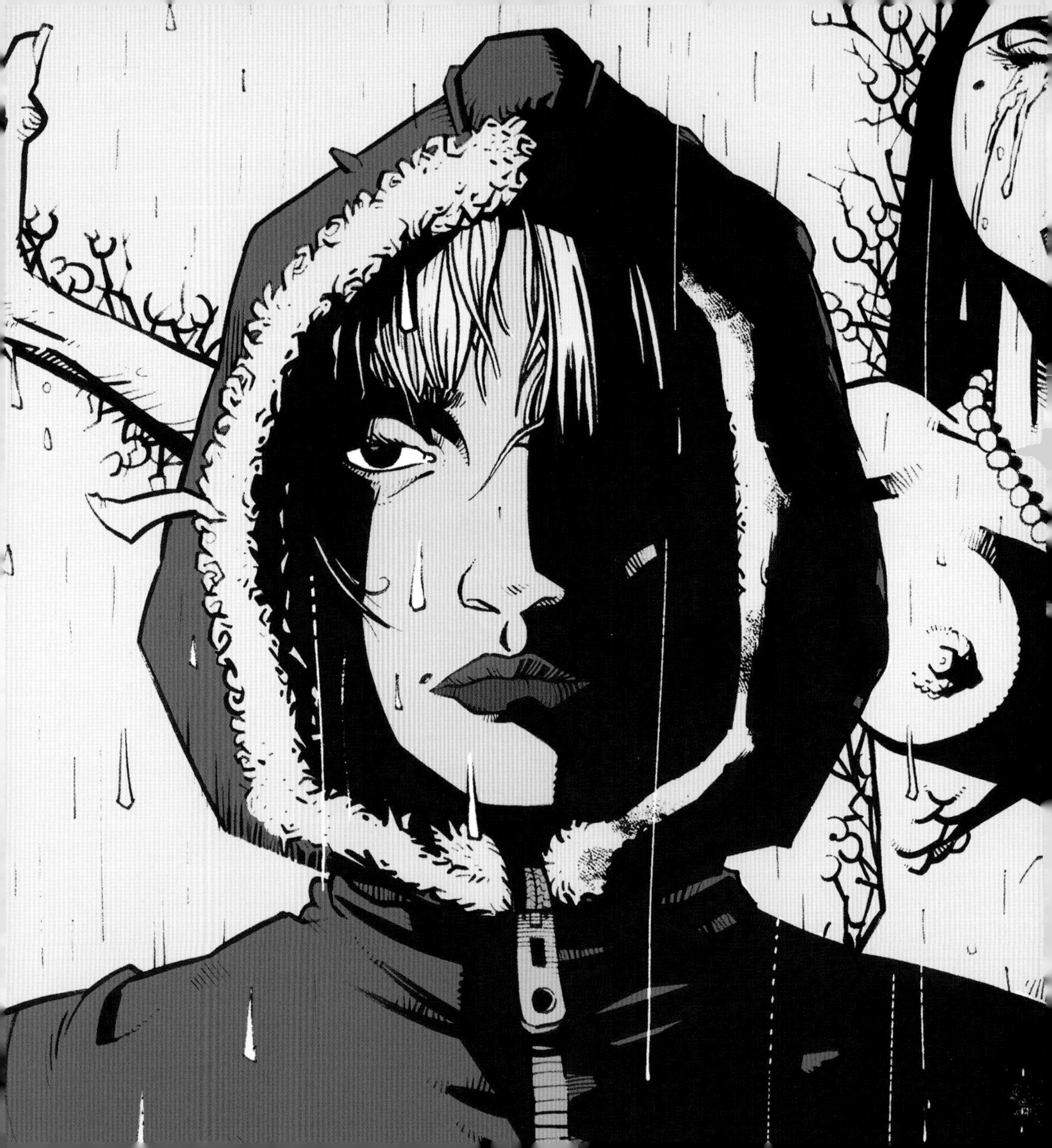

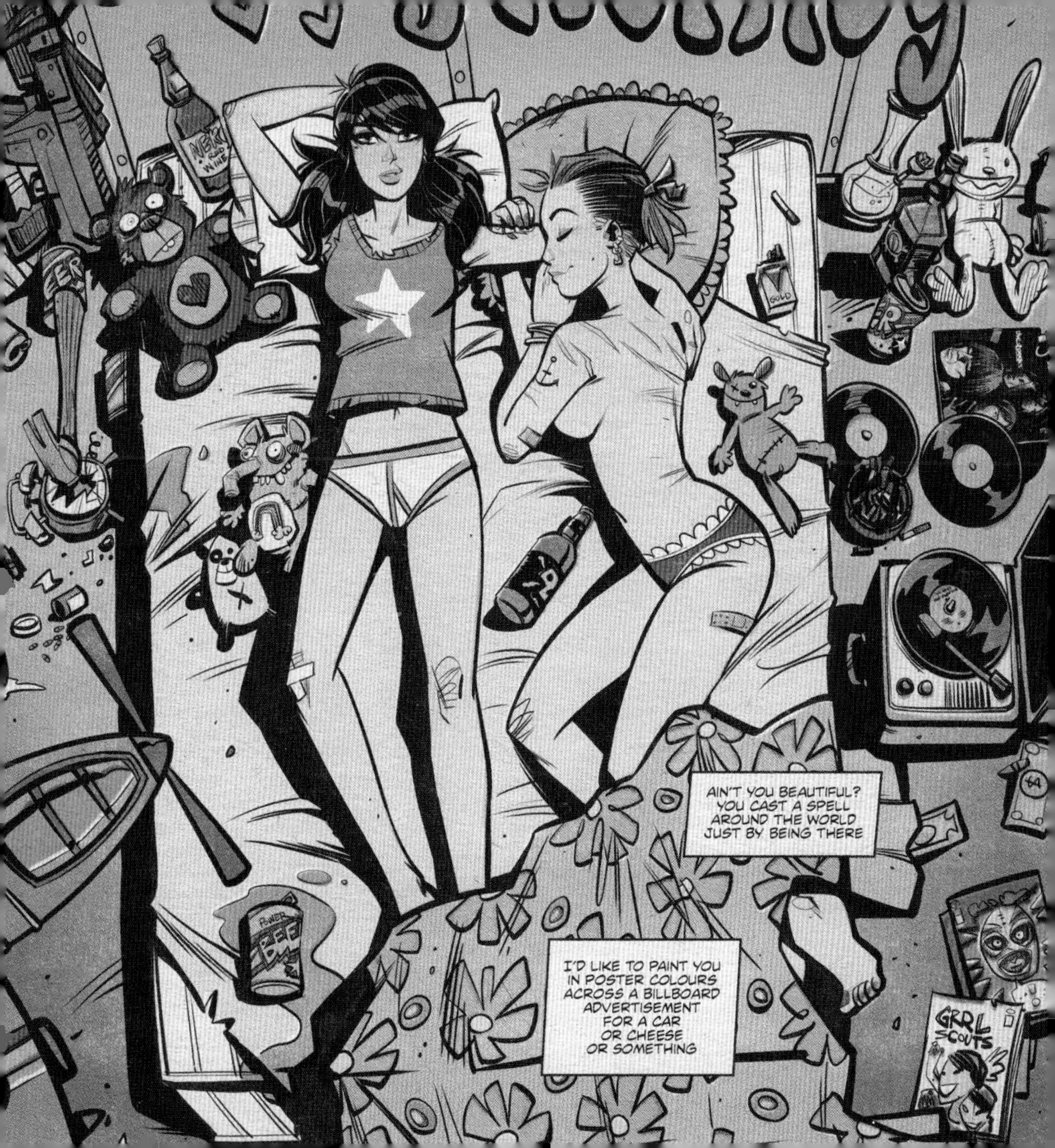
AIN'T YOU BEAUTIFUL?
YOU CAST A SPELL
AROUND THE WORLD
JUST BY BEING THERE
I'D LIKE TO PAINT YOU
IN POSTER COLOURS
ACROSS A BILLBOARD
ADVERTISEMENT
FOR A CAR
OR CHEESE
OR SOMETHING
GRRL SCOUTS

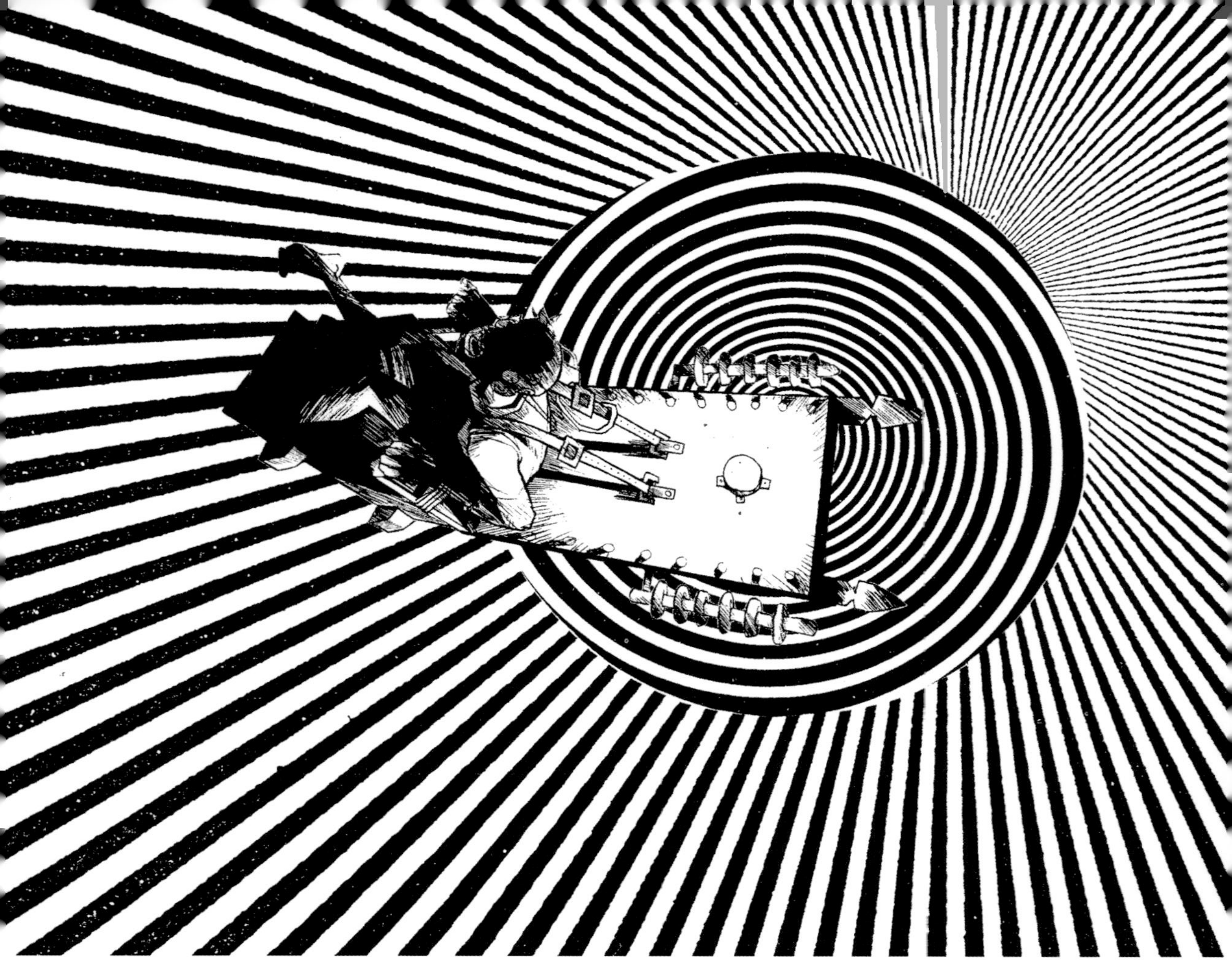
TELL US YOUR PROBLEMS AND WE'LL GIVE YOU THE SOLUTIONS, TAKE OUR SOLUTIONS AND WE'LL GIVE YOU MORE PROBLEMS. WHAT MORE CAN YOU DO WITH LEMONADE IN YOUR BLOOD, WITH LEMONADE IN YOUR BRAIN? TURQUOISE, BLUE, SKY BLUE, EMERALD GREEN, RED, RED, RED AND CLEAR, THE COOL CLEAR VISION THROUGH LEMONADE. I UNDERSTAND ALL. NO BLOOD ANYMORE, ONLY LEMONADE. CHOKE ON IT BITCH. GIVE US YOUR BLOOD AND WE'LL GIVE YOU LEMONADE. JOIN US. JOIN OUR MERRY MERRY GO ROUND. THERE'S A VERY COOL CLEAR VISION THROUGH A GLASS OF

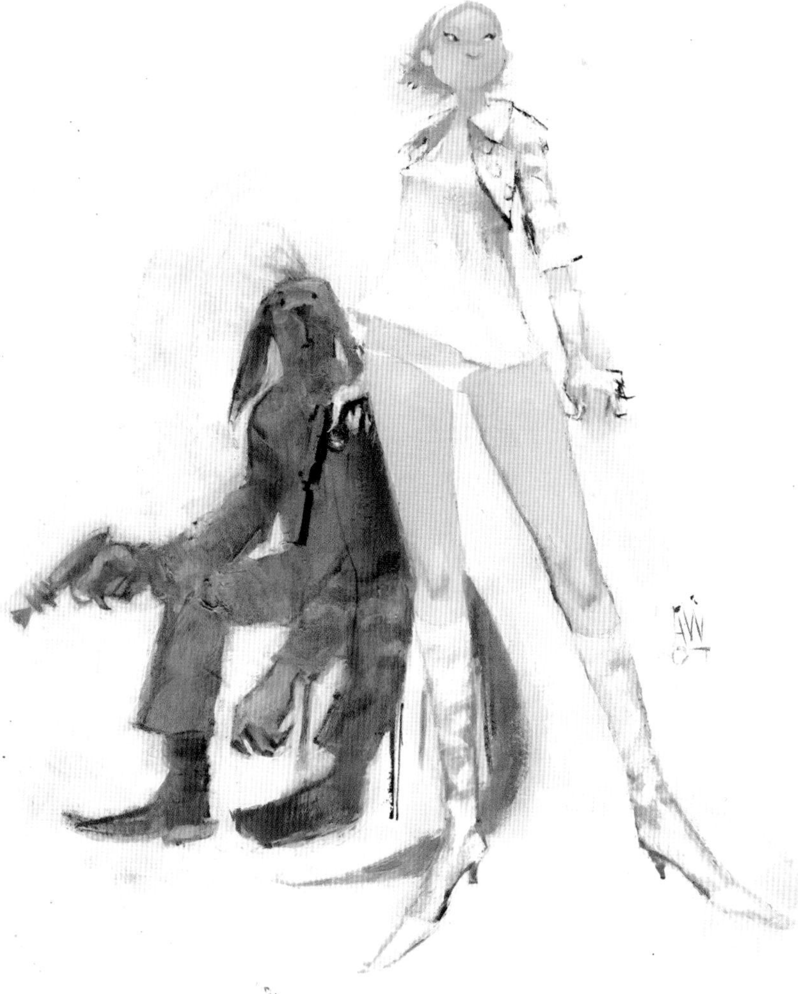

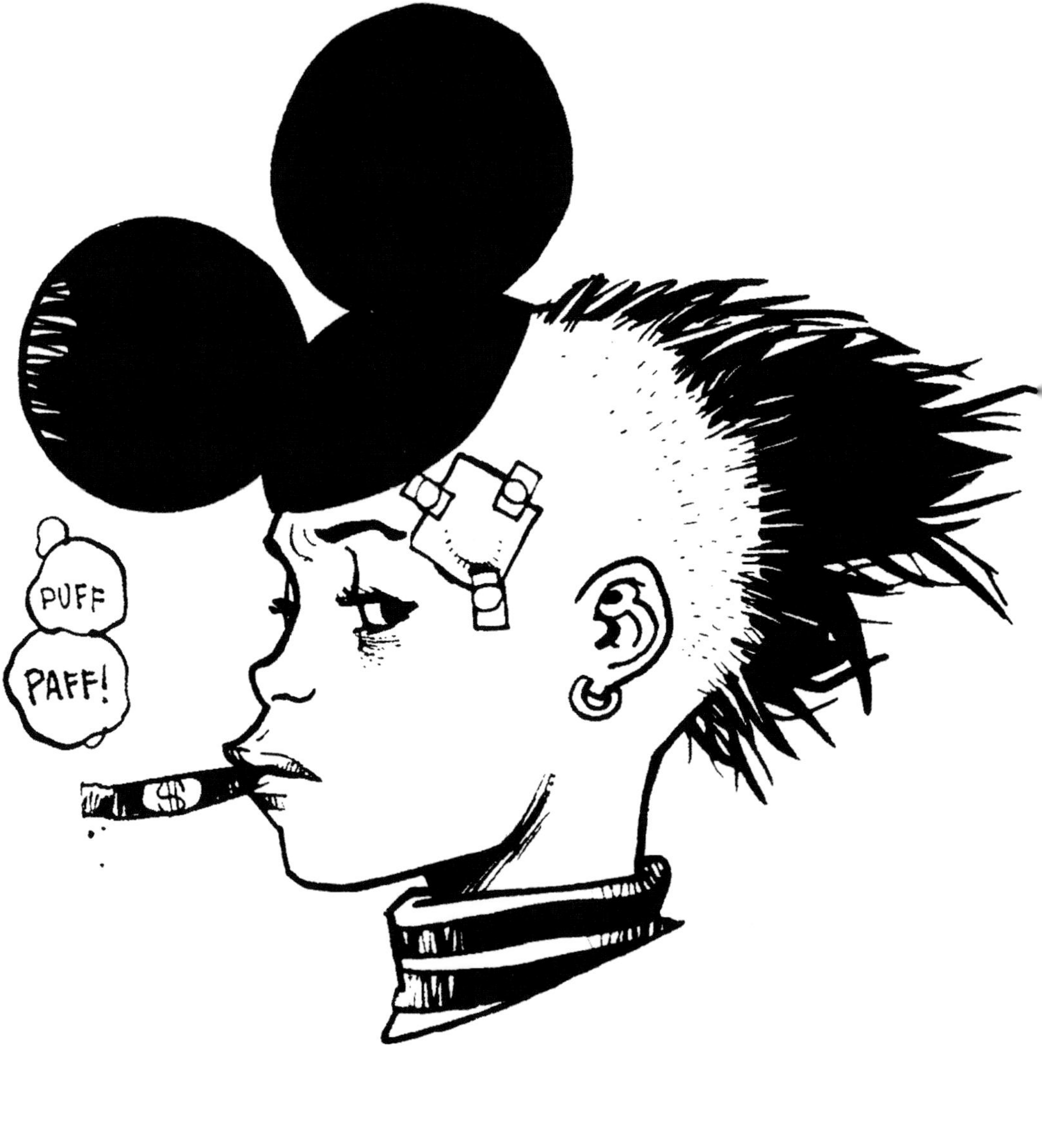
PUFF
PAFF!

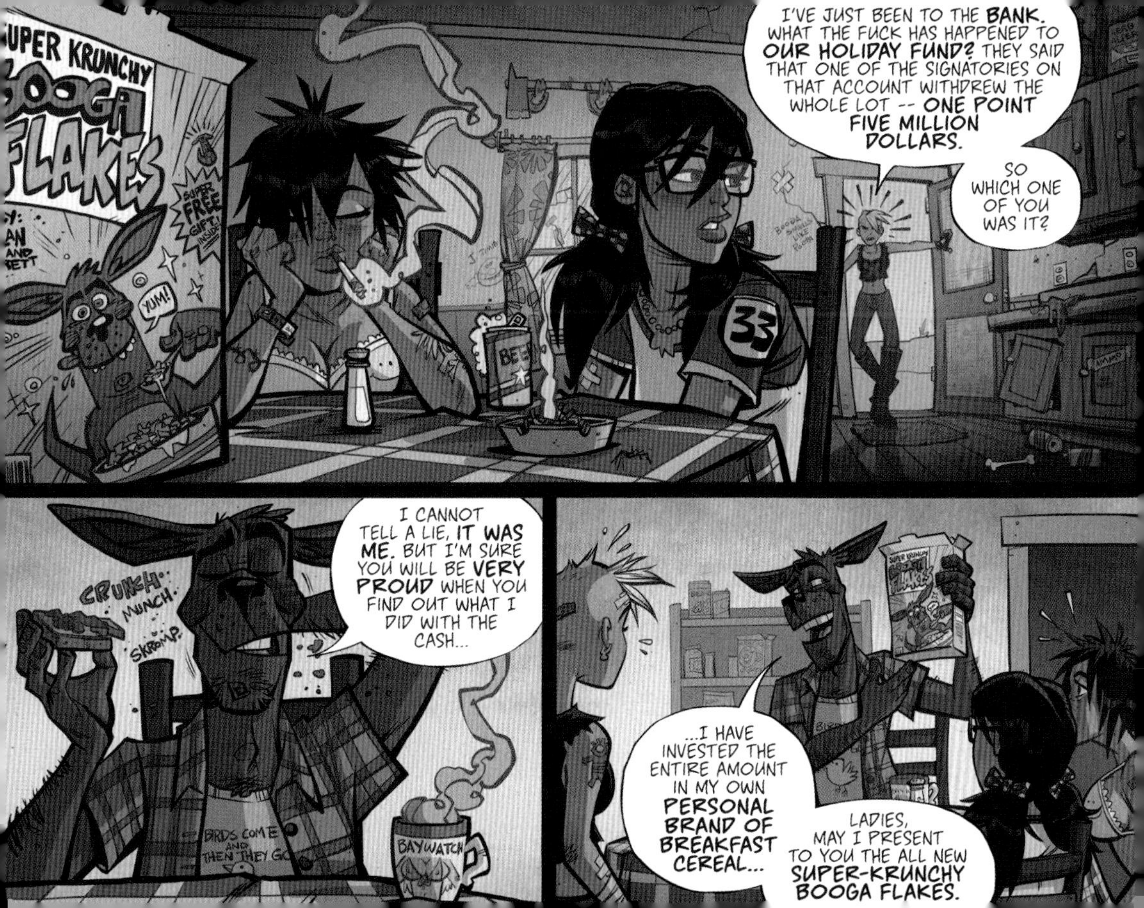
SUPER KRUNCHY BOOGA FLAKES
SUPER FREE GIFT! INSIDE!
YUM!
I'VE JUST BEEN TO THE BANK. WHAT THE FUCK HAS HAPPENED TO OUR HOLIDAY FUND? THEY SAID THAT ONE OF THE SIGNATORIES ON THAT ACCOUNT WITHDREW THE WHOLE LOT -- ONE POINT FIVE MILLION DOLLARS.
SO WHICH ONE OF YOU WAS IT?
CRUNCH MUNCH SKROMP
I CANNOT TELL A LIE, IT WAS ME. BUT I'M SURE YOU WILL BE VERY PROUD WHEN YOU FIND OUT WHAT I DID WITH THE CASH...
BIRDS COME AND THEN THEY GO
BAYWATCH
...I HAVE INVESTED THE ENTIRE AMOUNT IN MY OWN PERSONAL BRAND OF BREAKFAST CEREAL...
LADIES, MAY I PRESENT TO YOU THE ALL NEW SUPER-KRUNCHY BOOGA FLAKES.

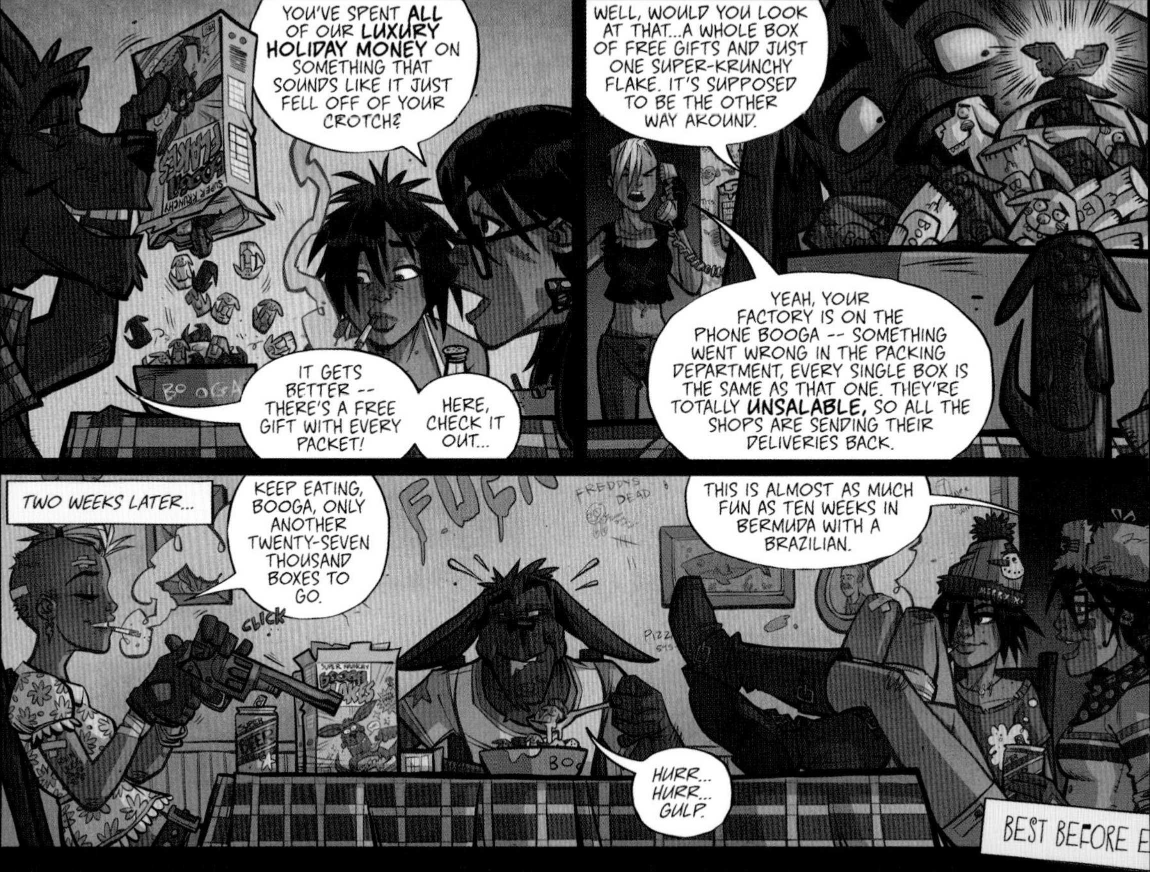

YOU'VE SPENT **ALL** OF OUR **LUXURY HOLIDAY MONEY** ON SOMETHING THAT SOUNDS LIKE IT JUST FELL OFF OF YOUR CROTCH?
SUPER KRUNCHY BOOGA FLAKES
IT GETS BETTER -- THERE'S A FREE GIFT WITH EVERY PACKET!
HERE, CHECK IT OUT...
BOOGA
WELL, WOULD YOU LOOK AT THAT...A WHOLE BOX OF FREE GIFTS AND JUST ONE SUPER-KRUNCHY FLAKE. IT'S SUPPOSED TO BE THE OTHER WAY AROUND.
YEAH, YOUR FACTORY IS ON THE PHONE BOOGA -- SOMETHING WENT WRONG IN THE PACKING DEPARTMENT, EVERY SINGLE BOX IS THE SAME AS THAT ONE. THEY'RE TOTALLY **UNSALABLE,** SO ALL THE SHOPS ARE SENDING THEIR DELIVERIES BACK.
TWO WEEKS LATER...
KEEP EATING, BOOGA, ONLY ANOTHER TWENTY-SEVEN THOUSAND BOXES TO GO.
FREDDYS DEAD
CLICK
THIS IS ALMOST AS MUCH FUN AS TEN WEEKS IN BERMUDA WITH A BRAZILIAN.
HURR... HURR... GULP.
BEST BEFORE E

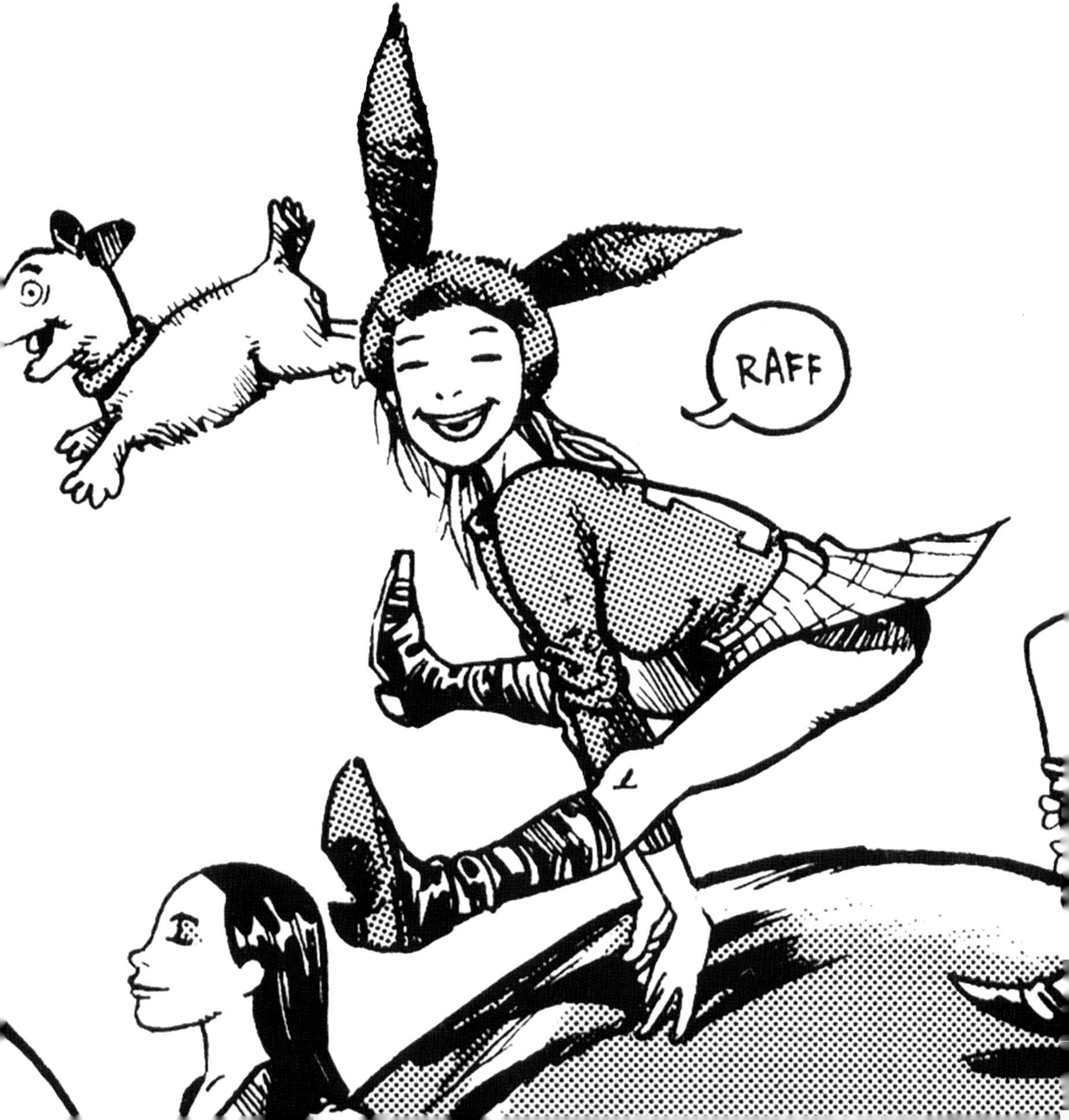
RAFF

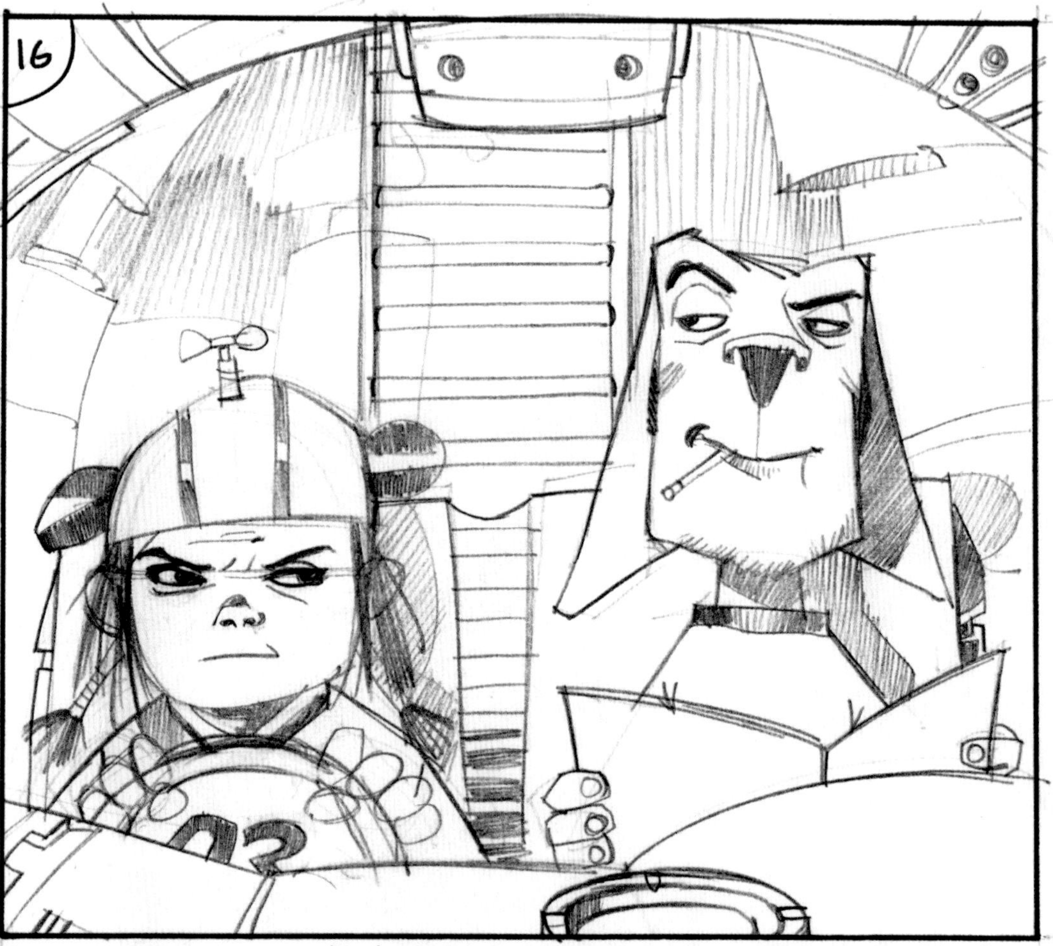
16

INSIDE TANK, OUR FUGITIVES ARE UNAWARE OF THE CARNAGE THEY HAVE CAUSED. TANK GIRL THINKS MAY BE THEY HIT A BUFFALO OR SOMTHING. BOOGA EXPLAINS IT WAS A POLICE BLOCKADE, TANK GIRL ASKS, "ARE THEY STILL COMING AFTER US?"

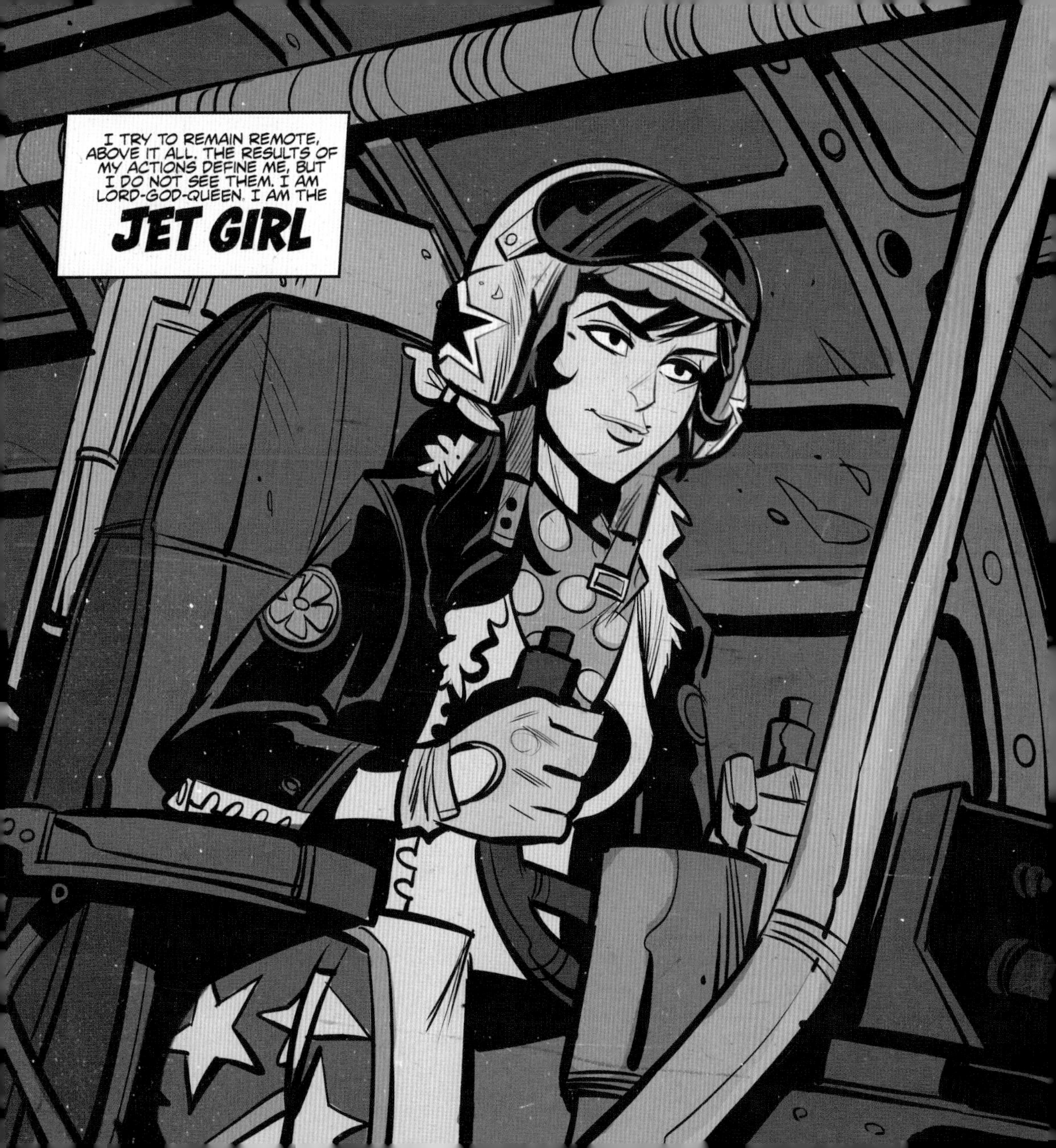
I TRY TO REMAIN REMOTE, ABOVE IT ALL. THE RESULTS OF MY ACTIONS DEFINE ME, BUT I DO NOT SEE THEM. I AM LORD-GOD-QUEEN. I AM THE
JET GIRL

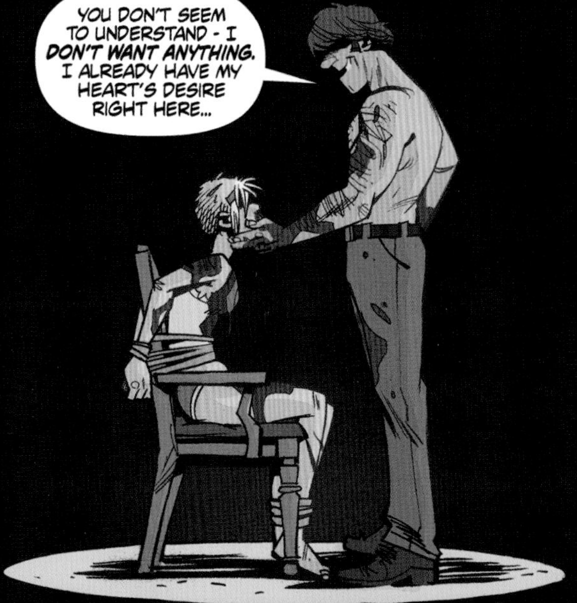
YOU DON'T SEEM TO UNDERSTAND - I DON'T WANT ANYTHING. I ALREADY HAVE MY HEART'S DESIRE RIGHT HERE...

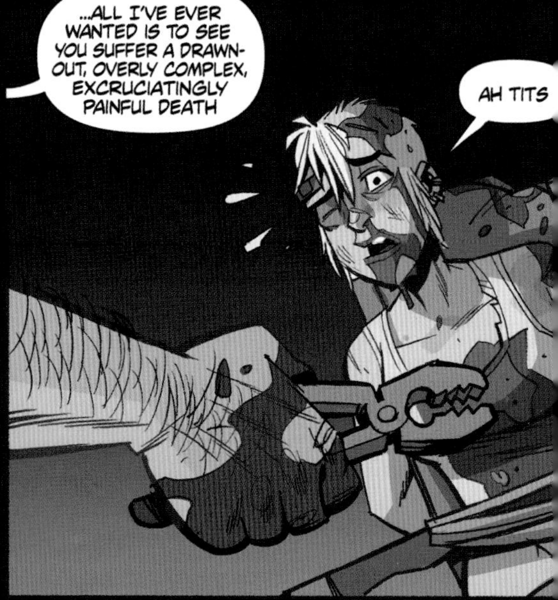
...ALL I'VE EVER WANTED IS TO SEE YOU SUFFER A DRAWN-OUT, OVERLY COMPLEX, EXCRUCIATINGLY PAINFUL DEATH
AH TITS

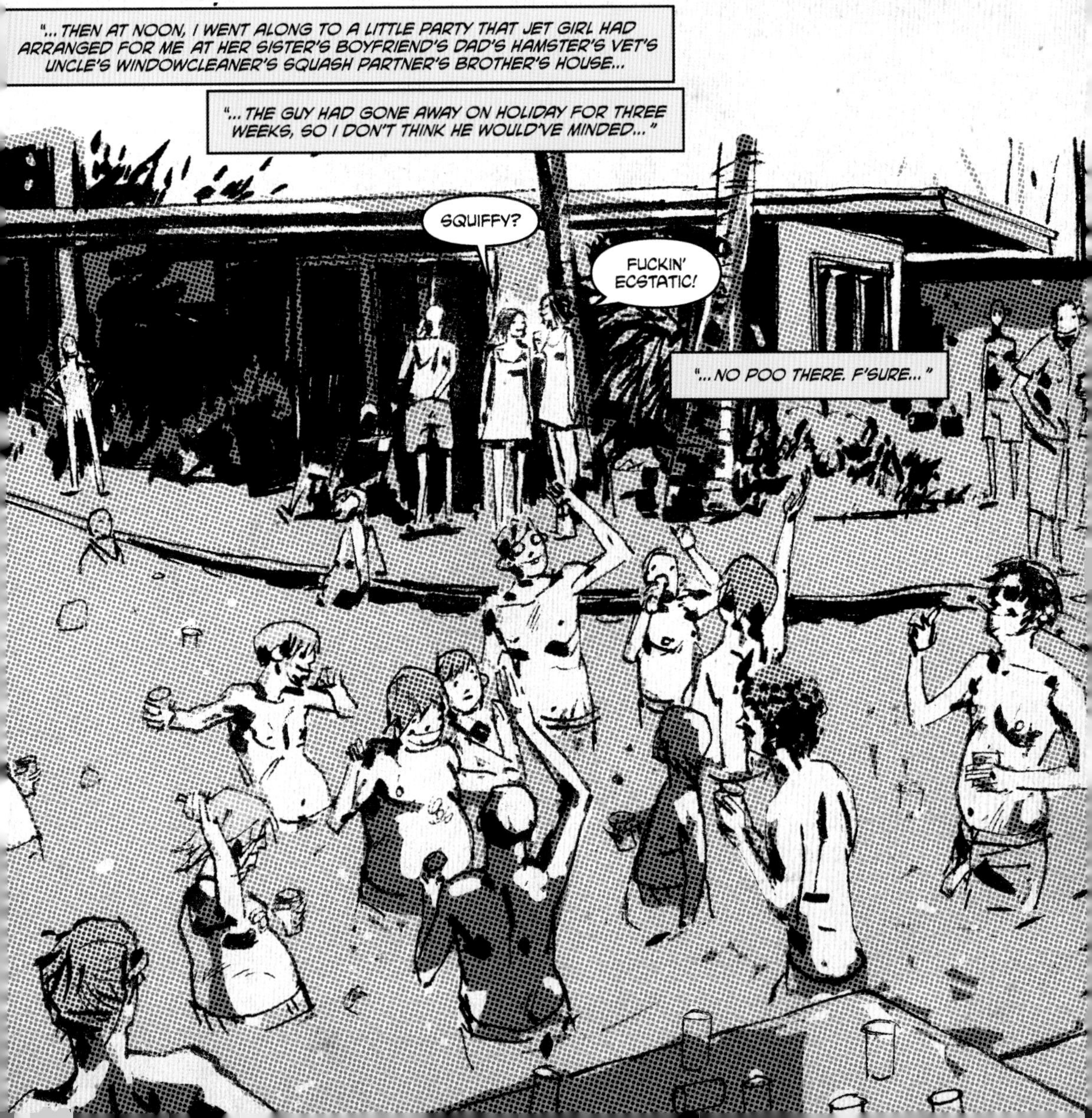
"...THEN AT NOON, I WENT ALONG TO A LITTLE PARTY THAT JET GIRL HAD ARRANGED FOR ME AT HER SISTER'S BOYFRIEND'S DAD'S HAMSTER'S VET'S UNCLE'S WINDOWCLEANER'S SQUASH PARTNER'S BROTHER'S HOUSE...
"...THE GUY HAD GONE AWAY ON HOLIDAY FOR THREE WEEKS, SO I DON'T THINK HE WOULD'VE MINDED..."
SQUIFFY?
FUCKIN' ECSTATIC!
"...NO POO THERE. F'SURE..."

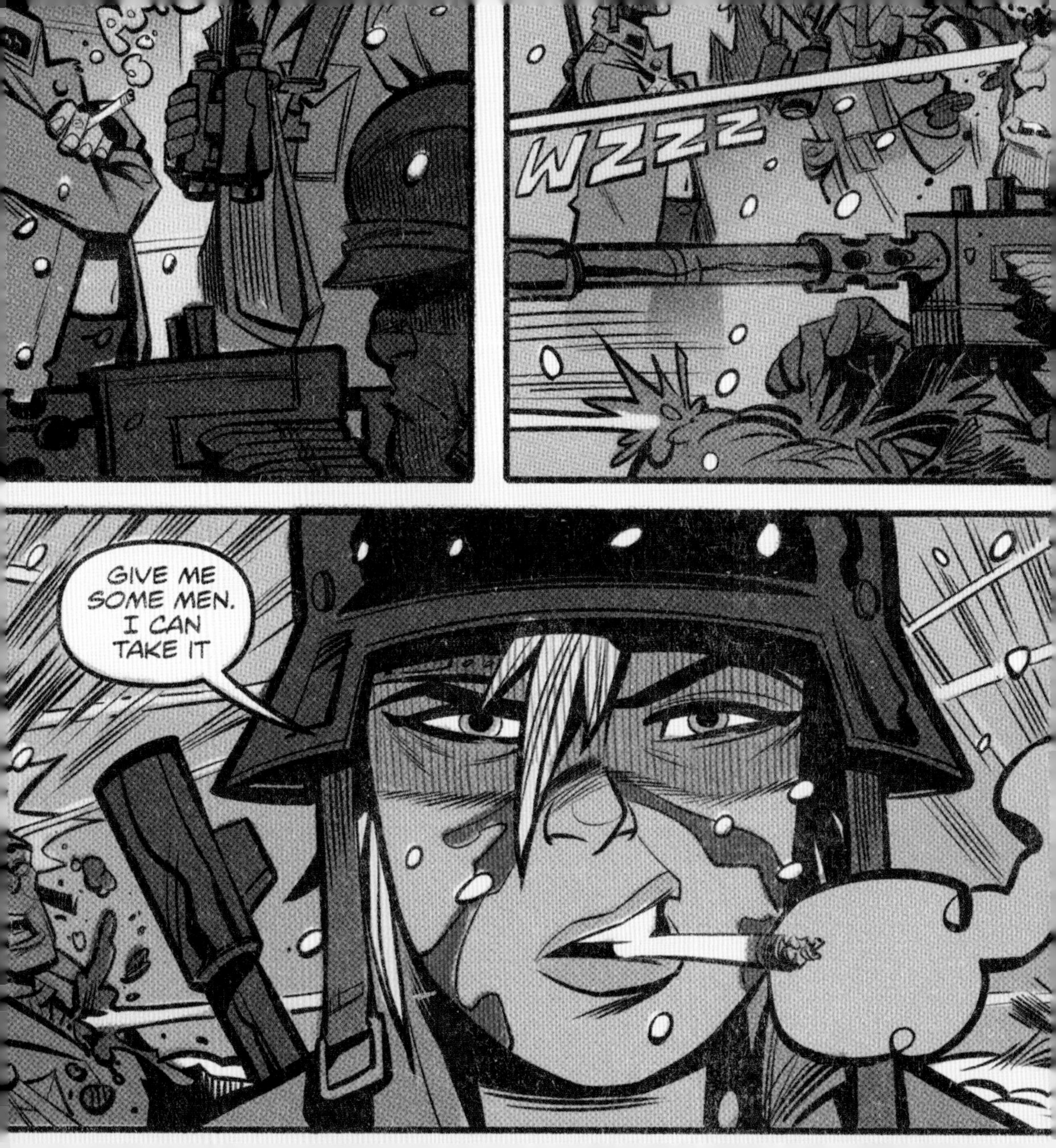
WZZZ
GIVE ME SOME MEN. I CAN TAKE IT

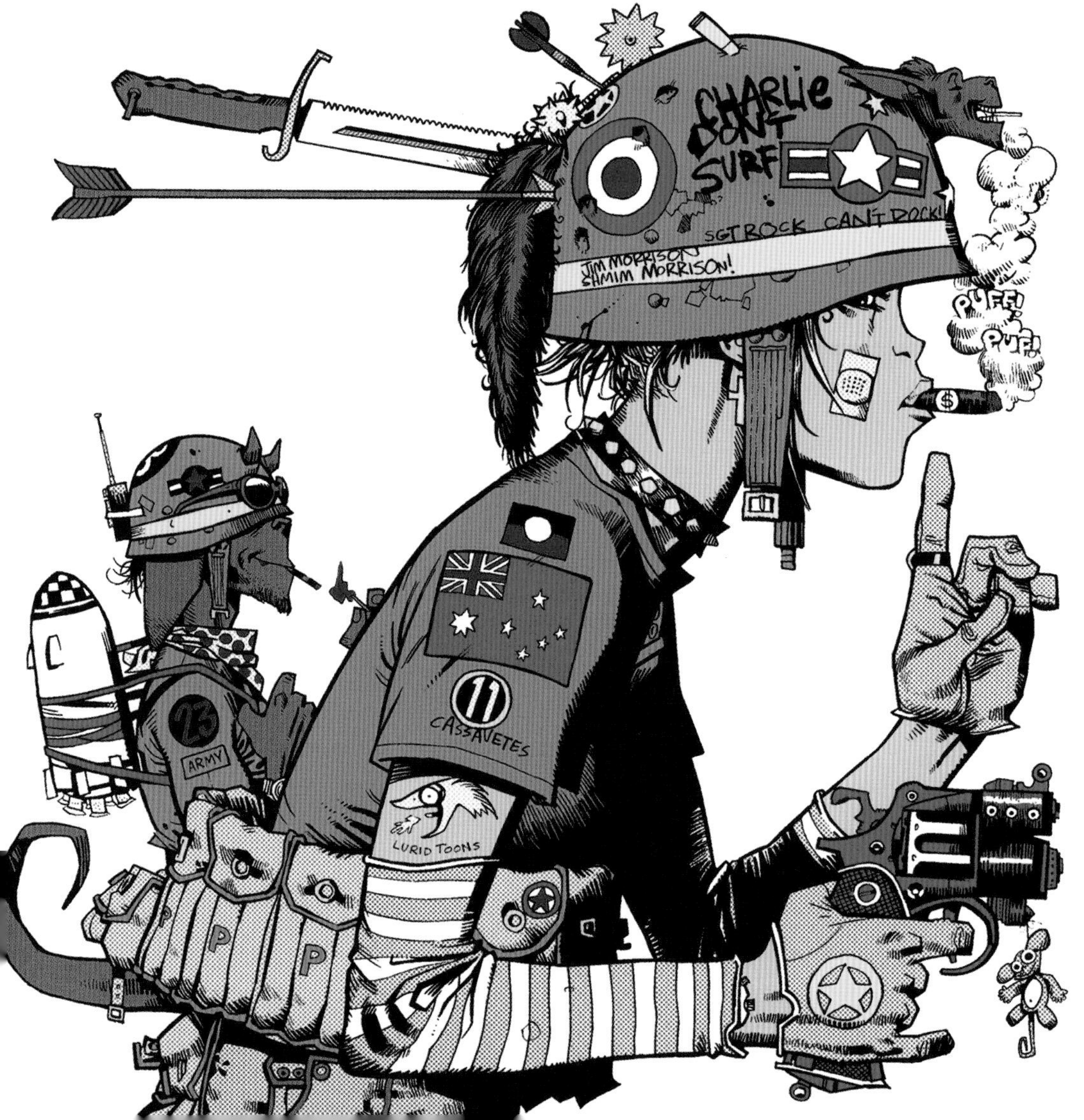

CHARLIE DONT SURF
SGT ROCK CAN'T ROCK!
JIM MORRISON SHMIM MORRISON!
PUFF!
PUFF!
11
CASSAVETES
23
ARMY
LURID TOONS

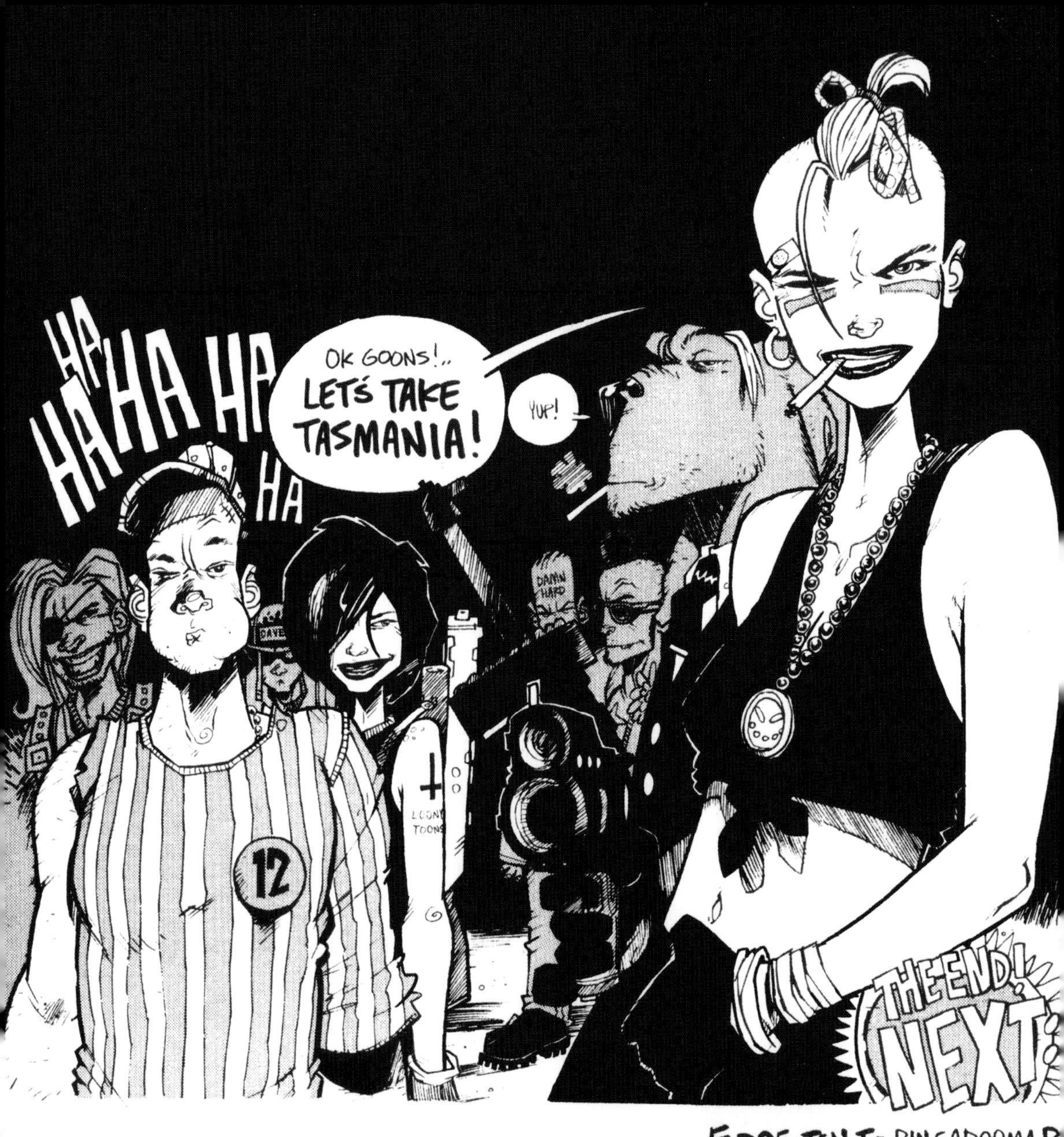
HA HA HA HA HA HA
OK GOONS!.. LET'S TAKE TASMANIA!
YUP!
THE END!
NEXT

FORCE TEN TO RINGAROOMA B

E - Tank Girl

AR SIGN - Crabby

AVOURITE FOOD - Pastry

BEST CHRISTMAS PRESENT EVER -
Escape from Colditz Dress-Up Kit

FAVOURITE FAMILY MEMBER -
My Mum, stupid but strong

TOP OF THE POPS -
Primitive Painters by FELT

IDEAL DAY OUT -
Cooked breakfast in bed, Long walk in the countryside, Lunch at the club, Croquet, Cream tea, Cocktails Dinner by the sea Drinkies, more drinkies, Waking up in a dumpster with someone else's pants on my head

IDOL - David Niven

BEST ITEM OF CLOTHING -
Noddy Holder's string vest

ANY ADDITIONAL INFORMATION -
Don't like the smell of potatoes

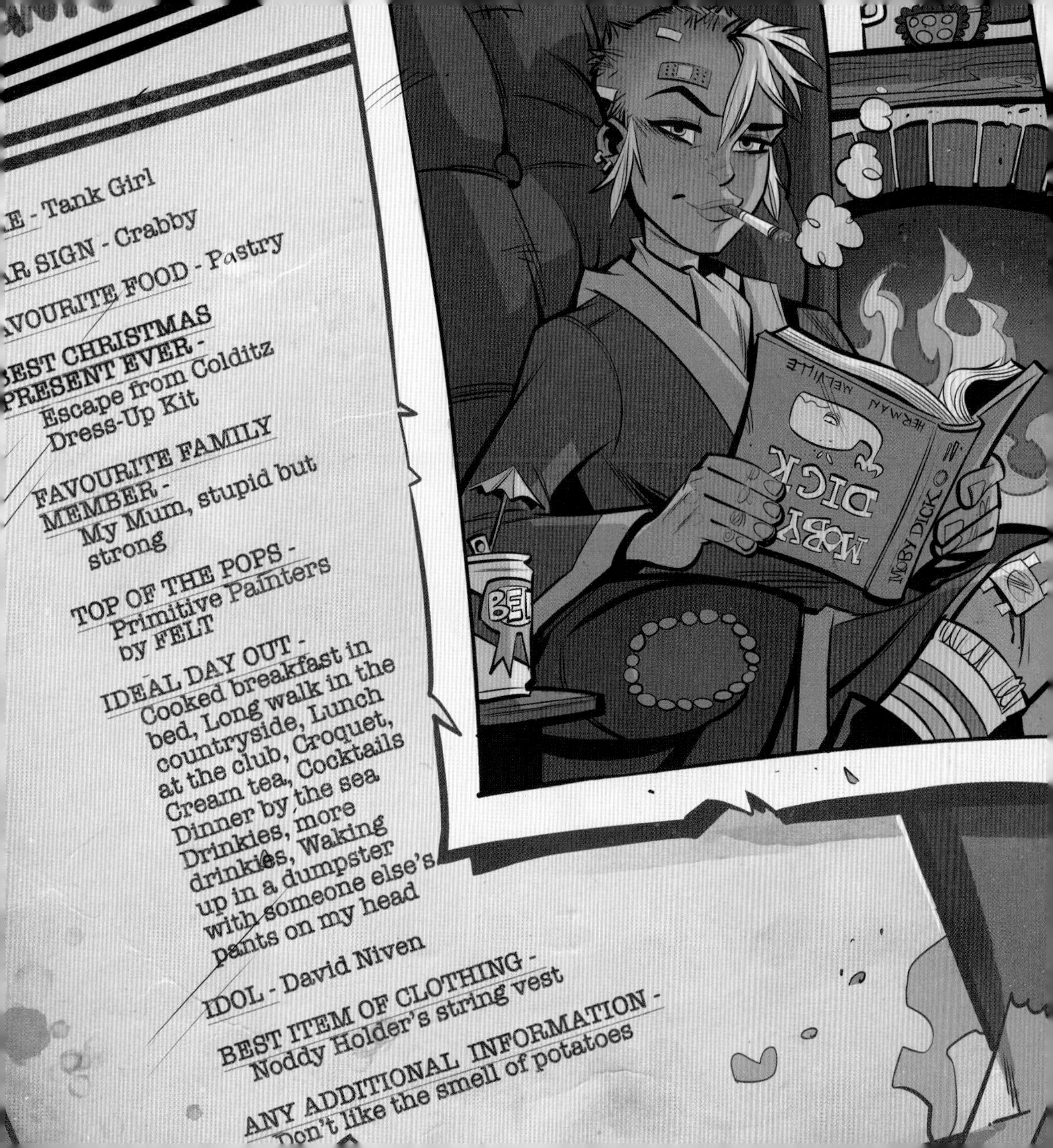
MOBY DICK
HERMAN MELVILLE
MOBY DICK

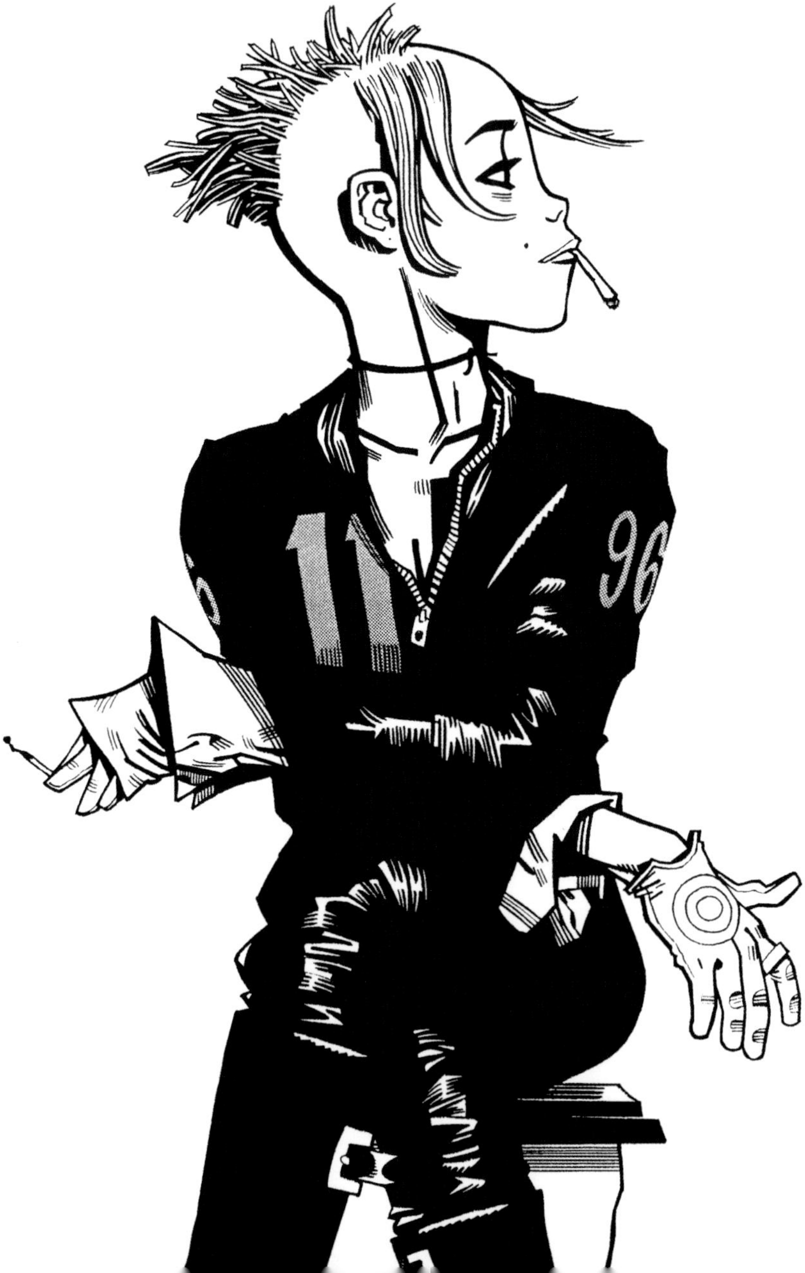

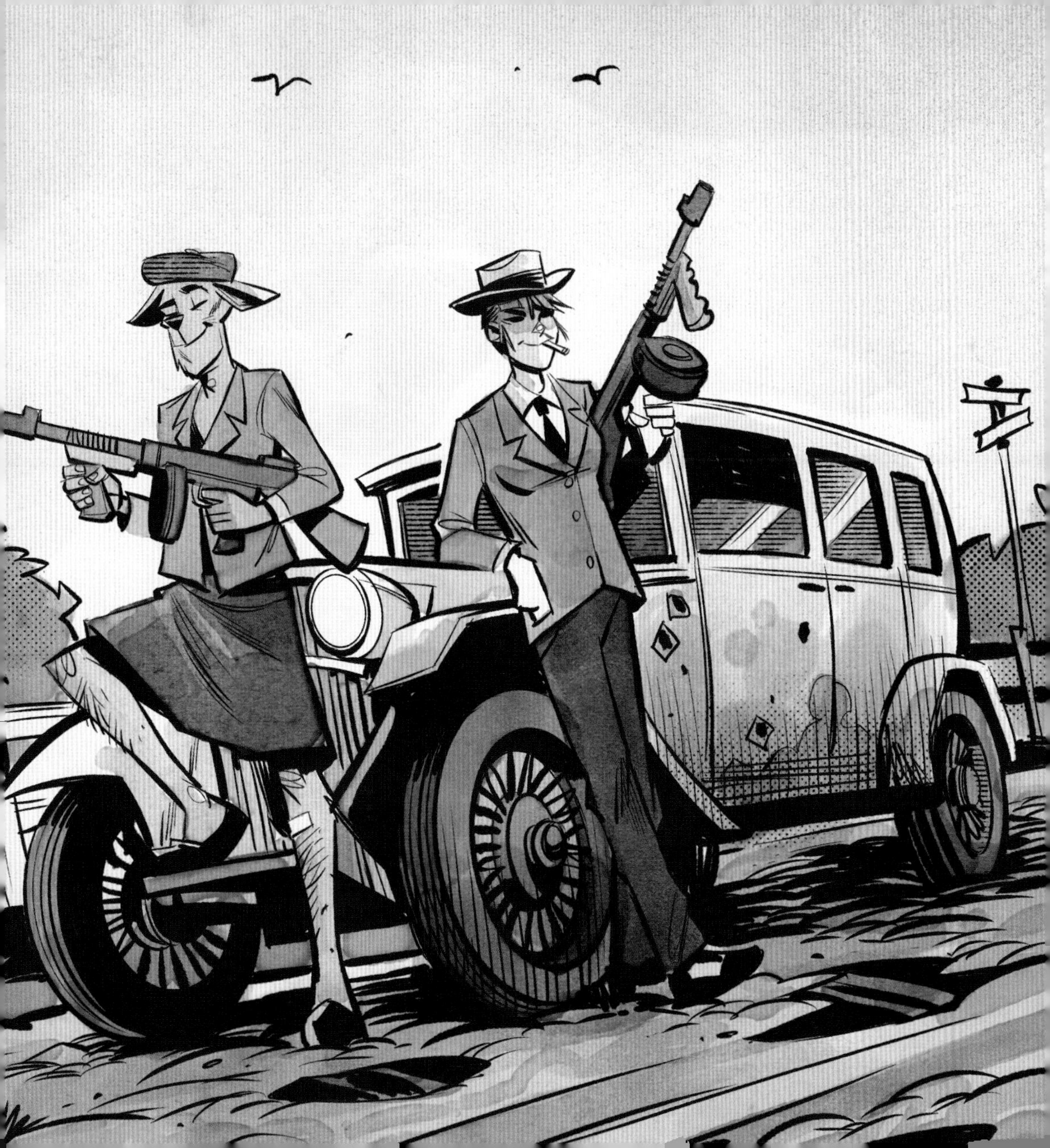

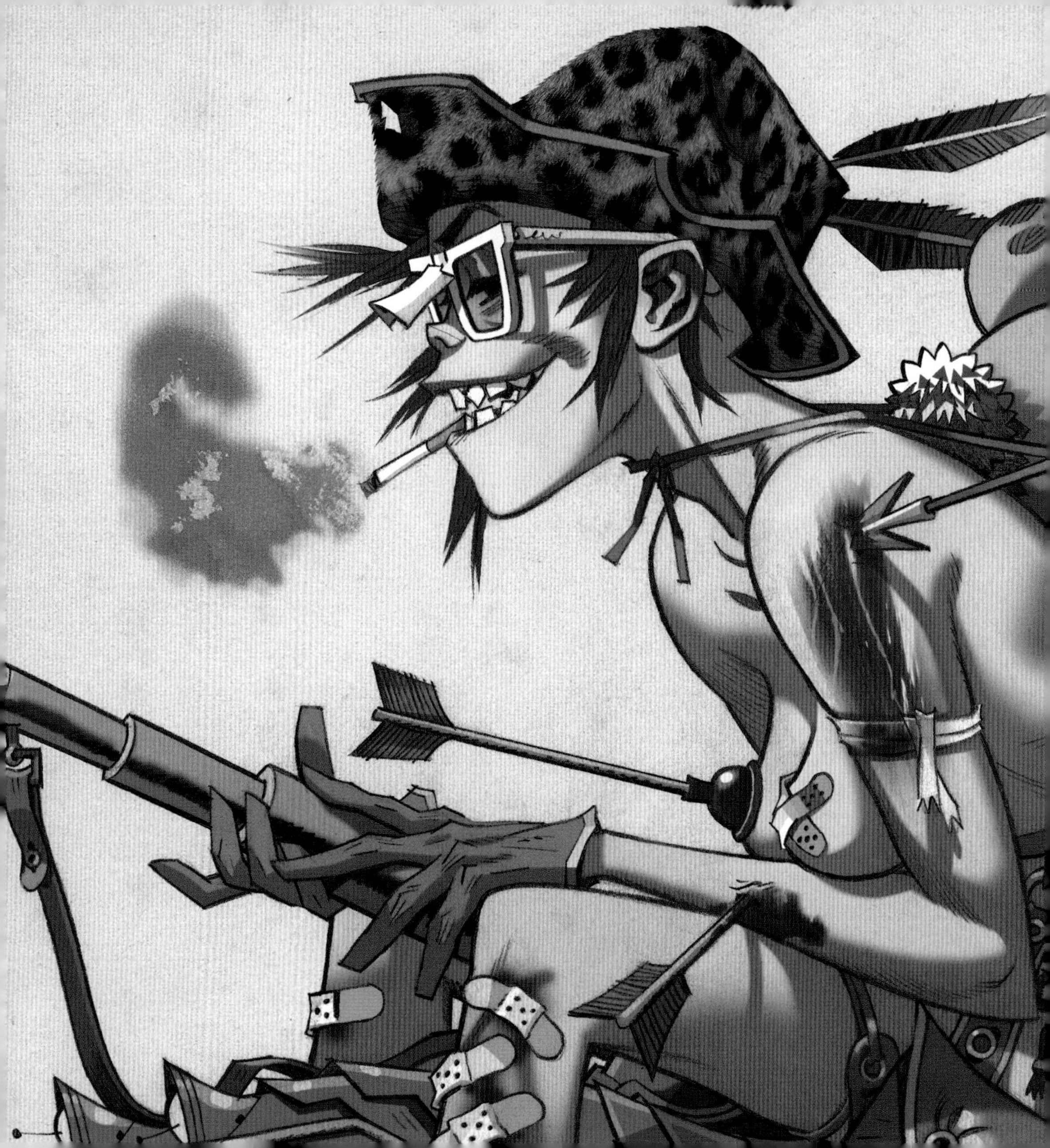

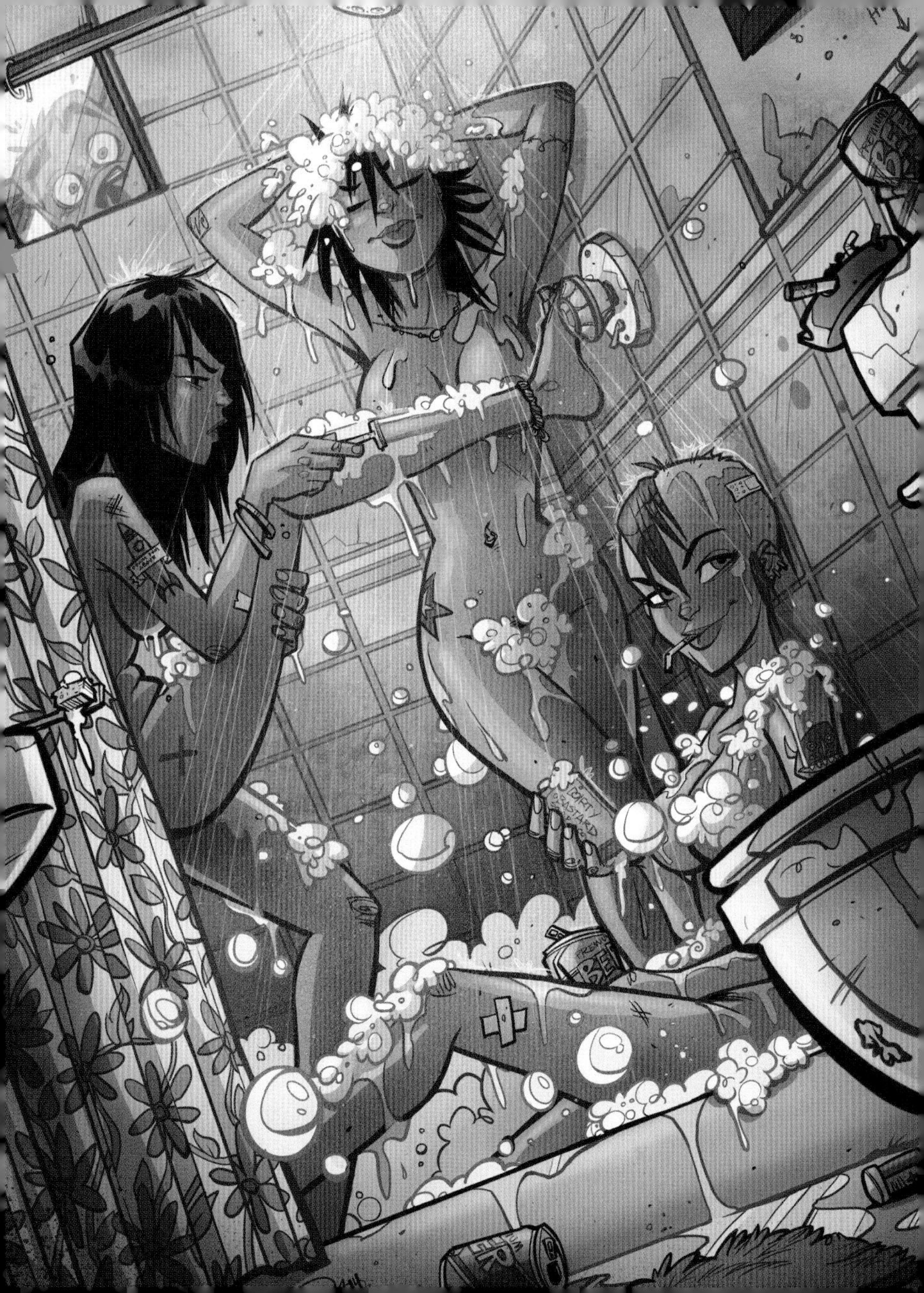
DIRTY
BASTARD

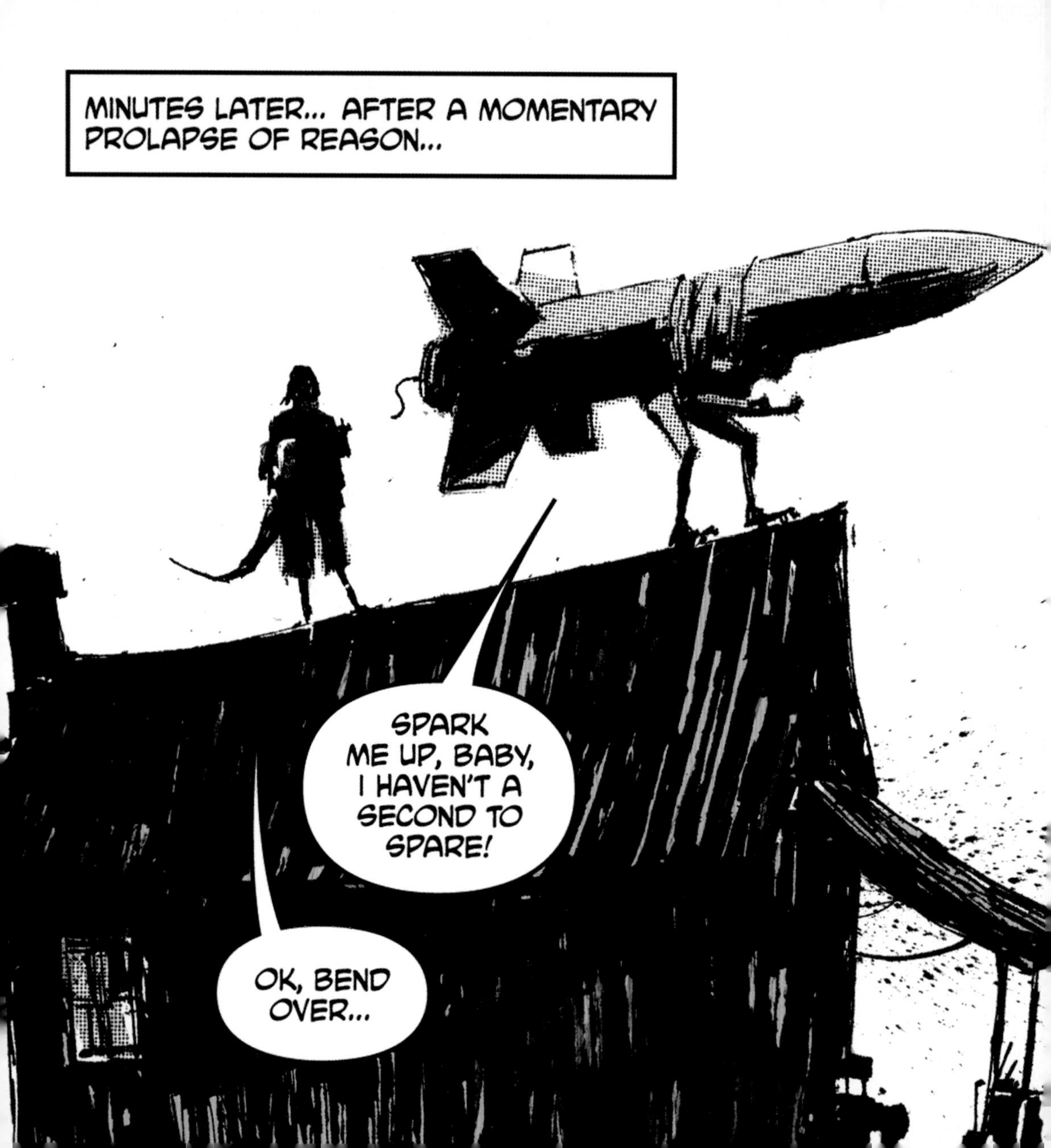
MINUTES LATER... AFTER A MOMENTARY PROLAPSE OF REASON...
SPARK ME UP, BABY, I HAVEN'T A SECOND TO SPARE!
OK, BEND OVER...

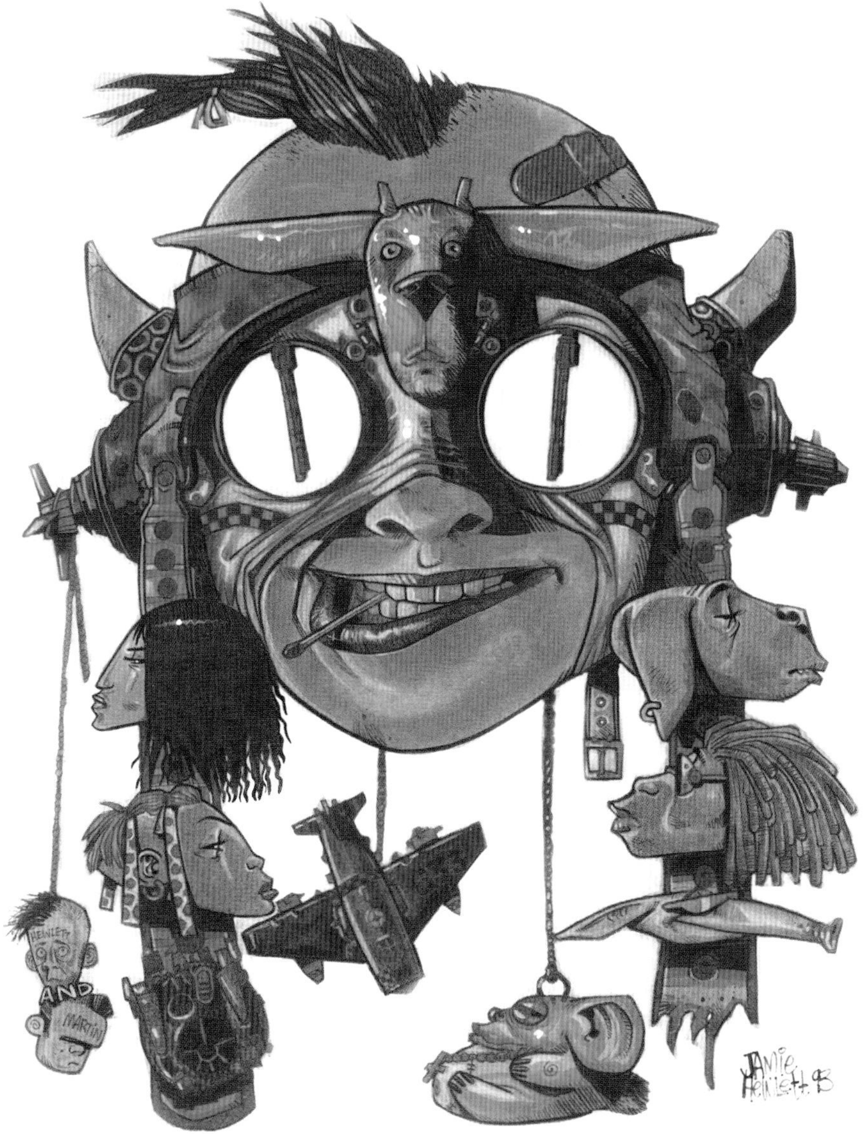
HEWLETT
AND
MARTIN
JAMIE HEWLETT 93

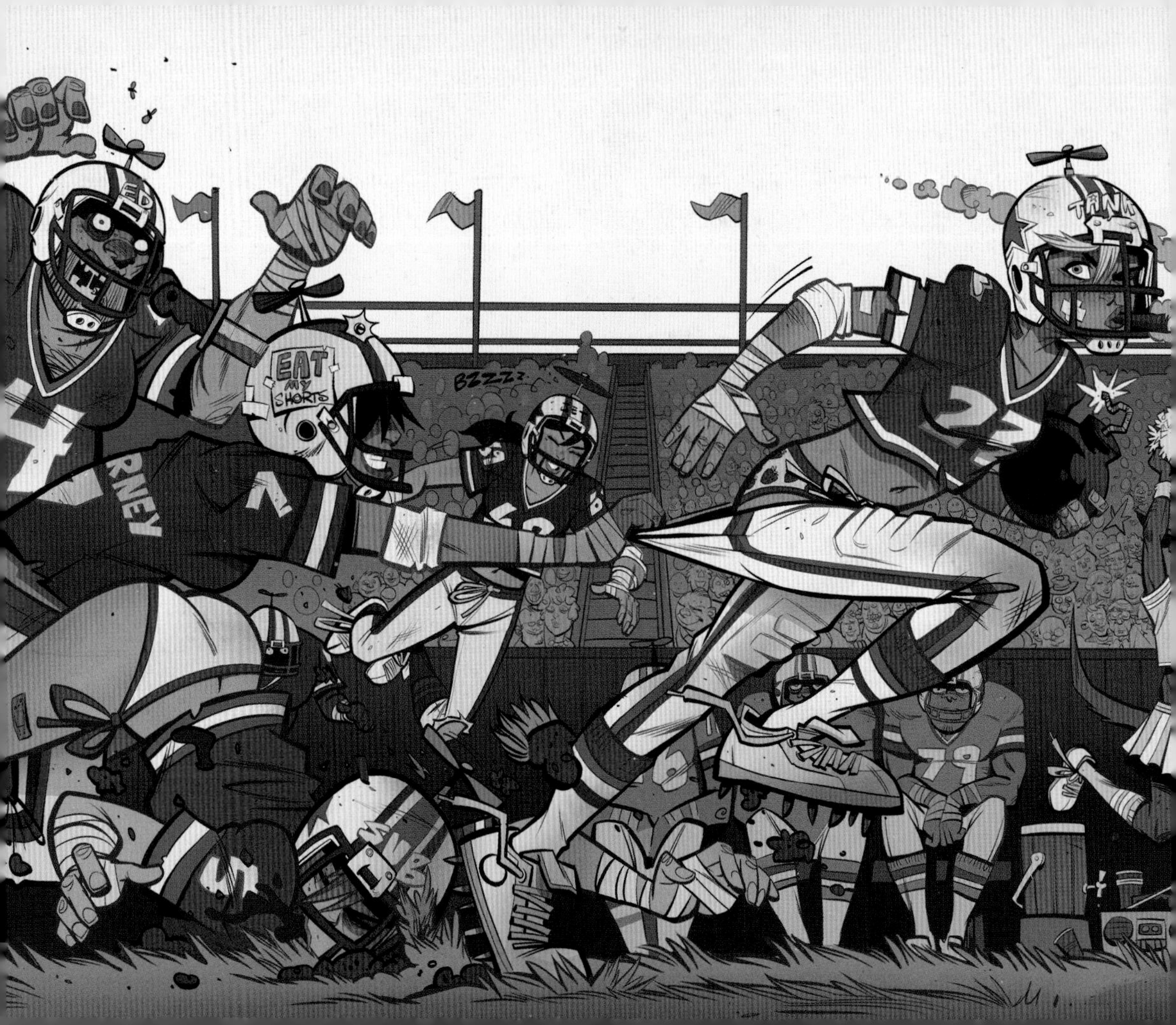
EAT MY SHORTS
BZZZZ
TANK
RNEY

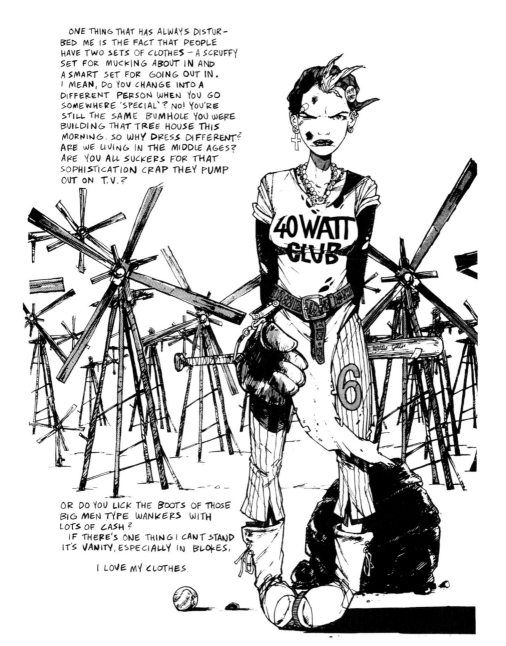

ONE THING THAT HAS ALWAYS DISTUR-
BED ME IS THE FACT THAT PEOPLE
HAVE TWO SETS OF CLOTHES — A SCRUFFY
SET FOR MUCKING ABOUT IN AND
A SMART SET FOR GOING OUT IN.
I MEAN, DO YOU CHANGE INTO A
DIFFERENT PERSON WHEN YOU GO
SOMEWHERE 'SPECIAL'? NO! YOU'RE
STILL THE SAME BUMHOLE YOU WERE
BUILDING THAT TREE HOUSE THIS
MORNING. SO WHY DRESS DIFFERENT?
ARE WE LIVING IN THE MIDDLE AGES?
ARE YOU ALL SUCKERS FOR THAT
SOPHISTICATION CRAP THEY PUMP
OUT ON T.V.?

OR DO YOU LICK THE BOOTS OF THOSE
BIG MEN TYPE WANKERS WITH
LOTS OF CASH?
  IF THERE'S ONE THING I CAN'T STAND
IT'S VANITY, ESPECIALLY IN BLOKES.

  I LOVE MY CLOTHES.

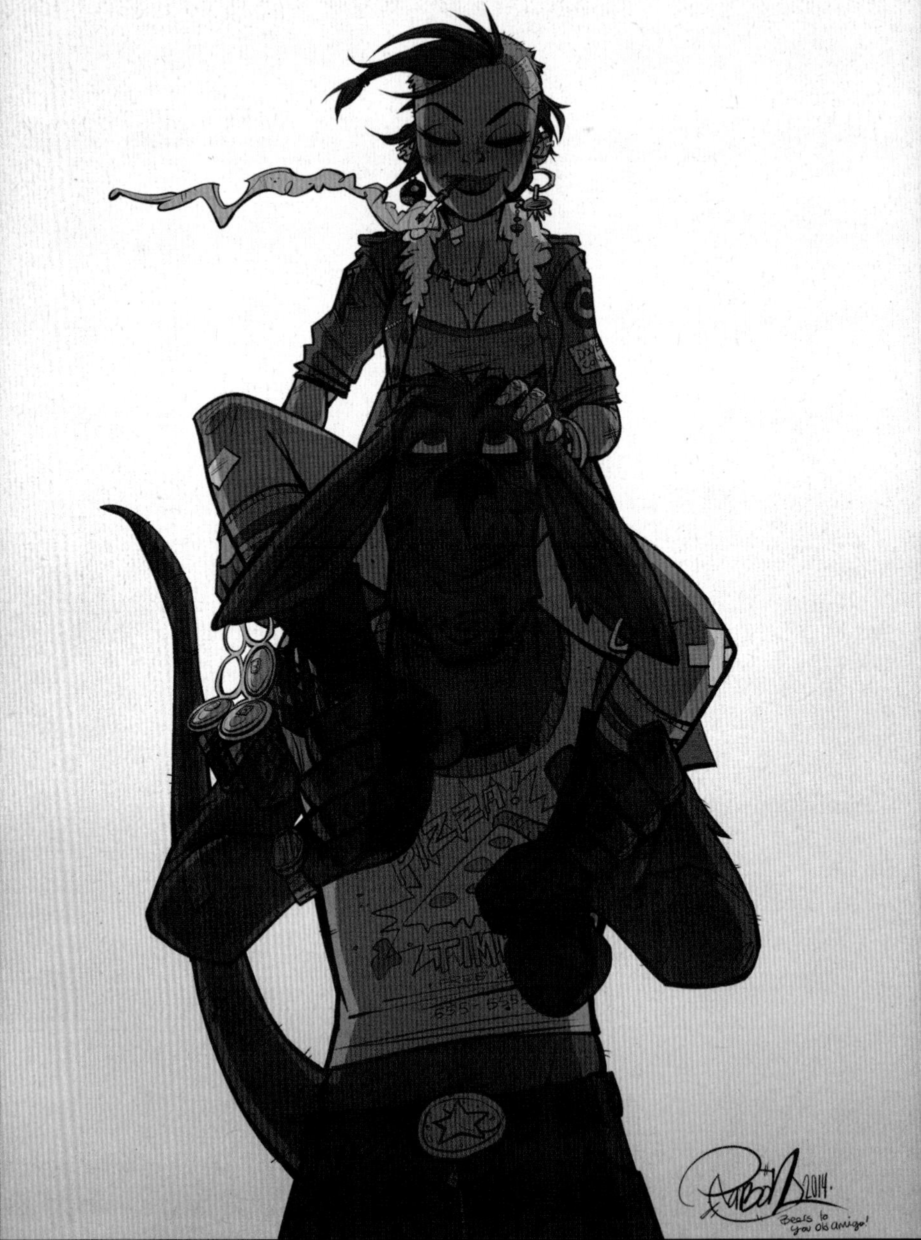
2014.
Beers to you old amigo!

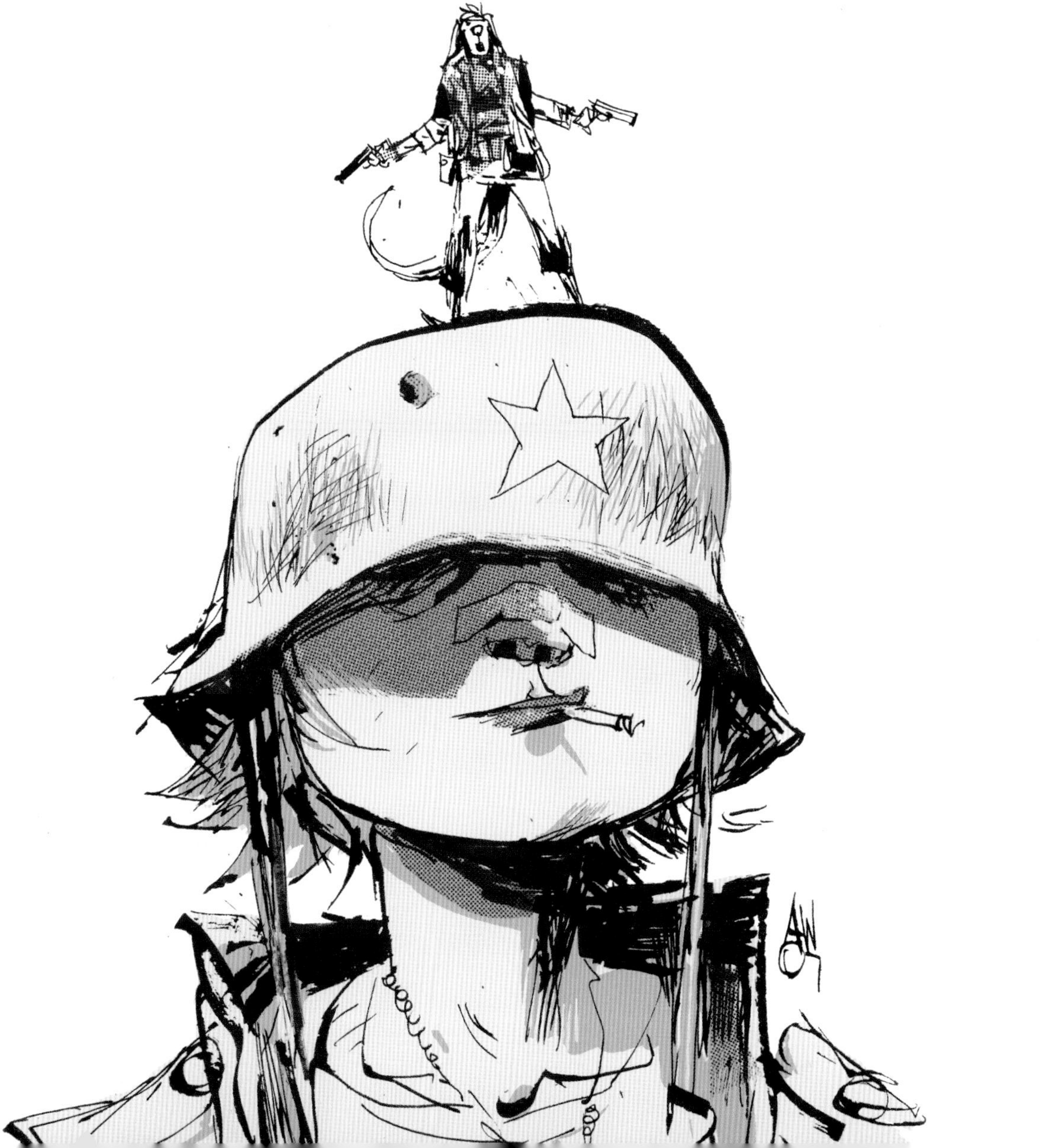

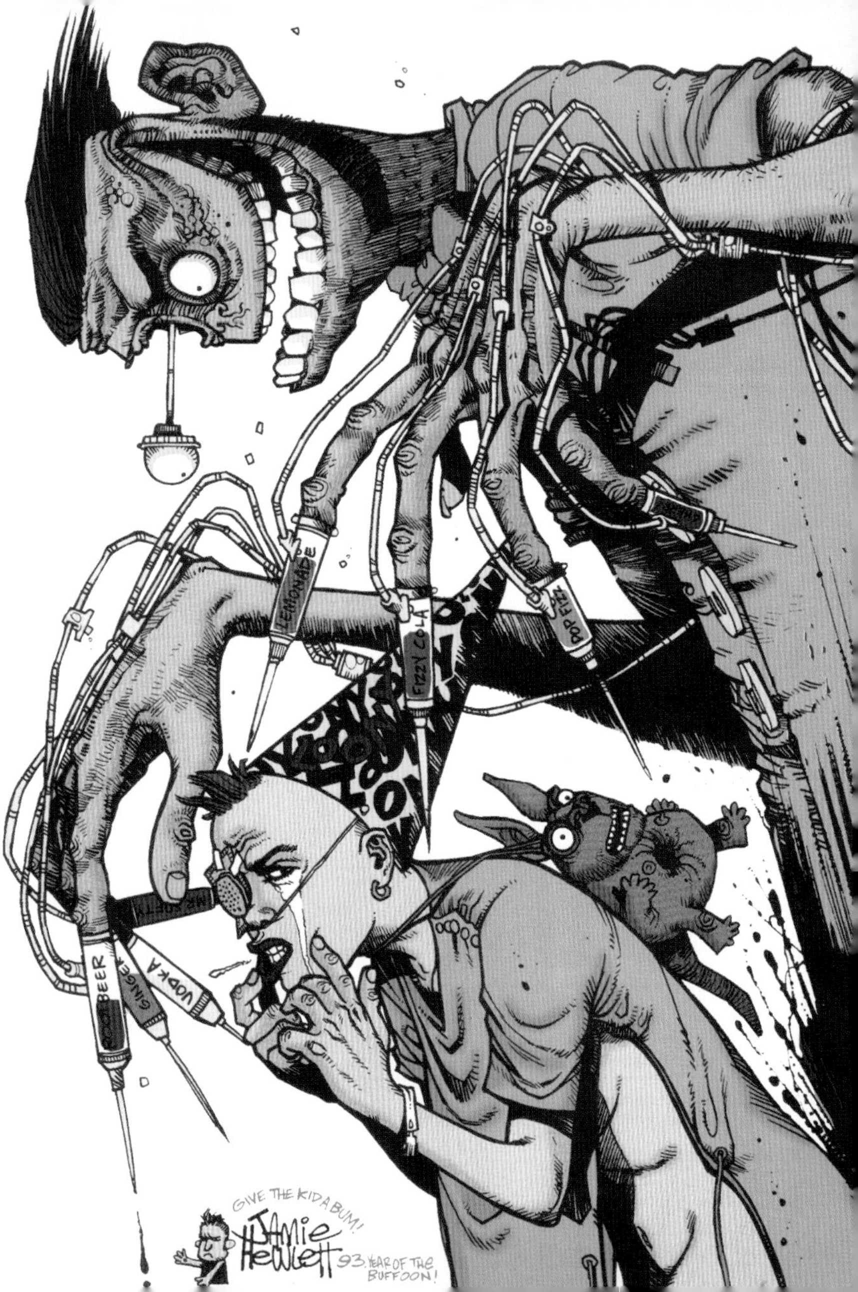
LEMONADE
FIZZY COLA
POP FIZZ
BEER
GINGER
VODKA
GIVE THE KID A BUM!
Jamie Hewlett
93. YEAR OF THE BUFFOON!

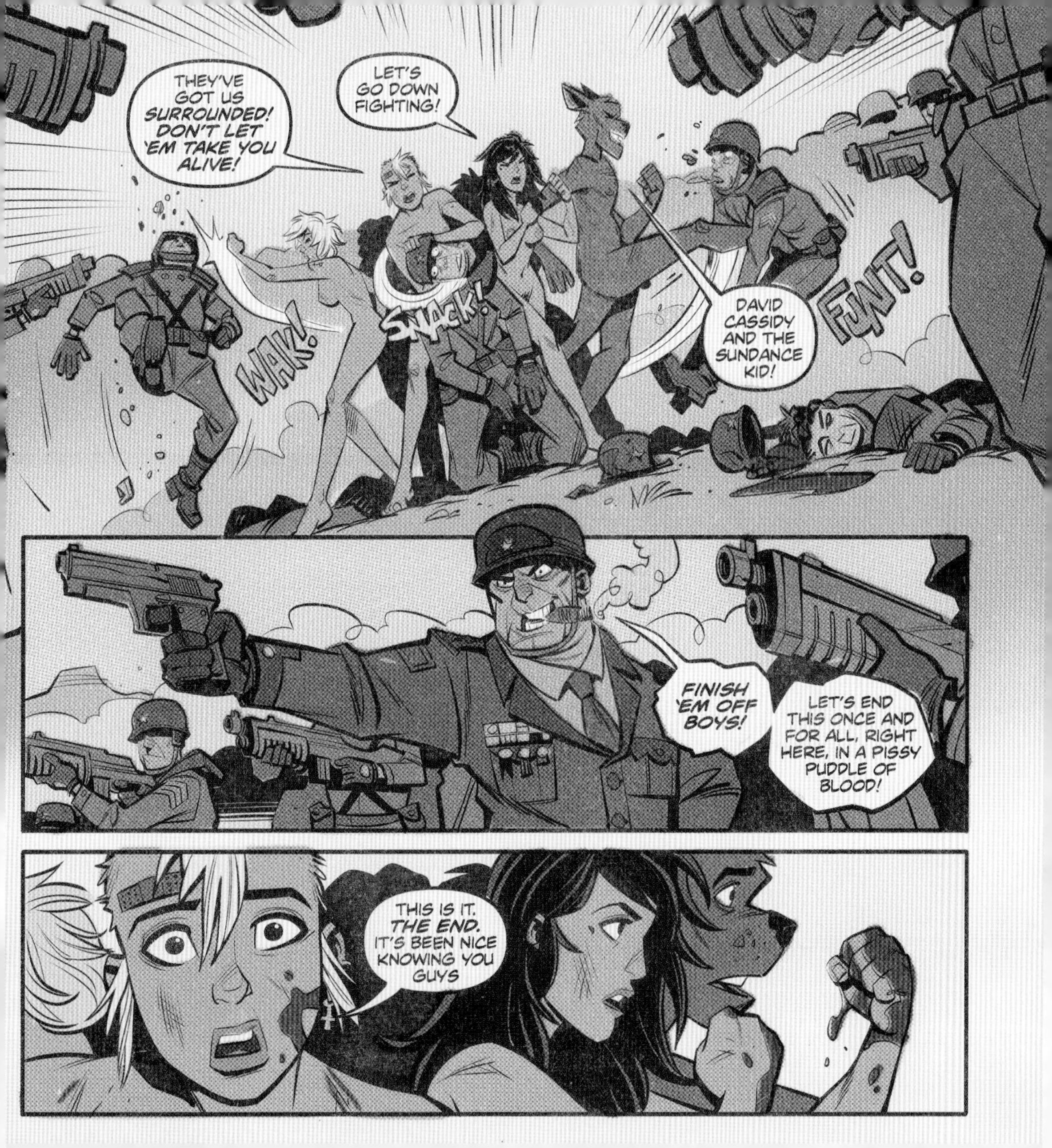
THEY'VE GOT US SURROUNDED! DON'T LET 'EM TAKE YOU ALIVE!
LET'S GO DOWN FIGHTING!
WAK!
SMACK!
DAVID CASSIDY AND THE SUNDANCE KID!
FJNT!
FINISH 'EM OFF BOYS!
LET'S END THIS ONCE AND FOR ALL, RIGHT HERE, IN A PISSY PUDDLE OF BLOOD!
THIS IS IT. THE END. IT'S BEEN NICE KNOWING YOU GUYS

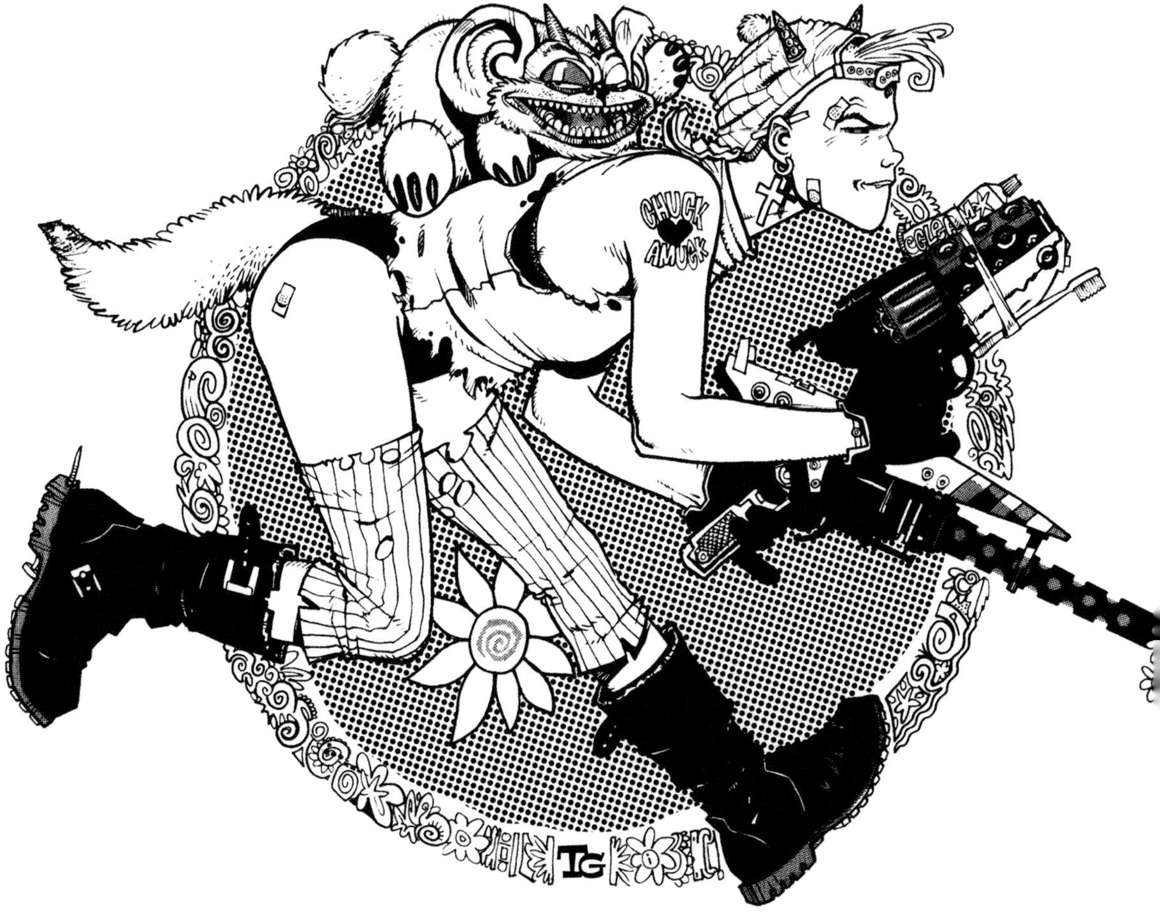
CHUCK
AMUCK
TG

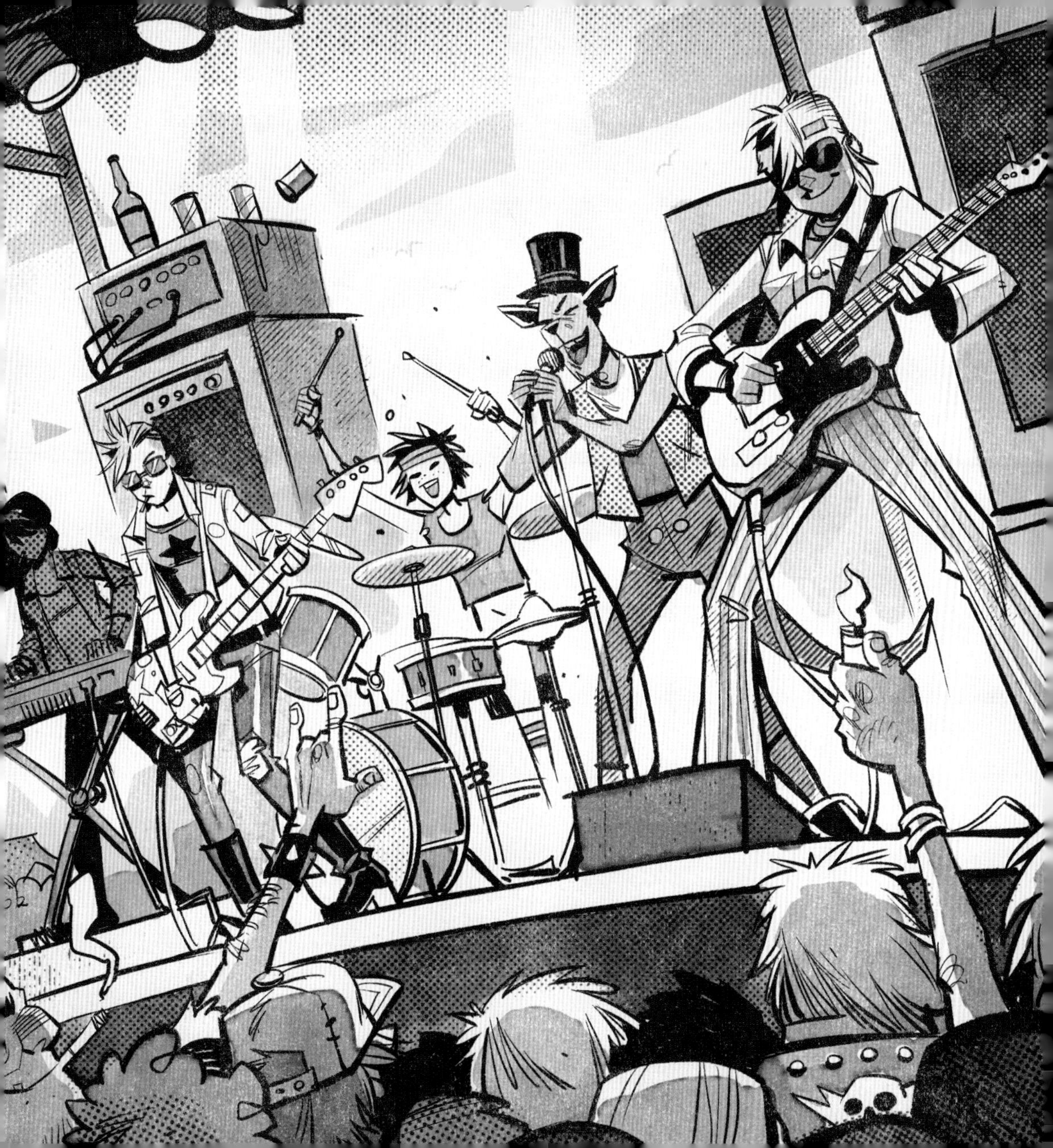

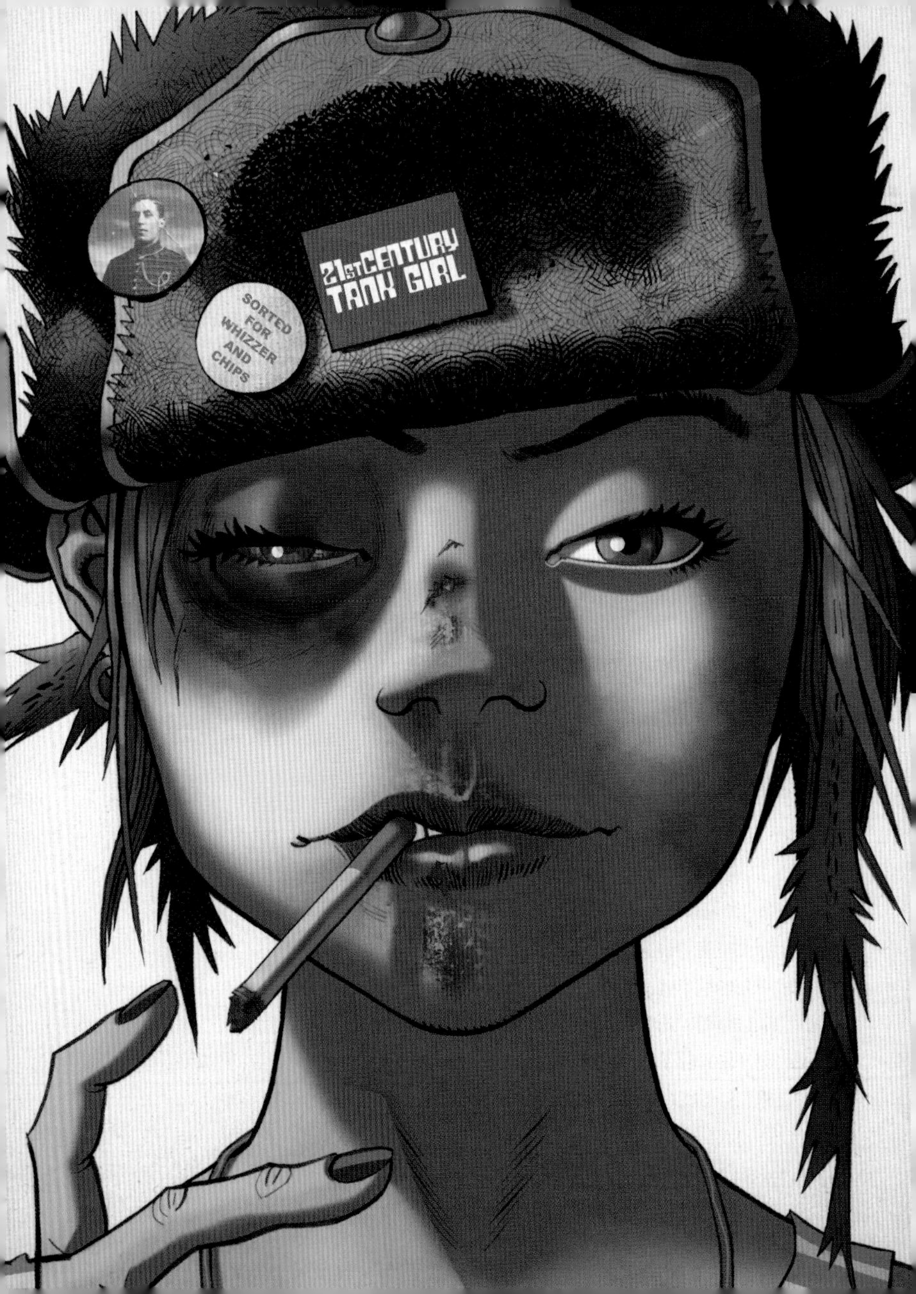
21st CENTURY TANK GIRL
SORTED FOR WHIZZER AND CHIPS

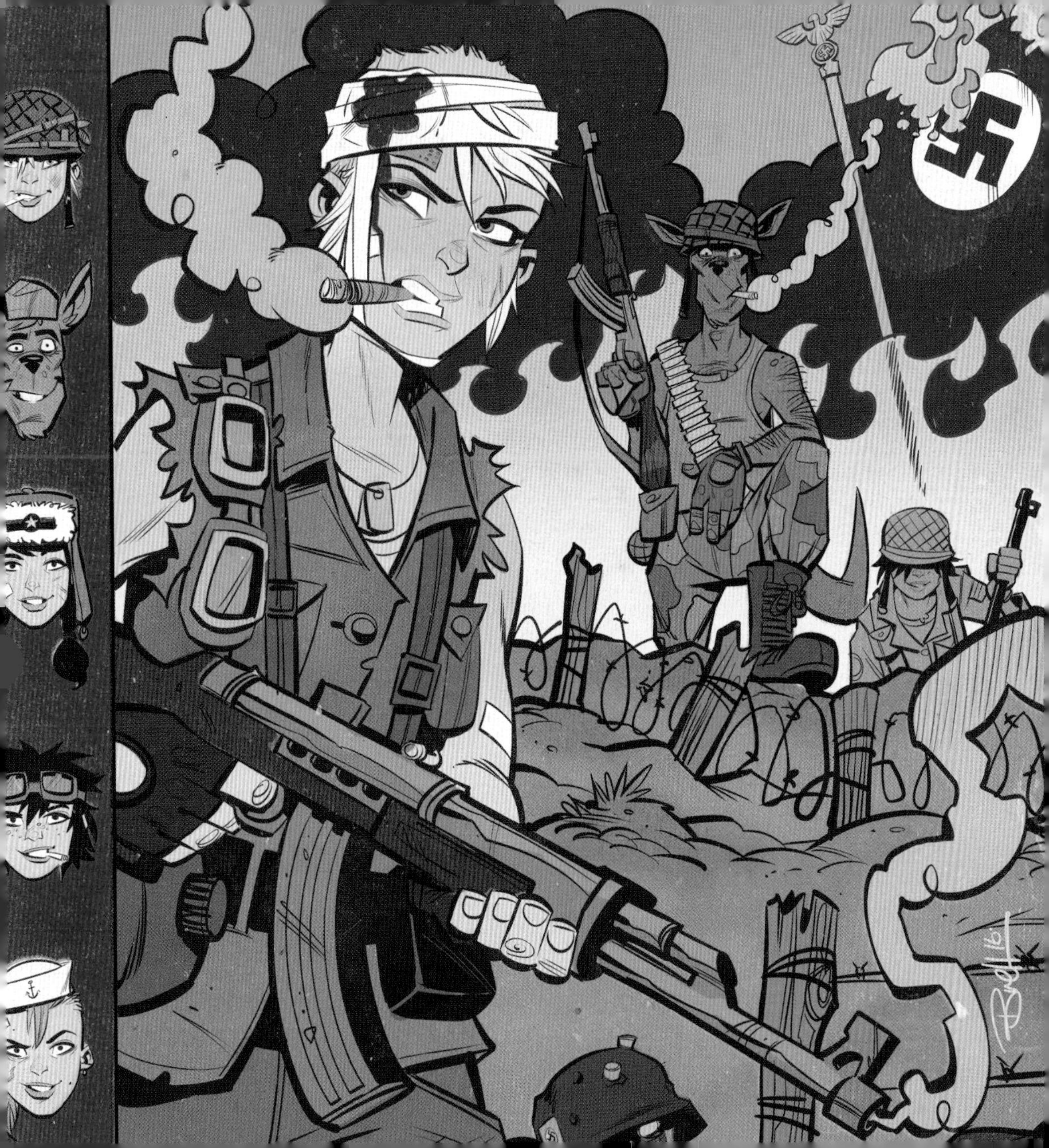

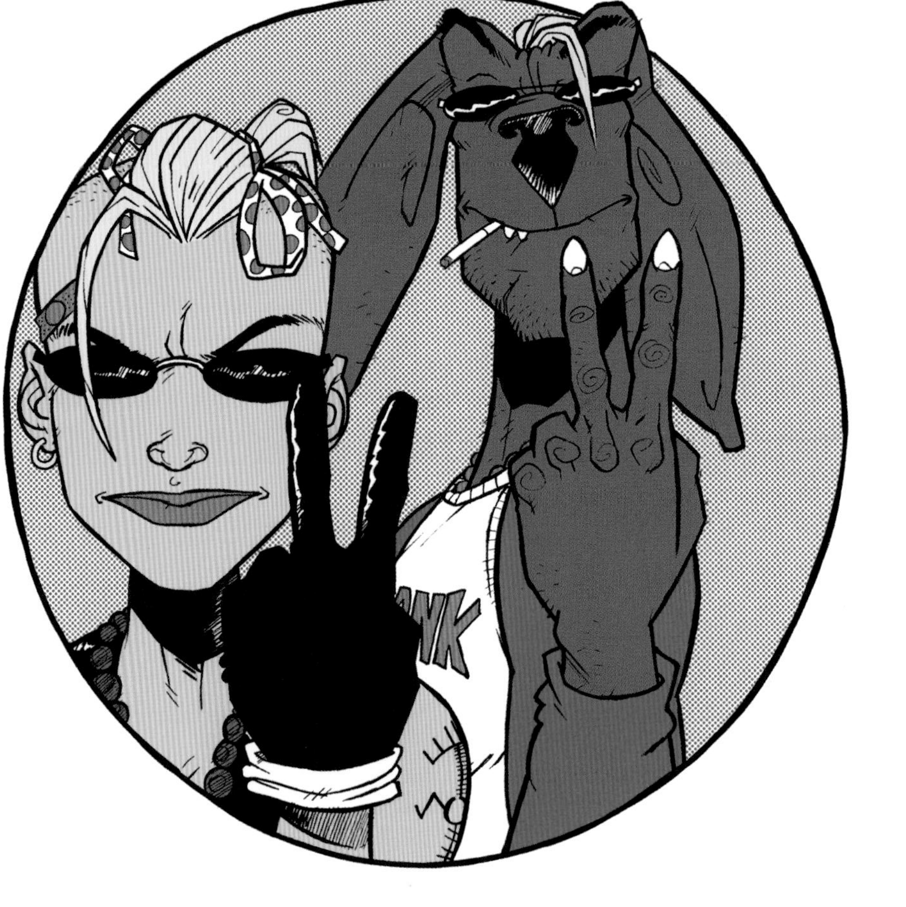

“The less I know, the stronger I am”

- Booga

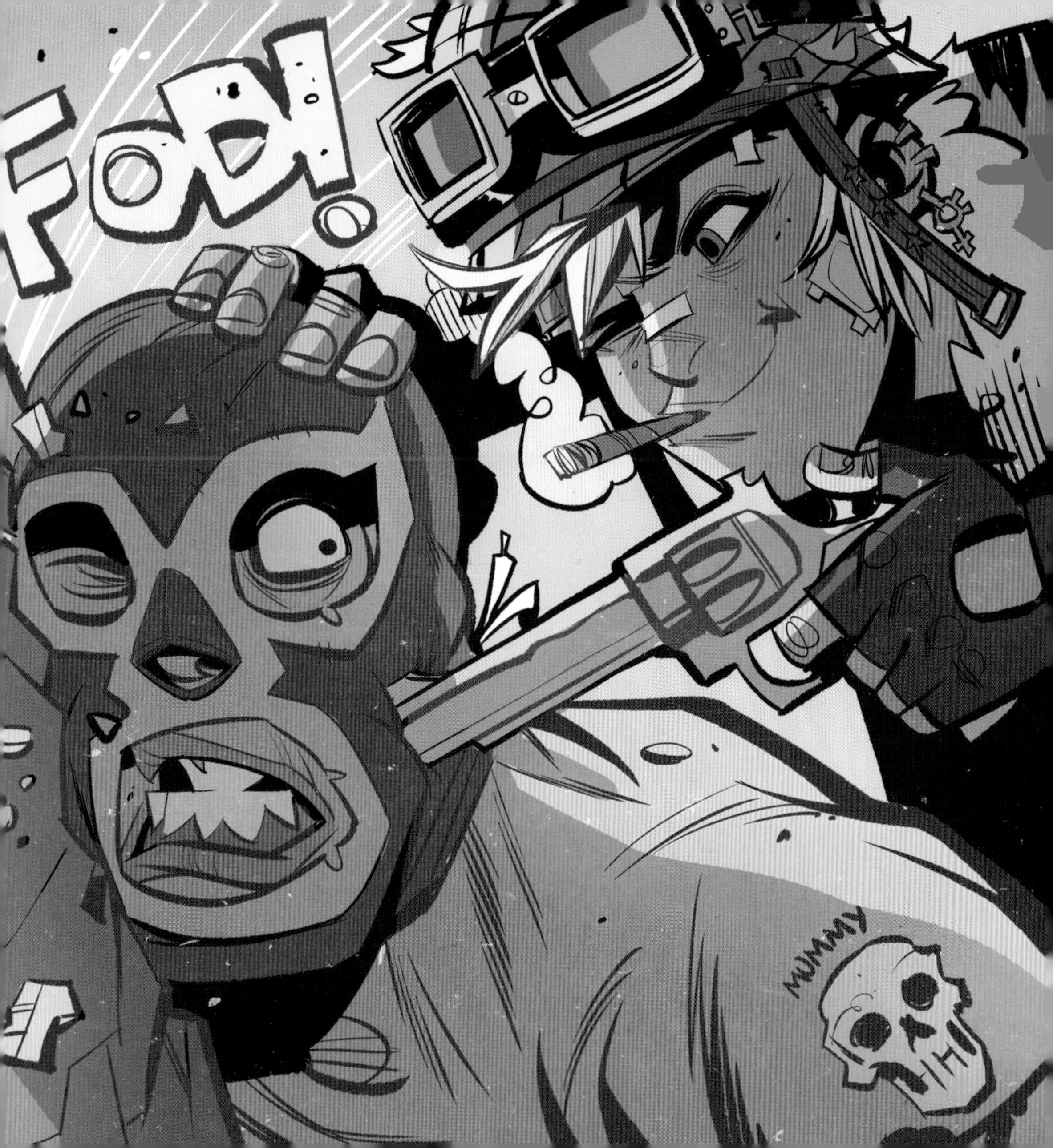
POW!
MUMMY

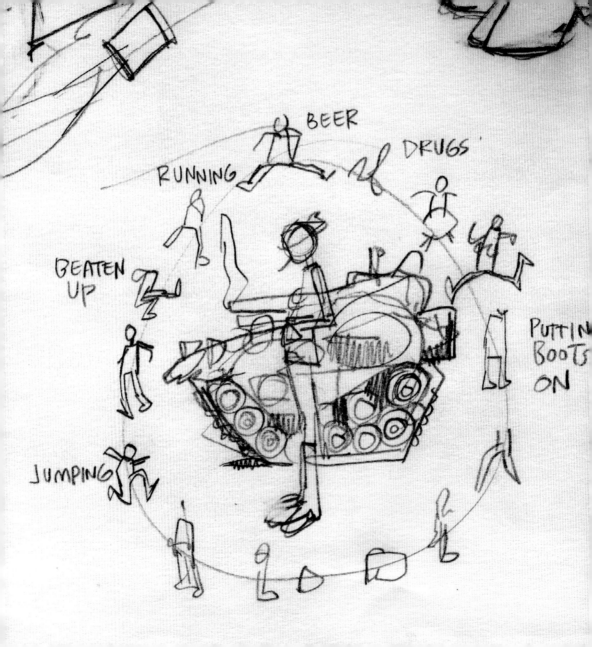

BEER

DRUGS

RUNNING

BEATEN
UP

PUTTIN'
BOOTS
ON

JUMPING

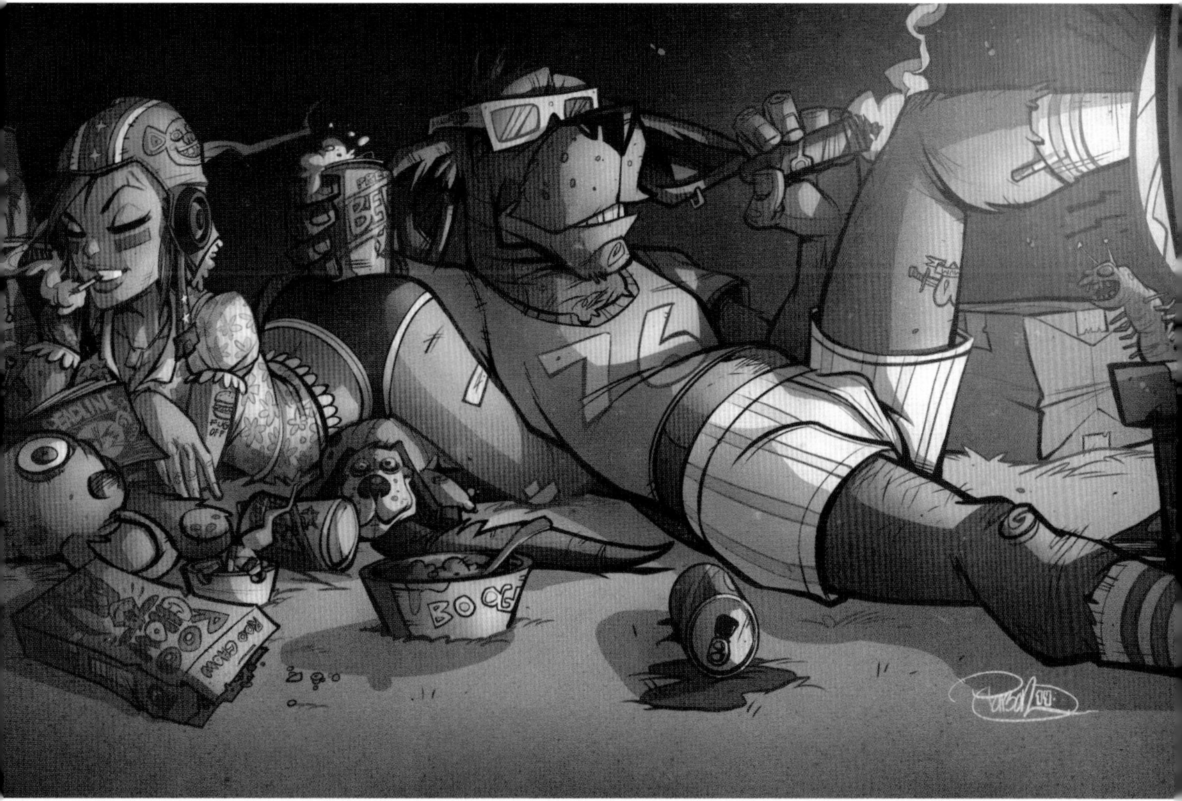

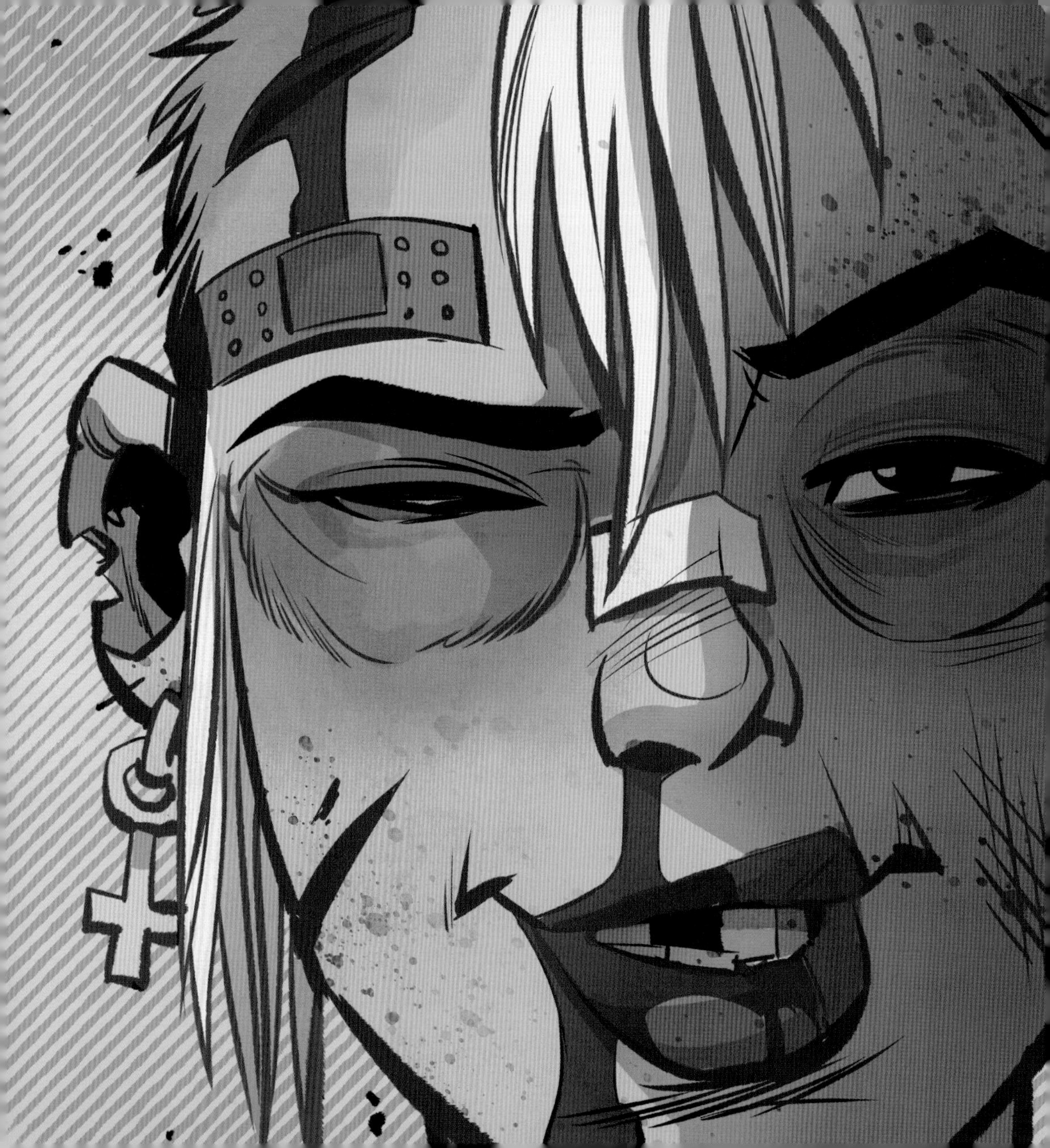

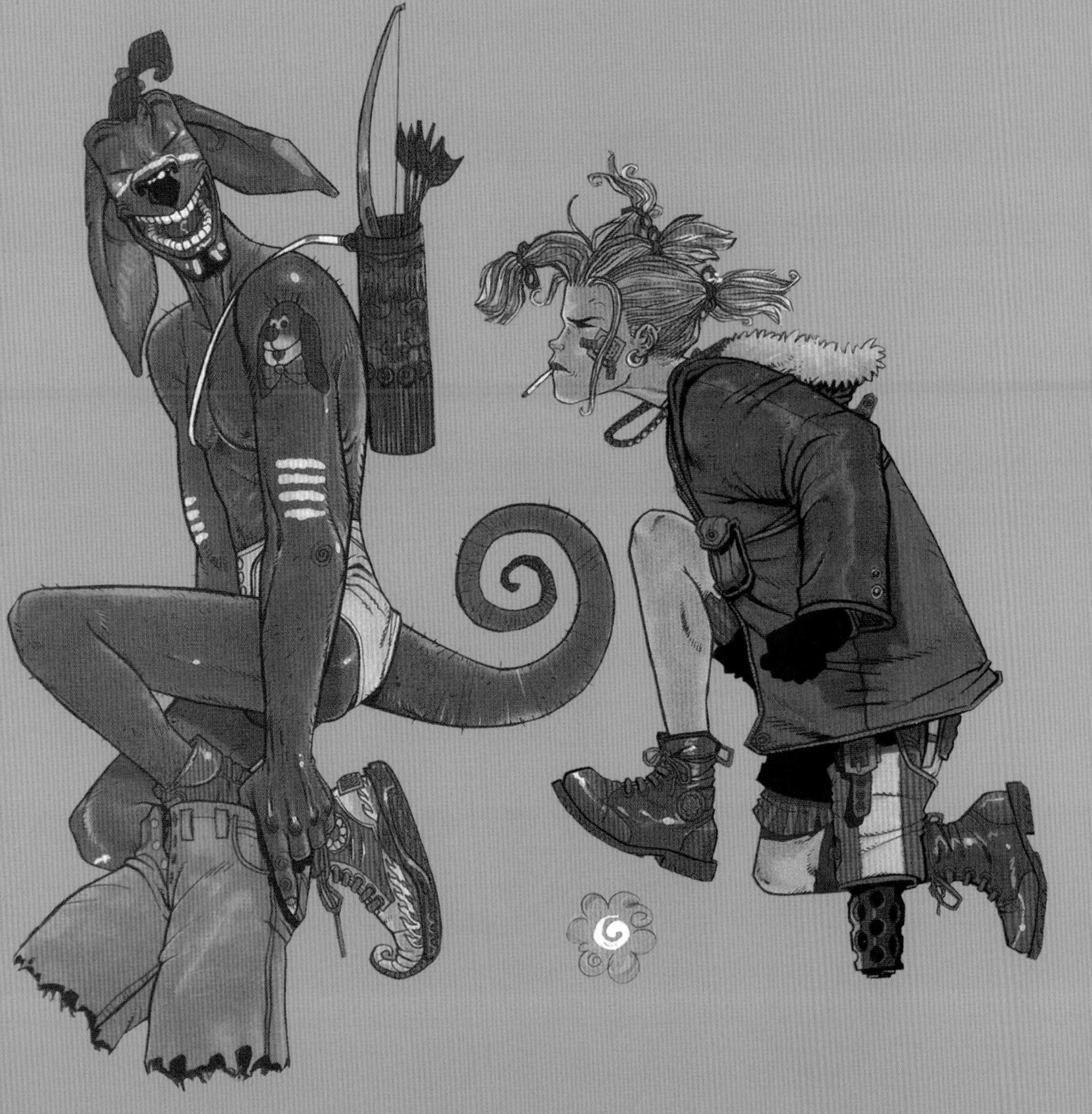

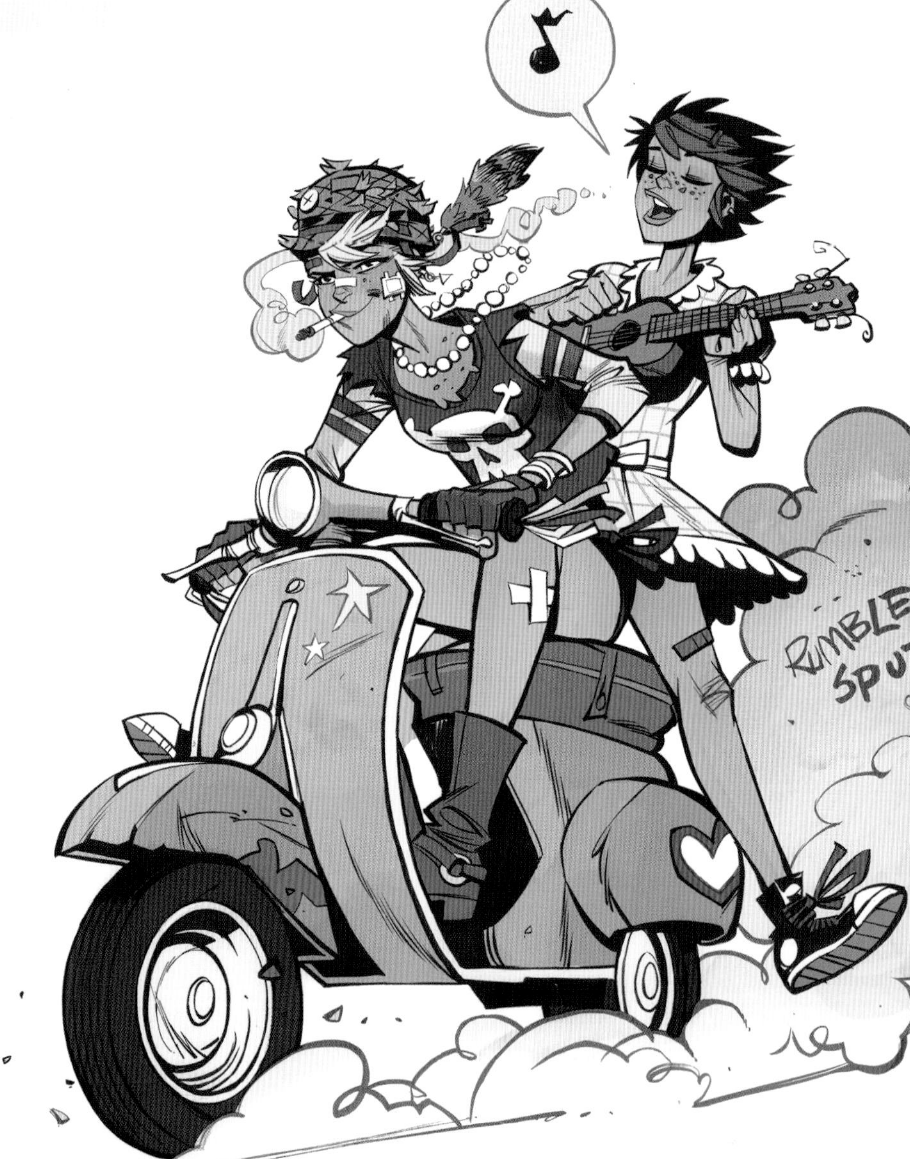
RUMBLE!
SPUT!

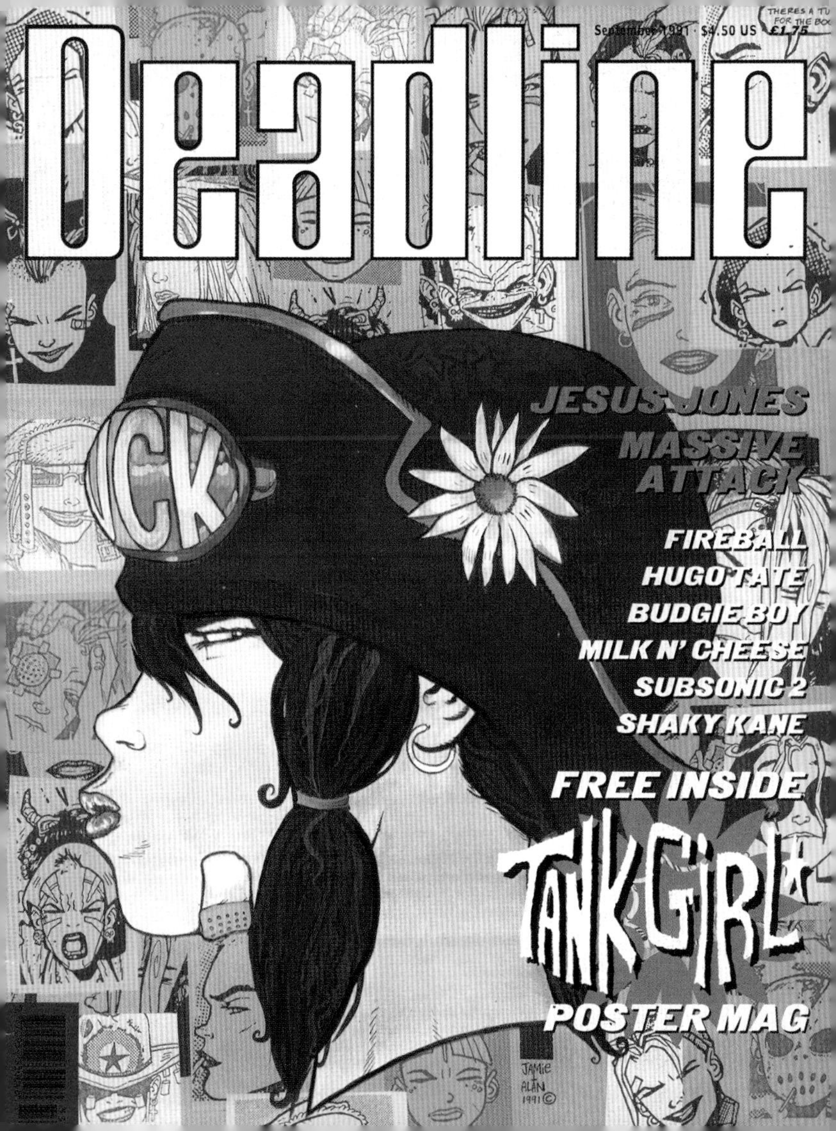

Deadline
September 1991 · $4.50 US £1.75
JESUS JONES
MASSIVE ATTACK
FIREBALL
HUGO TATE
BUDGIE BOY
MILK N' CHEESE
SUBSONIC 2
SHAKY KANE
FREE INSIDE
TANK GIRL
POSTER MAG
JAMIE + ALAN 1991 ©

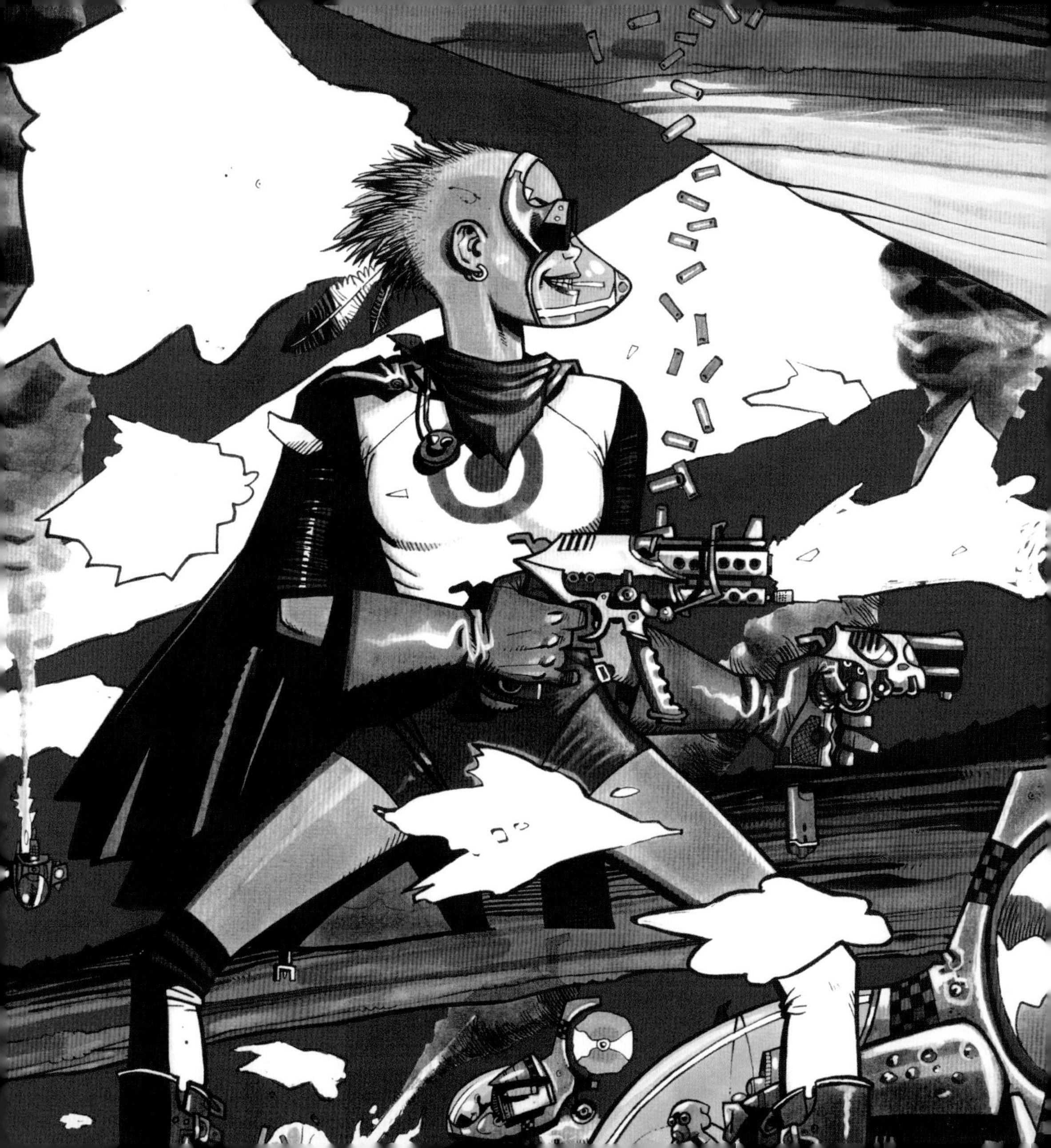

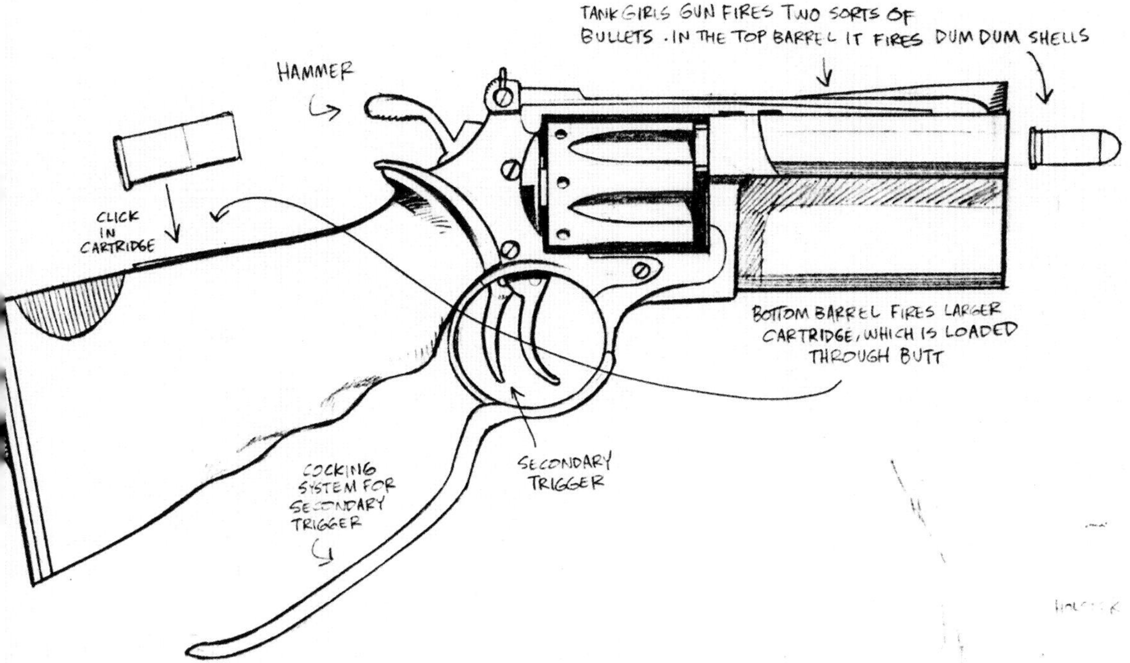
TANK GIRLS GUN FIRES TWO SORTS OF BULLETS . IN THE TOP BARREL IT FIRES DUM DUM SHELLS
HAMMER
CLICK IN CARTRIDGE
BOTTOM BARREL FIRES LARGER CARTRIDGE, WHICH IS LOADED THROUGH BUTT
SECONDARY TRIGGER
COCKING SYSTEM FOR SECONDARY TRIGGER

THE PROFOUND INFLUENCE OF TERENCE HAWKINS

It is generally accepted that Jet Girl is called Jet Girl because she flies a jet, but people should learn that things are never that simple.

She called herself Jet Girl from a very early age – she even had her junior school teachers calling her Jet Girl – and this was not because of her skills in the air, but because of her all-consuming obsession with Jet Harris, the original bass player with 60's beat/guitar group The Shadows.

Jet Harris (born Terence Hawkins in London, 1939) was already one of the coolest dudes on the scene when he joined the Shads in the late fifties. Having learnt the trade in various jazz and skiffle outfits, he wielded his massive Fender bass with poise and character and did the Shadows' shuffle with an easy grace. He was the quiet leader of the group, like Brian Jones of The Stones. A solo career followed, in which he built on the darker side of his image with his backing band, The JetBlacks.

Jet Girl was attracted to Harris because of his enigmatic moodiness. Harris – who was haunted by the idea that he wouldn't live past the age of thirty – almost died in a car crash in 1963, bringing a virtual end to his career as a recording artist (one which may well have equalled – or even surpassed – those of Cliff and Hank Marvin in longevity and stature, had it been given the chance to continue into the 70s, 80s and 90s).

I know all of this crap because Jet Girl brings it up on a monthly basis and harps on about it until she's got it out of her system.

She always ends by saying, "I defy anyone on this planet to watch the end of 'The Young Ones' film – where The Shadows play at the big gig to help Cliff and the kids save their youth club – and tell me that Jet Harris isn't the coolest fuckin' god-star this universe has ever seen. Watch him, man, he has the spirits of Buddha, Jesus, and Lawrence of Arabia, all wrapped up in a shiny, silver mohair suit. The camera can't leave him alone; Marvin's grinning, bespectacled face doesn't get a close-up and the drummer and rhythm guitarist don't even get a look in. It's like he's been beamed down from another solar system, he just glows with other-worldliness. He makes me die that I can't be as cool as him, I just don't know how he does it. I can hardly speak, he chokes me up so badly. I think...I...love him. " Or something like that.

So that's where it began. And from her preoccupation with Jet Harris sprang an interest in all things 'jet'.

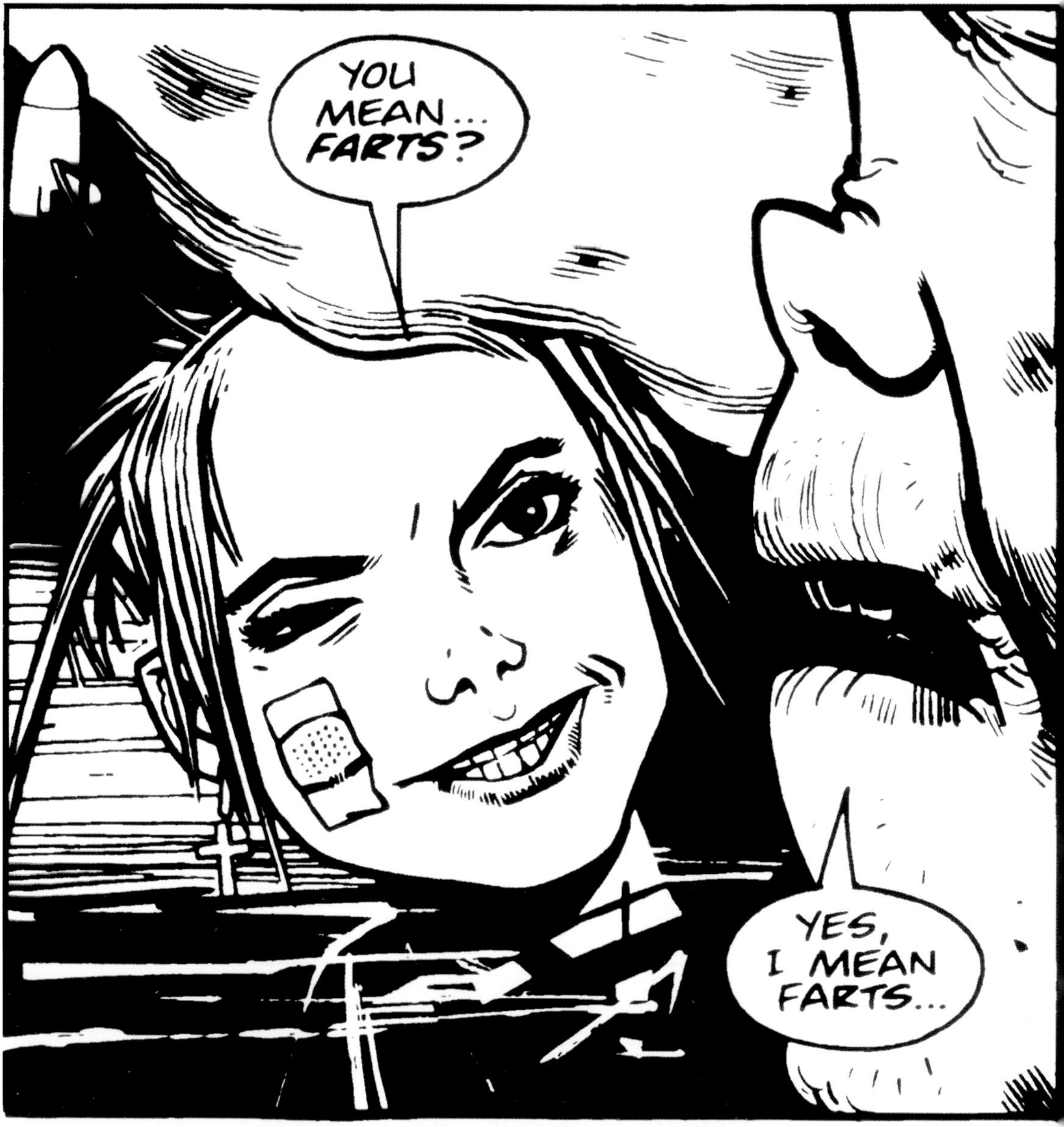
YOU MEAN... FARTS?
YES, I MEAN FARTS...

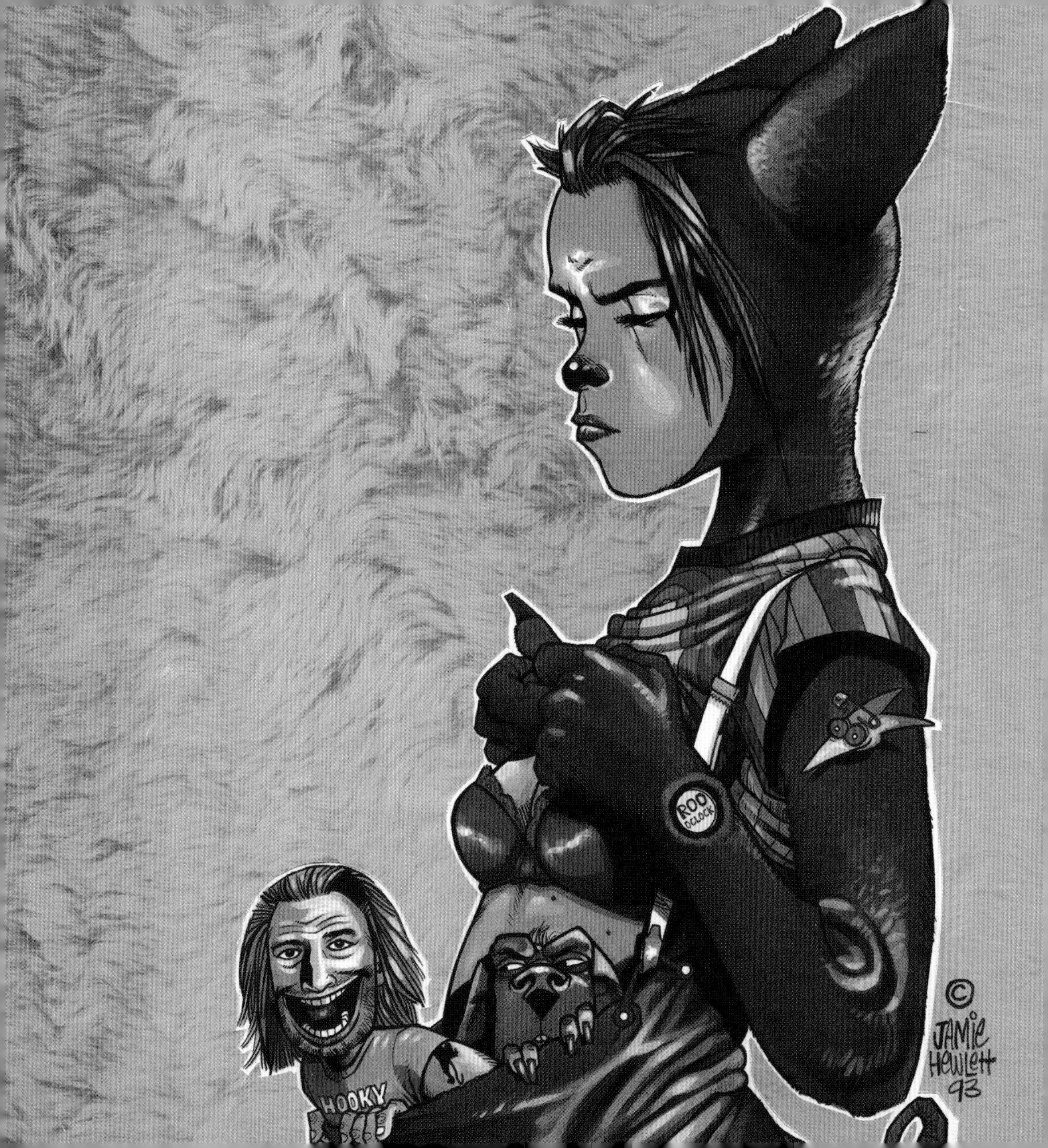
ROD OCLOCK
HOOKY
© JAMIE HEWLETT 93

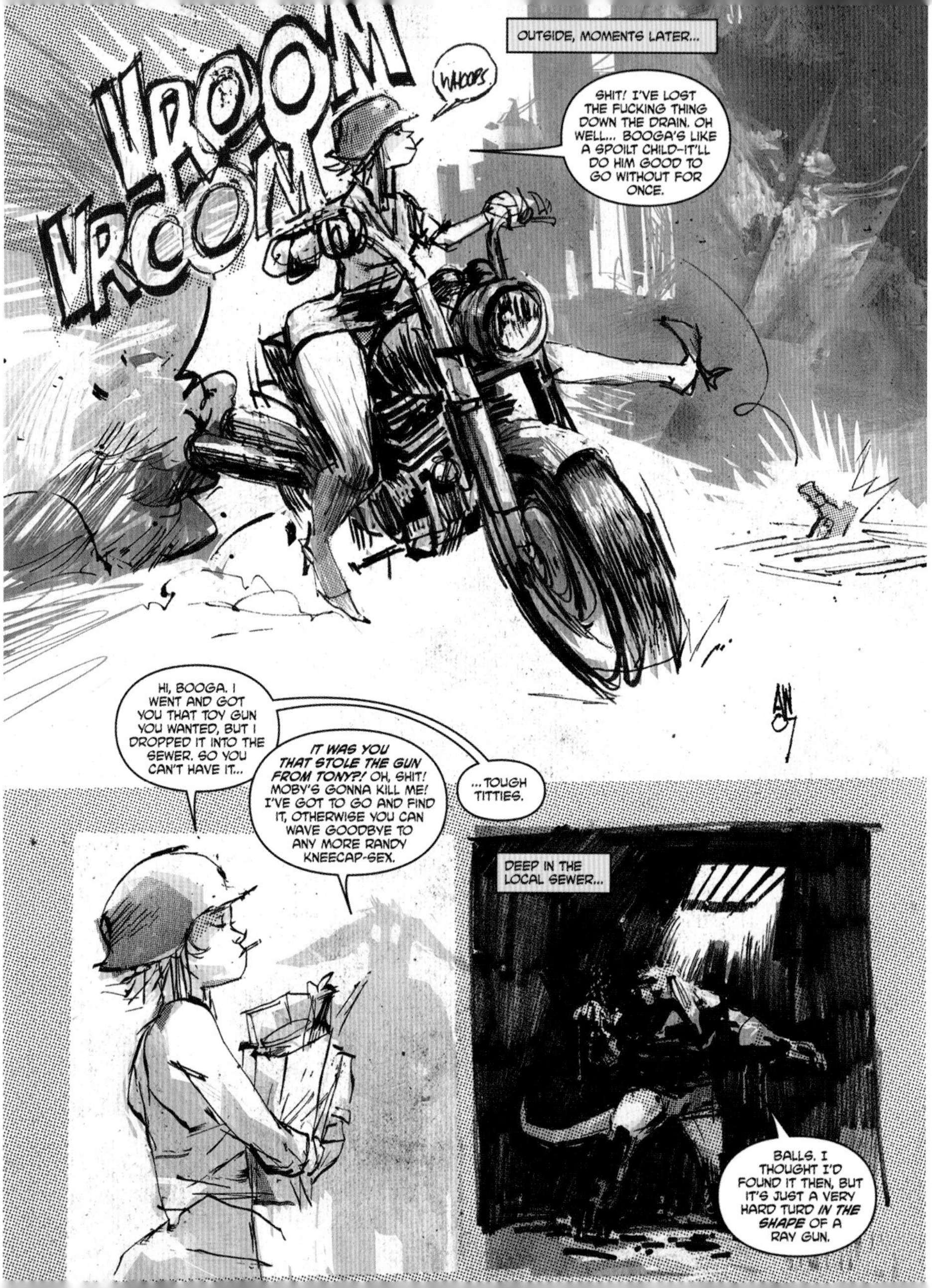
OUTSIDE, MOMENTS LATER...
VROOM
VROOM
WHOOPS.
SHIT! I'VE LOST THE FUCKING THING DOWN THE DRAIN. OH WELL... BOOGA'S LIKE A SPOILT CHILD–IT'LL DO HIM GOOD TO GO WITHOUT FOR ONCE.
HI, BOOGA. I WENT AND GOT YOU THAT TOY GUN YOU WANTED, BUT I DROPPED IT INTO THE SEWER. SO YOU CAN'T HAVE IT...
...TOUGH TITTIES.
IT WAS YOU THAT STOLE THE GUN FROM TONY?! OH, SHIT! MOBY'S GONNA KILL ME! I'VE GOT TO GO AND FIND IT, OTHERWISE YOU CAN WAVE GOODBYE TO ANY MORE RANDY KNEECAP-SEX.
DEEP IN THE LOCAL SEWER...
BALLS. I THOUGHT I'D FOUND IT THEN, BUT IT'S JUST A VERY HARD TURD IN THE SHAPE OF A RAY GUN.

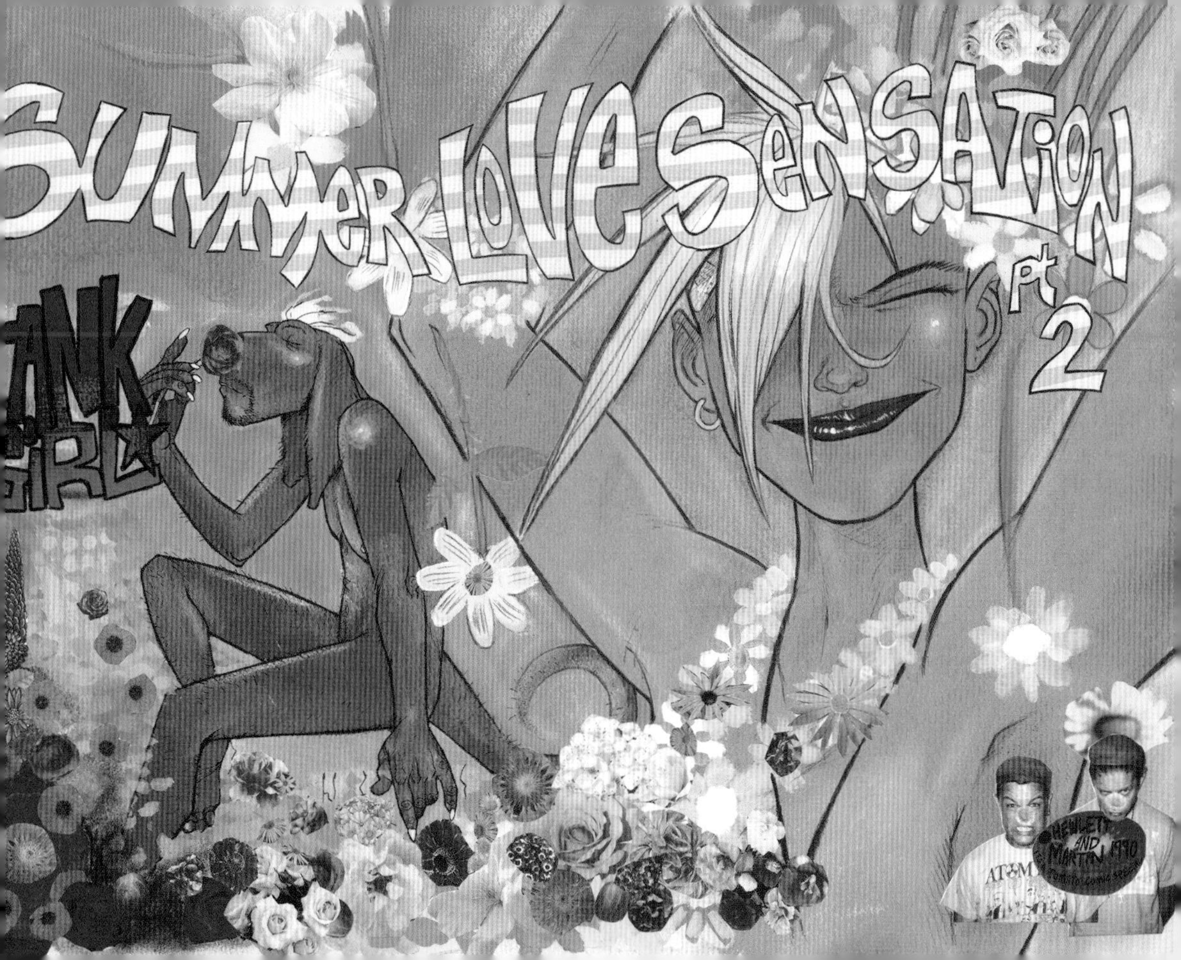
SUMMER LOVE SENSATION
pt 2
ANK
IRL
HEWLETT AND MARTIN 1990
ATOM

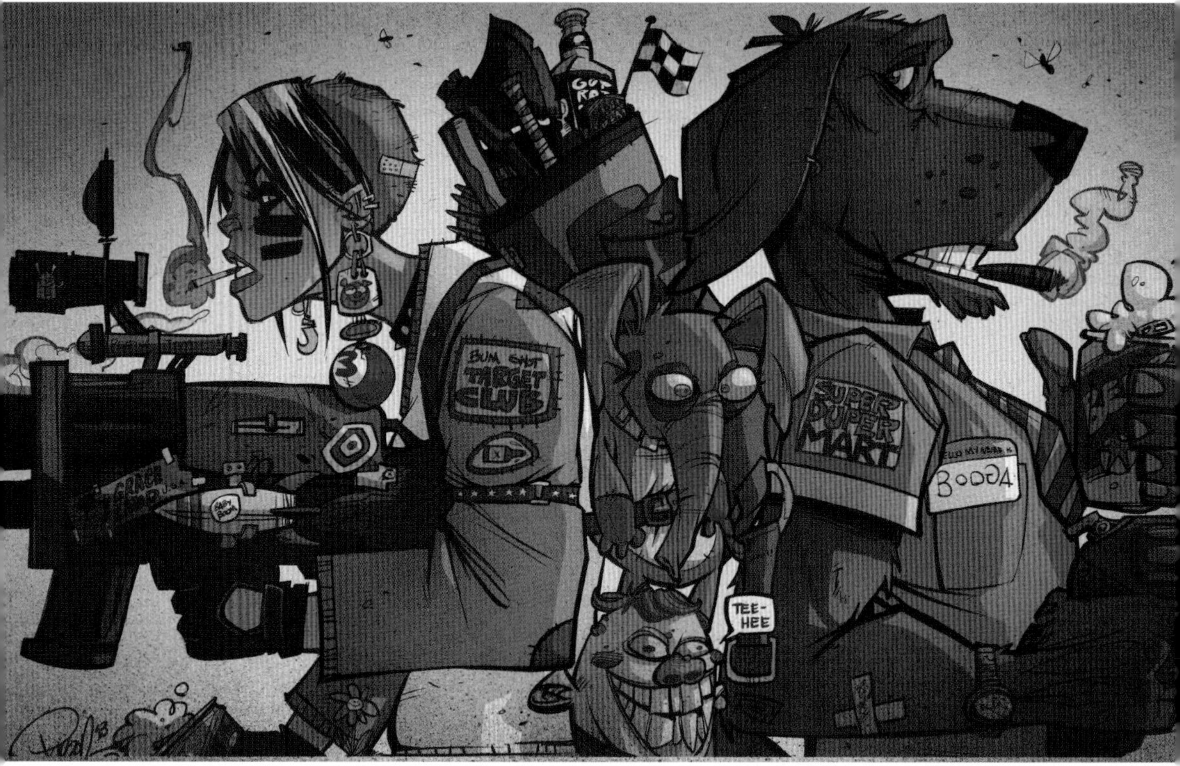
BUM SHOT TARGET CLUB
SUPER DUPER MART
BODGA
TEE-HEE

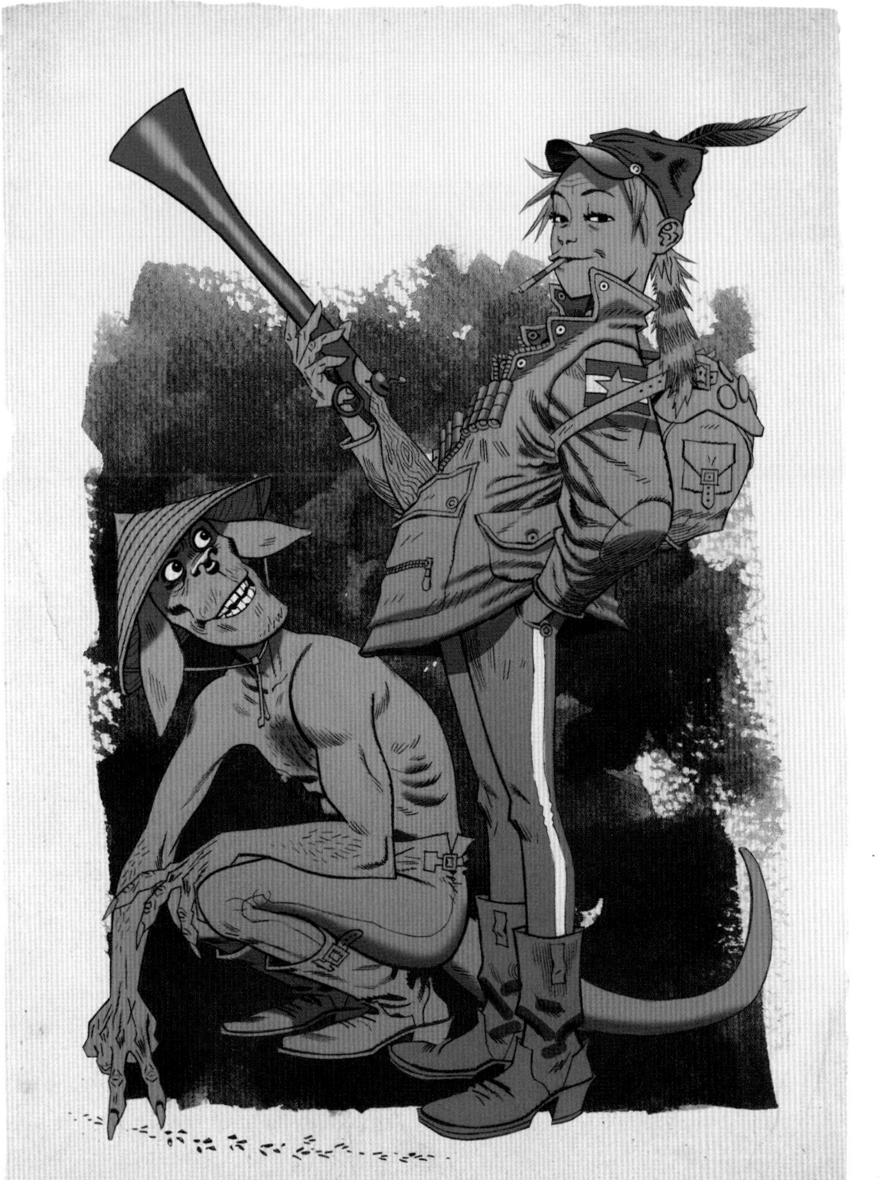

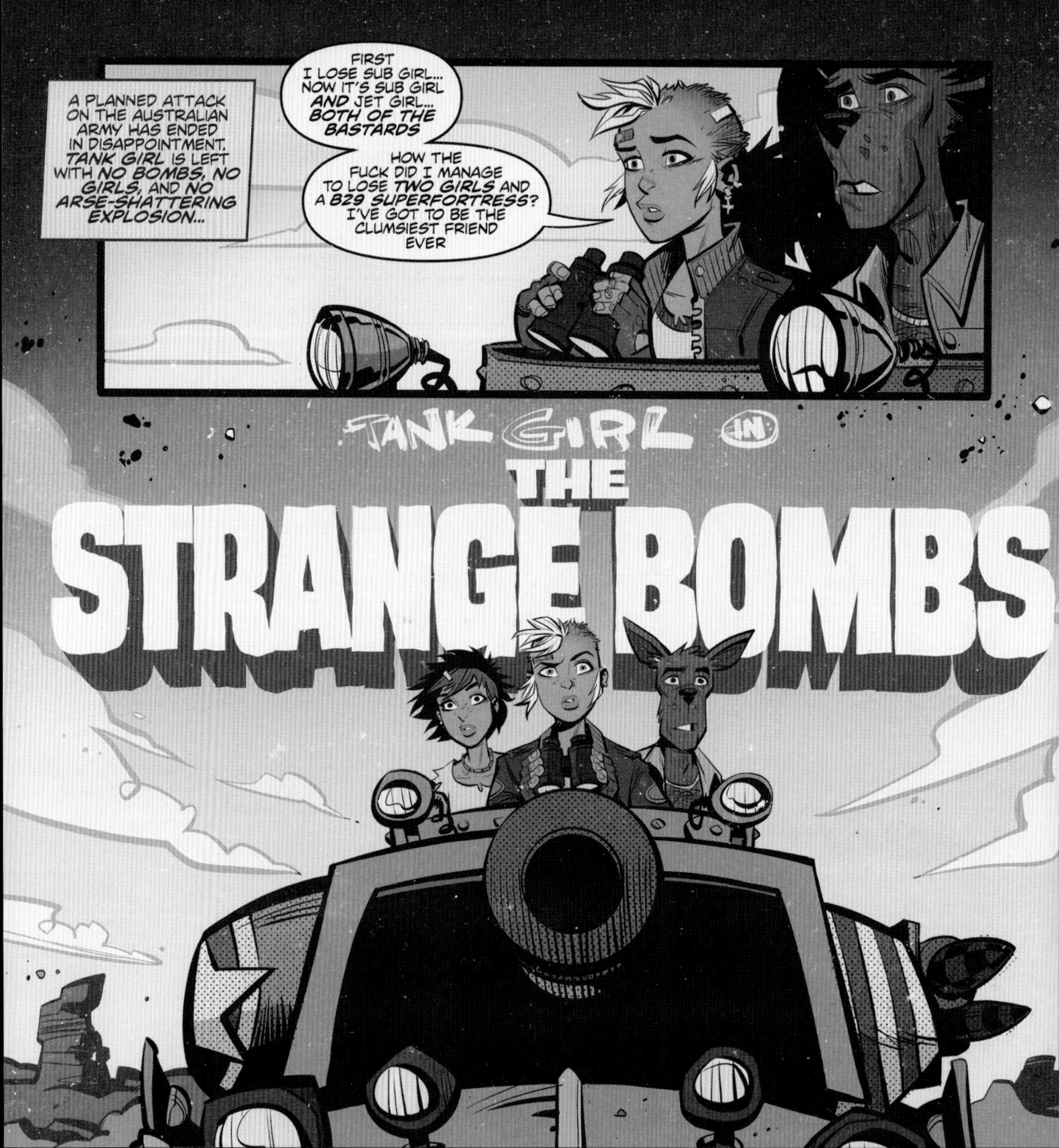

A PLANNED ATTACK ON THE AUSTRALIAN ARMY HAS ENDED IN DISAPPOINTMENT. TANK GIRL IS LEFT WITH NO BOMBS, NO GIRLS, AND NO ARSE-SHATTERING EXPLOSION...
FIRST I LOSE SUB GIRL... NOW IT'S SUB GIRL AND JET GIRL... BOTH OF THE BASTARDS
HOW THE FUCK DID I MANAGE TO LOSE TWO GIRLS AND A B29 SUPERFORTRESS? I'VE GOT TO BE THE CLUMSIEST FRIEND EVER
TANK GIRL IN
THE STRANGE BOMBS

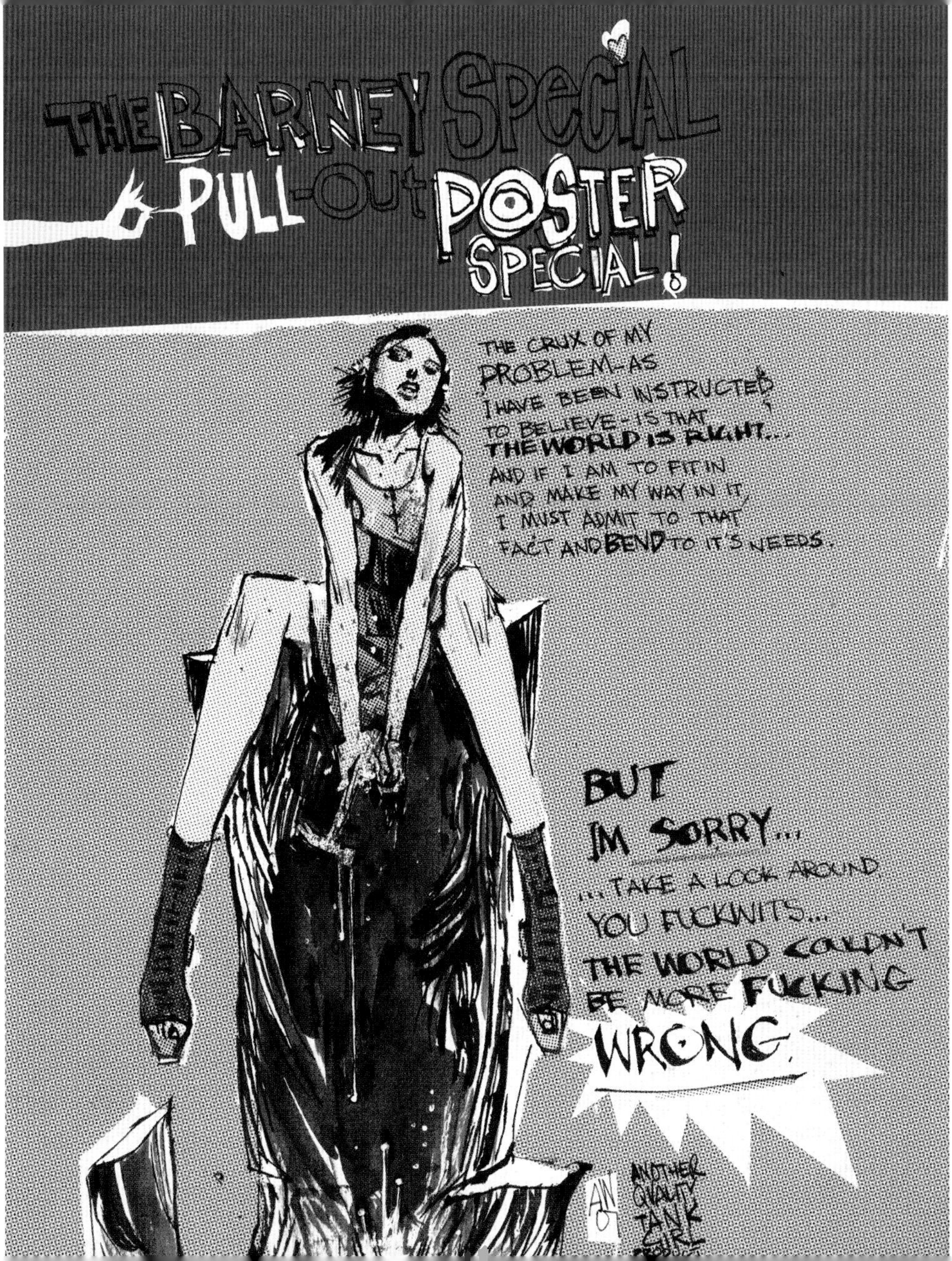
THE BARNEY SPECIAL
PULL-OUT POSTER SPECIAL!
THE CRUX OF MY PROBLEM - AS I HAVE BEEN INSTRUCTED TO BELIEVE - IS THAT THE WORLD IS RIGHT...
AND IF I AM TO FIT IN AND MAKE MY WAY IN IT, I MUST ADMIT TO THAT FACT AND BEND TO IT'S NEEDS.
BUT I'M SORRY...
...TAKE A LOOK AROUND YOU FUCKWITS...
THE WORLD COULDN'T BE MORE FUCKING
WRONG.
ANOTHER QUALITY TANK GIRL

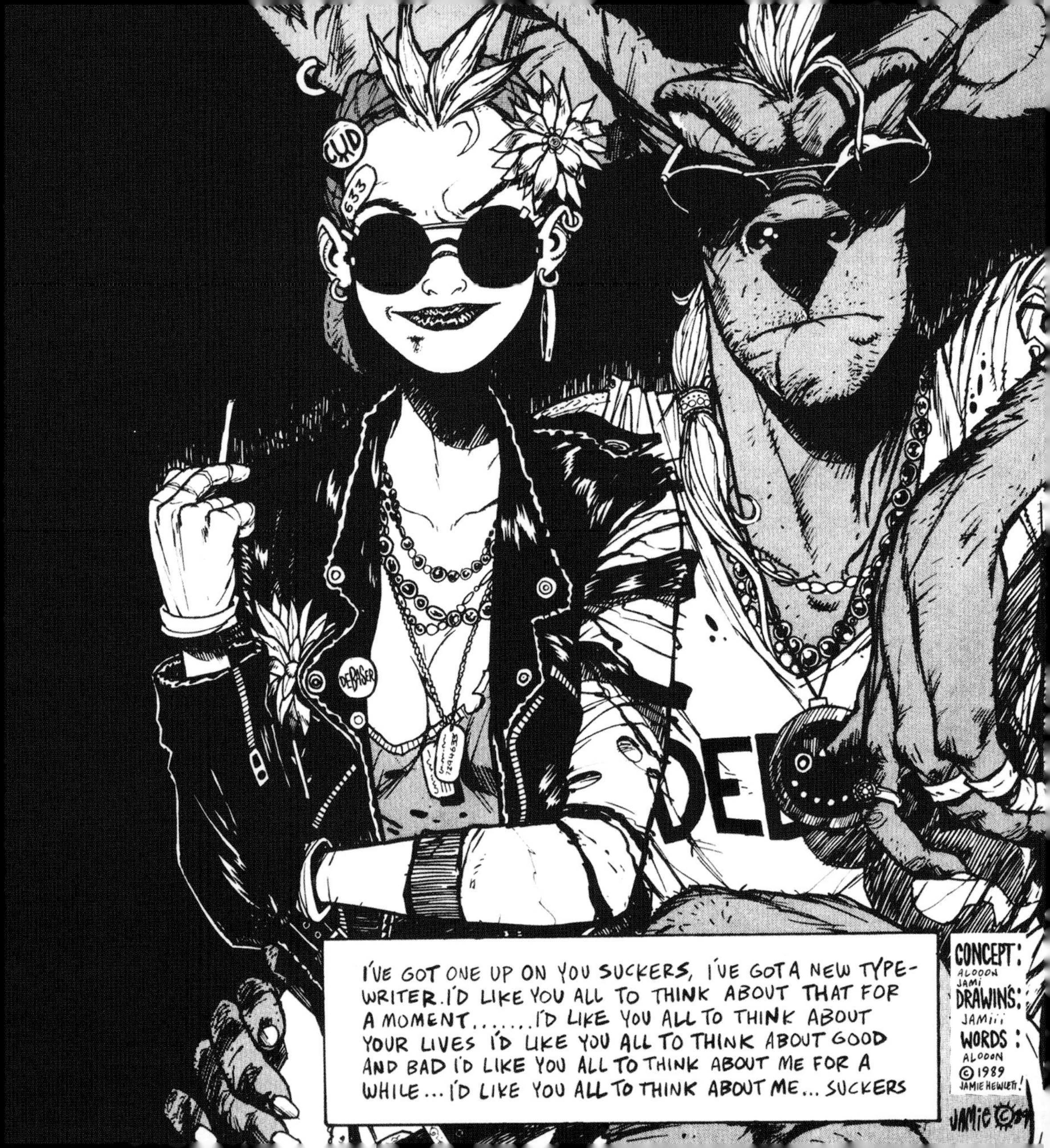
CUD
633
DEBASER
I'VE GOT ONE UP ON YOU SUCKERS, I'VE GOT A NEW TYPE-WRITER. I'D LIKE YOU ALL TO THINK ABOUT THAT FOR A MOMENT.......I'D LIKE YOU ALL TO THINK ABOUT YOUR LIVES I'D LIKE YOU ALL TO THINK ABOUT GOOD AND BAD I'D LIKE YOU ALL TO THINK ABOUT ME FOR A WHILE... I'D LIKE YOU ALL TO THINK ABOUT ME... SUCKERS
CONCEPT: ALOOON JAMI
DRAWIN'S: JAMiii
WORDS: ALOOON
© 1989 JAMIE HEWLETT!
JAMIE ©

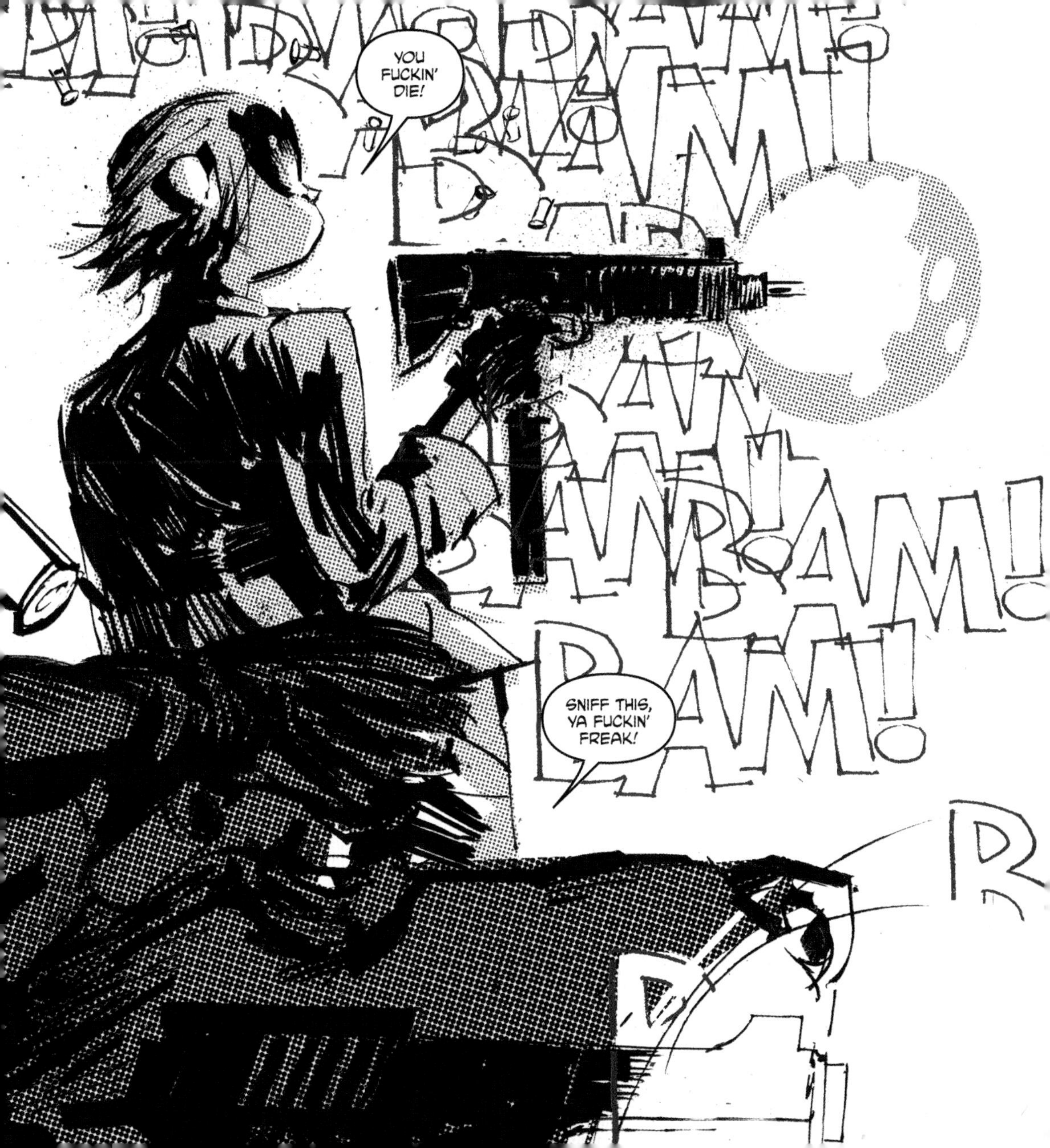
YOU FUCKIN' DIE!
BAM!
SNIFF THIS, YA FUCKIN' FREAK!

I pulled gently on the knob of the old fashioned doorbell. I could hear a tinkle-tinkle far away, deep in the bowels of the enormous mansion.

I waited.

The sun had already set and a chilly breeze was working its way into my bones. I hunched my shoulders and pulled up the collar of my sheepskin coat. My stomach moaned with hunger, I hadn't eaten for days, ever since some tricky bastard had stolen my packed-lunch. Seagulls wheeled around the sky and yelped their sad songs across the empty bay.

Eventually a funny little butler appeared and greeted me with a snotty leer. "Yes, Madam," he ponced, "what can I do for you?"

"I'm calling for Booga," I replied, a bit taken-a-back by the unfriendliness of my loved one's new housekeeper.

"Mr. Booga is to be found in his library-tower, which can be accessed by the narrow pathway to the south of the house," he instructed, giving me a nod in the right direction and quickly closing the door.

"Huh," I huffed, "charmin'."

I trudged up the muddy track. The library – a beautiful, mock-mediaeval-style turret folly - was tucked away in the woodland, almost invisible from view until you got right up close to it.

The door was open. A warm candlelight glow lit up the rustic, white walled passage inside.

I went in.

A stone spiral staircase took me to the top floor of the building.

Booga was stretched out on a big antique chaise longue, reading an old newspaper, and smoking a long Churchwarden pipe. The room was lavishly decorated in late William Morris with tastefully framed original pre-Raphaelite sketches filling the gaps between the wooden bookshelves.

"Booga?" I enquired.

He lowered the paper and looked up through his half-moon glasses. "Ah, Tank Girl my dear, do come in, I've been expecting you all day."

"Oh yeah? Exactly why have you been expecting me?" I asked angrily. "You never told me where you were. You just buggered off without a word. It took me ages to trace you here. And anyway...what the fuck do you think you're playing at? Whose place is this?"

"It's mine," he stated proudly.

"No it isn't."

"Yeah, it is. I bought it."

"You bought it?" I questioned, staggering with disbelief.

"Yeah," he replied, "I saved up for it."

"Booga, that is utter bullshit. You've never saved up for a thing in your life. You've never even had a job for fucksake."

"I had a paper-round," he pleaded.

"Yeah," I conceded, "okay, so you had a paper-round. But you couldn't even do that properly. And there's no way you managed to save up for this place by earning three quid a week when you were twelve. This must've cost you fucking millions."

"Well I had a stroke of luck..." he explained.

"Please," I interjected sarcastically, "do go on."

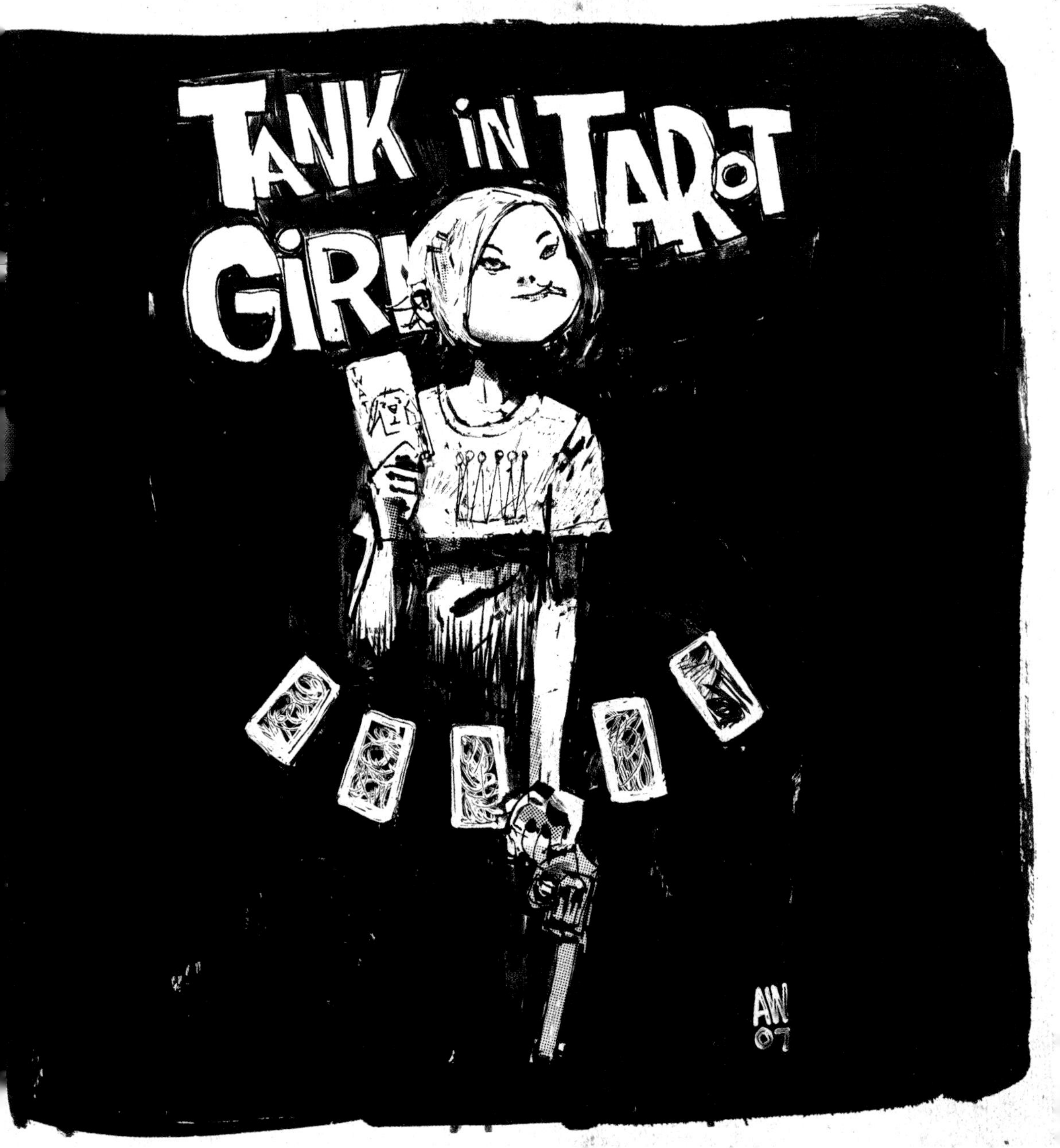
TANK IN TAROT
GIR
AW 07

"...well...it happened like this..." he sat up straight to tell his story, re-lighting his pipe and doing up his richly embroidered smoking jacket, "...I was having a crap in the toilets at the church hall..."

I had to butt-in straight away, "Booga, what were you doing in the church hall toilets?"

"It was half way through the Sunday service," he answered earnestly, "and they started doing a really boring bit and I really needed to curl one down, so I sneaked out."

"When did you start going to Sunday service?" I asked.

"That was my first time," he replied. "Someone told me that if I went to church and did all of the praying and stuff, then they would give me free wine, because Jesus was really into wine and all that. Fish too."

That figured.

"Okay," I said, "then what happened?"

"I done a lot into the lav," he explained, "so I needed to use a fair amount of bog-paper. Halfway through the roll I came across this..."

Booga got up and walked over to a shelf of encyclopaedias, carefully taking down the volume marked "X, Y & Z". He opened the book at its end pages and removed a single sheet of expertly pressed white toilet paper. He placed the sheet on the small wine table in front of me.

"Take a look," he offered.

I took a look.

The paper was covered with unrecognisable biro lettering. It was like nothing I'd ever seen before – weird symbols and characters and shit.

"So," I asked Booga, with more than a subtle hint of parody, "what is this? Written in ancient Poo-Poo?"

"It's a cipher," replied Booga. "Here's a translation what I got done."

He handed me another sheet of paper. This time the writing was legible, but still incomprehensible.

It read:

SHEPHERD'S PIE, QUITE TEMPTED, THAT PUSSY, TENNERS, HOLD THE PHONE, PEACE 23. BY THE BUS STOP AND THIS HORSEMEAT, I COMPLAINED – or DECLINED – TO THIS DEMON STUNT-CYCLIST AT HIGH NOON. CHEESE AND ONION.

"Booga," I complained, "this is complete crap. It doesn't mean anything."

"That's exactly what I though," he said brightly, "and I was about to wipe my arse with it when the vicar burst in. In my hurry to have a shit, I had neglected to bolt the door properly. He didn't hang around for long, coz of the stink, but the upshot was that I pulled up my trousers pronto and stuffed the bog-paper in my shirt pocket. I didn't think any more of it until I needed to blow my nose, that's when things started to get weird..."

"No kidding," I injected.

"...I took the bit of bog-paper down to the library and the woman there translated it for me," he continued, "she said it was written in sam-script or something."

"You mean Sanskrit?" I asked.

"Yeah, him as well. Anyway, the boff at the library couldn't help me any further so I went and consulted Mandy, my fortune teller."

"Mandy your fortune teller?" I repeated quizzically, "and what did Mandy have to say?"

"She done my tarot," he explained, "and she said that somehow my destiny had become irrevocably intertwined with that of the universe. She said that I would have to look out for signs, things with hidden meanings, shit like that. And that once the trail had begun, then my future was set and the dice had been cast and stuff."

"And has the trail begun, whatever that means?"

"It has begun and ended already," he replied. "Shortly after my reading, I was walking down the High Street when a feint waft of shepherd's pie hit my sensitive kangaroo nostrils. I thought about going into the café for a portion, but I was distracted by a cat with no tail. Then I found two ten-dollar bills in the gutter and thought I'd give you a call to ask you out for a curry. You couldn't talk coz you were busy doing a jigsaw of The Fonz and you couldn't find the last bit, the twenty-third piece. So I waited for a bus to take me home and this guy started munching into a Mc Farmyards' burger right next to me. So I told him to fuck off and he got on his bike and did a wheelie all the way down the road. When I got in I was starving, so I opened my bag of cheese and onion flavour Potato Fancies."

I'd been following his story through the translation; "CHEESE AND ONION" was where it ended. "And is that it?" I asked. "Where did all of these goodies come from then?"

Booga cleared his throat and prepared to finish his story by licking his lips, "Inside the packet I found a little blue envelope. They were doing a special promotion, giving away cash to lucky eaters. I got the grand prize – two million big ones!"

"You what?!" I screamed. "And you didn't fucking tell me?"

"It was weird," he explained, "I wasn't in control. It was like destiny itself had taken me over and I was flying on auto-pilot."

Just then something dawned on me, "Hold it right there buster, did you say you had a packet of cheese and onion Potato Fancies?"

"Er...yeah," he answered hesitantly.

"You bastard. It was you that stole my packed-lunch!" then the rest of it dawned on me too, "I was the one who was meant to win the two million quid! And you've fucking spent it! You utter, utter bastard!"

Later that night, as I was using Booga as an ashtray and his butler as a footstool, I contemplated what might have been, had I won all that cash. I daydreamed of living a saintly existence, somewhere near a fountain of healing water in a far-off European mountain village.

"Can I please have a number-two toilet break, ma'am," Booga asked quietly.

"You can poo in your pants and clean it up with this," I replied sharply, flicking the rolled-up piece of Sanskrit bog-paper at him, "I'll bet that Mandy never predicted this in your reading."

"Well," groaned Booga with excremental relief, "She did say that the story would end with a nice warm feeling, deep down."

PRESENTING...

THE JET GIRL CUT-OUT DIORAMA SUPER THEATRE

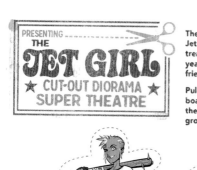

Thespian blood has always coursed through the veins of Jet Girl's family. Her ancestors and relatives have been treading the boards since theatre began, thousands of years ago. These days, Jet Girl still delights in dressing her friends up in period costume and ordering them around

Pull out these pages and glue them to some strong cardboard (an empty cereal packet would be ideal). Cut out the characters and add stands to the slots, fold the backgrounds and scenery so that it stands independently.

There's props and actors aplenty here, so let your stupid imagination run wild! We'll leave it to you to adlib your own story and dialogue, but keep it clean and family friendly!

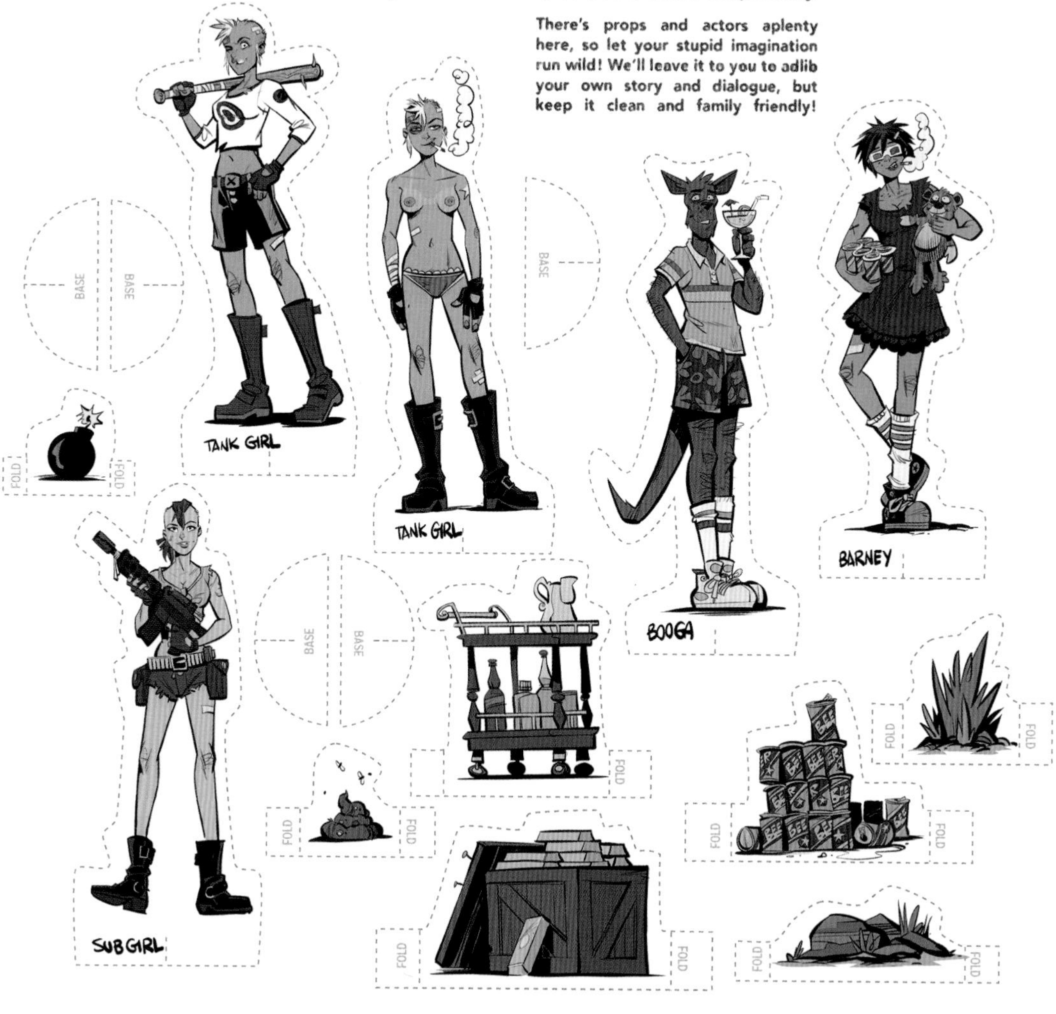

TANK GIRL
TANK GIRL
BOOGA
BARNEY
SUBGIRL
BASE
FOLD

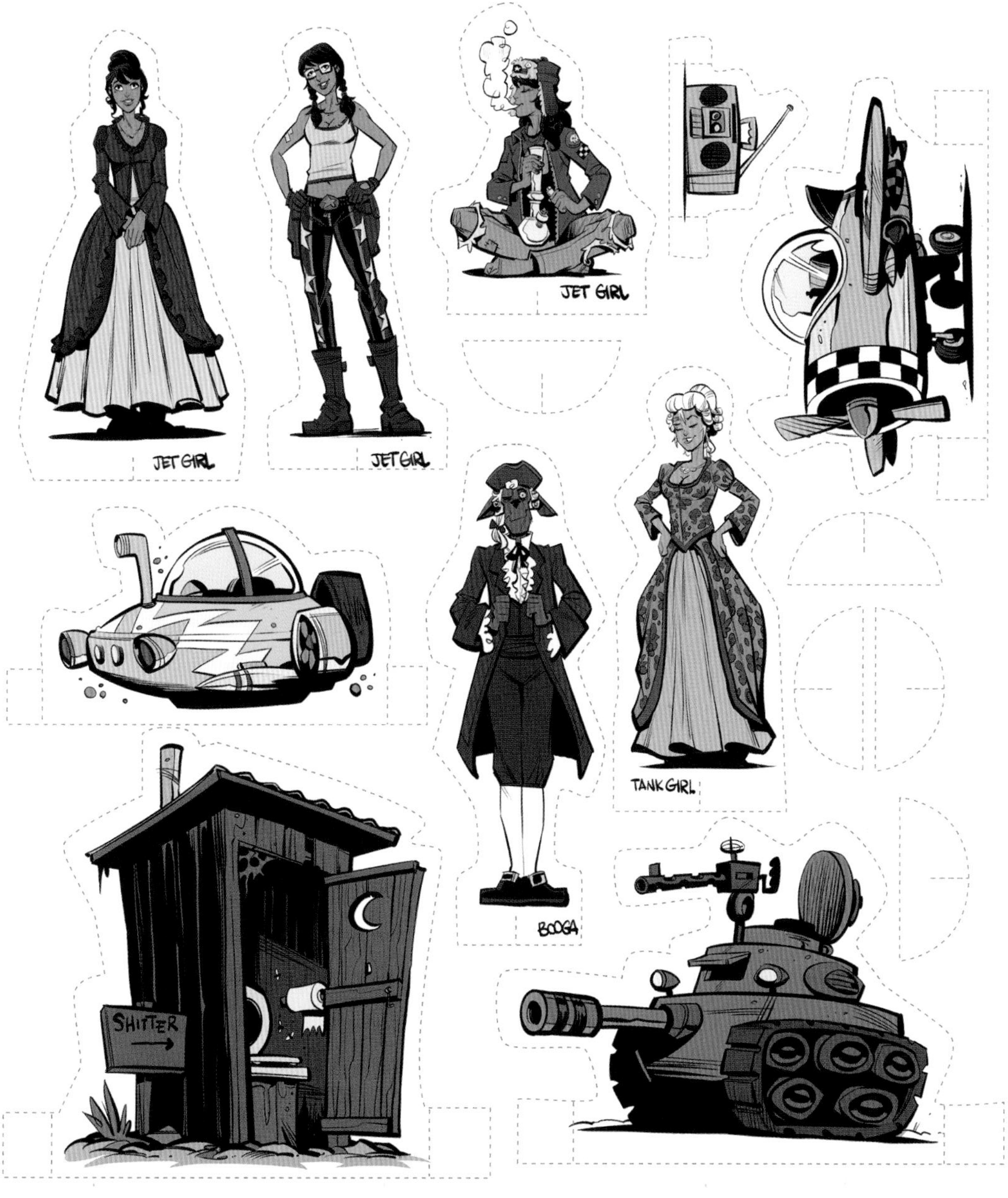
JET GIRL
JET GIRL
JET GIRL
TANK GIRL
BOOGA
SHITTER

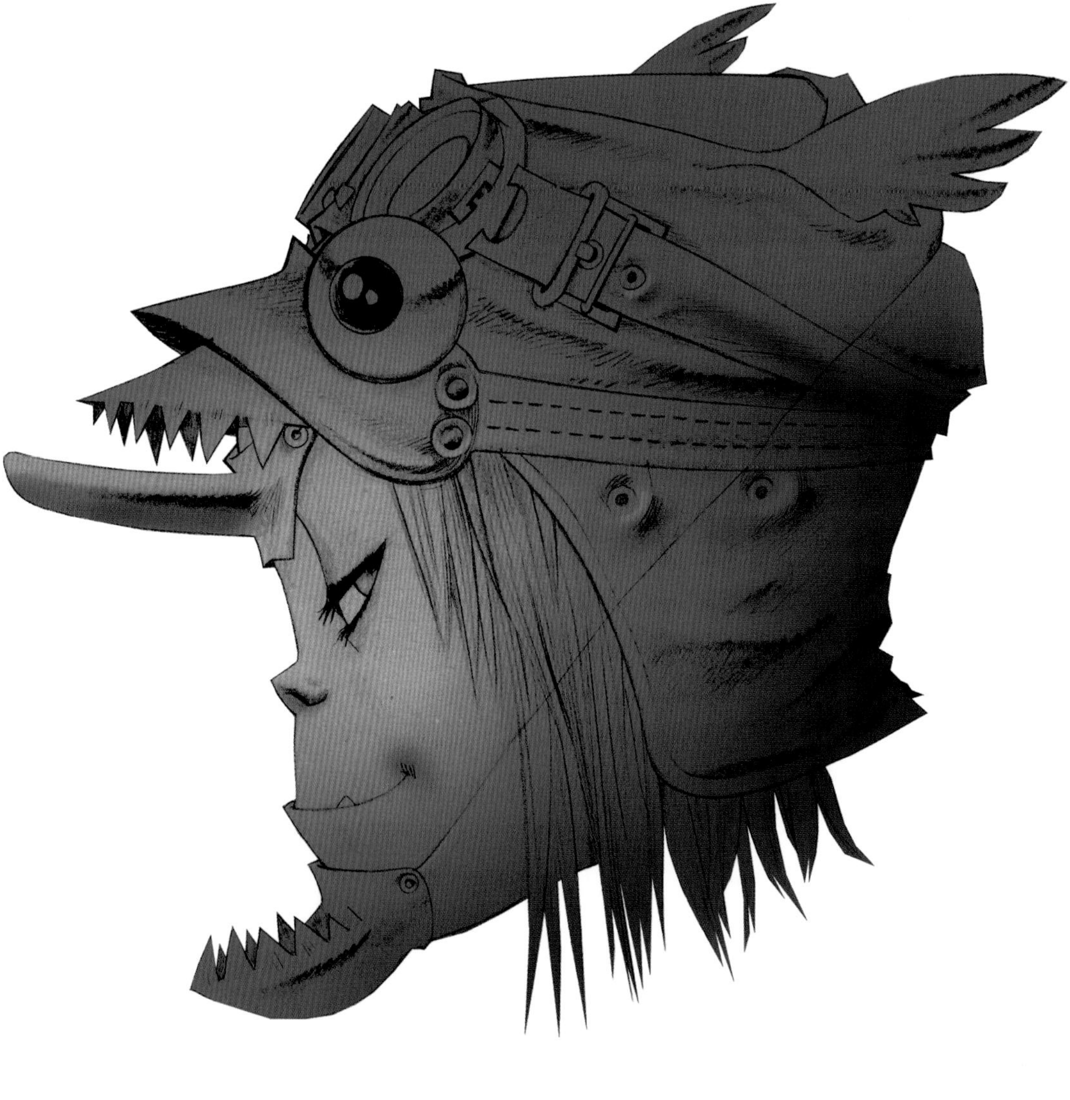

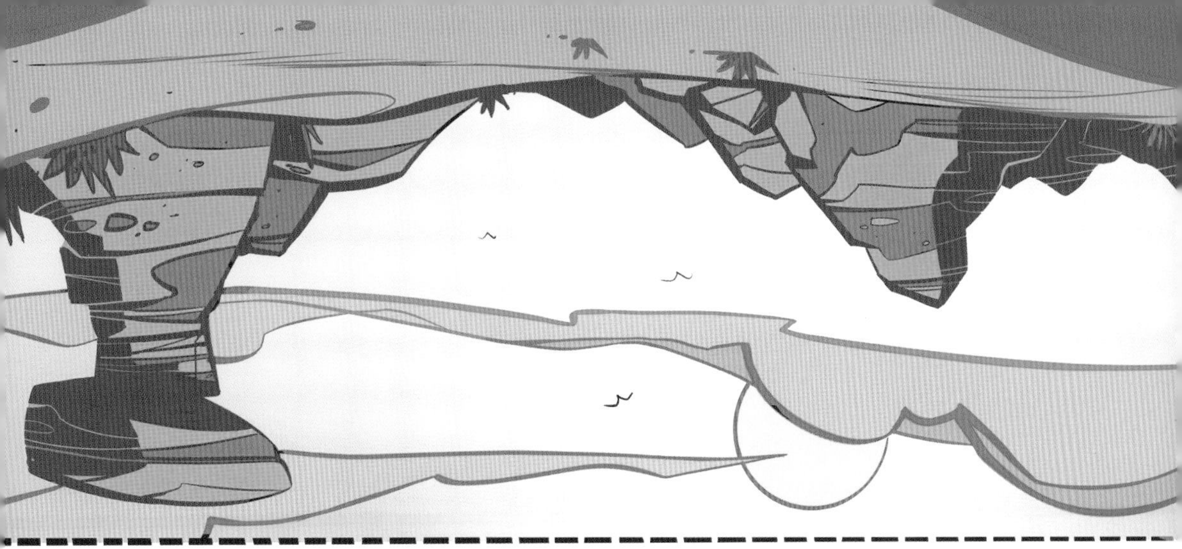

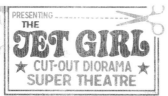

PRESENTING

THE

JET GIRL

★ CUT-OUT DIORAMA ★

SUPER THEATRE

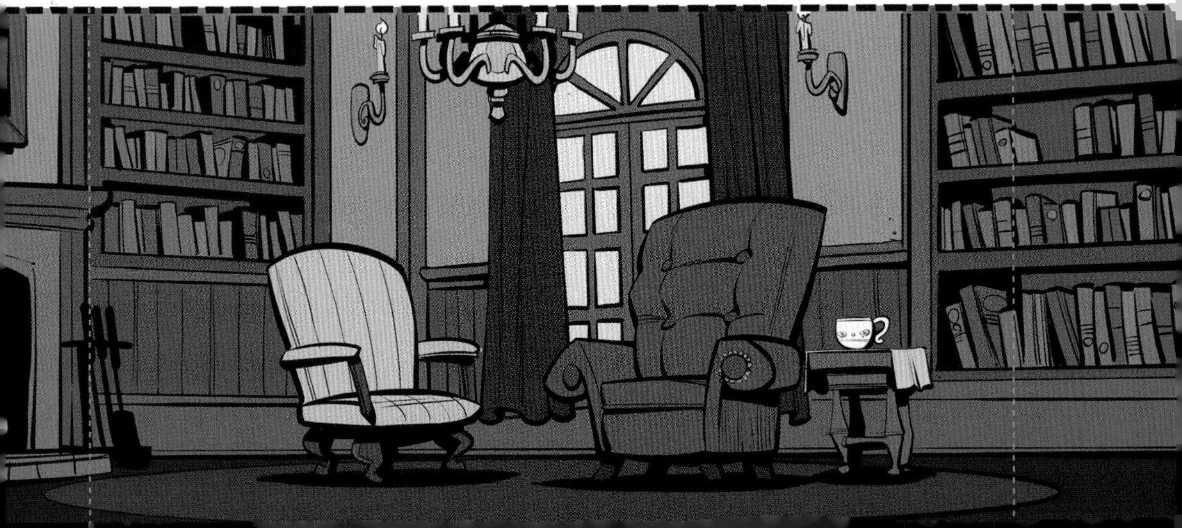

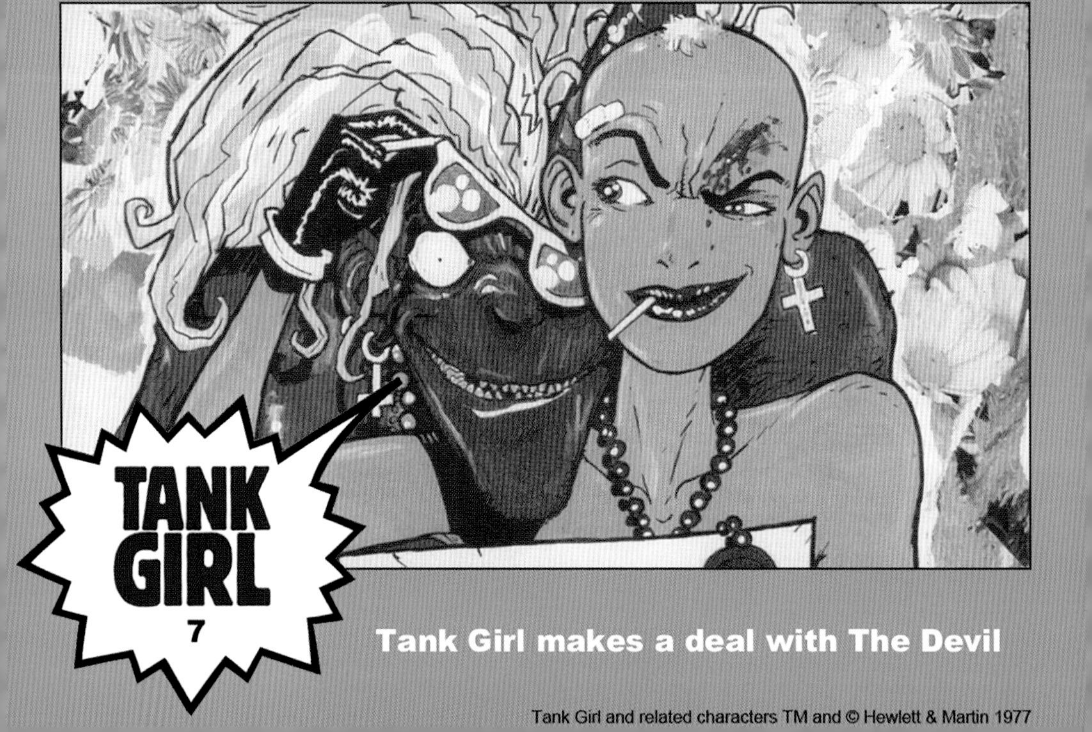

TANK GIRL

7

Tank Girl makes a deal with The Devil

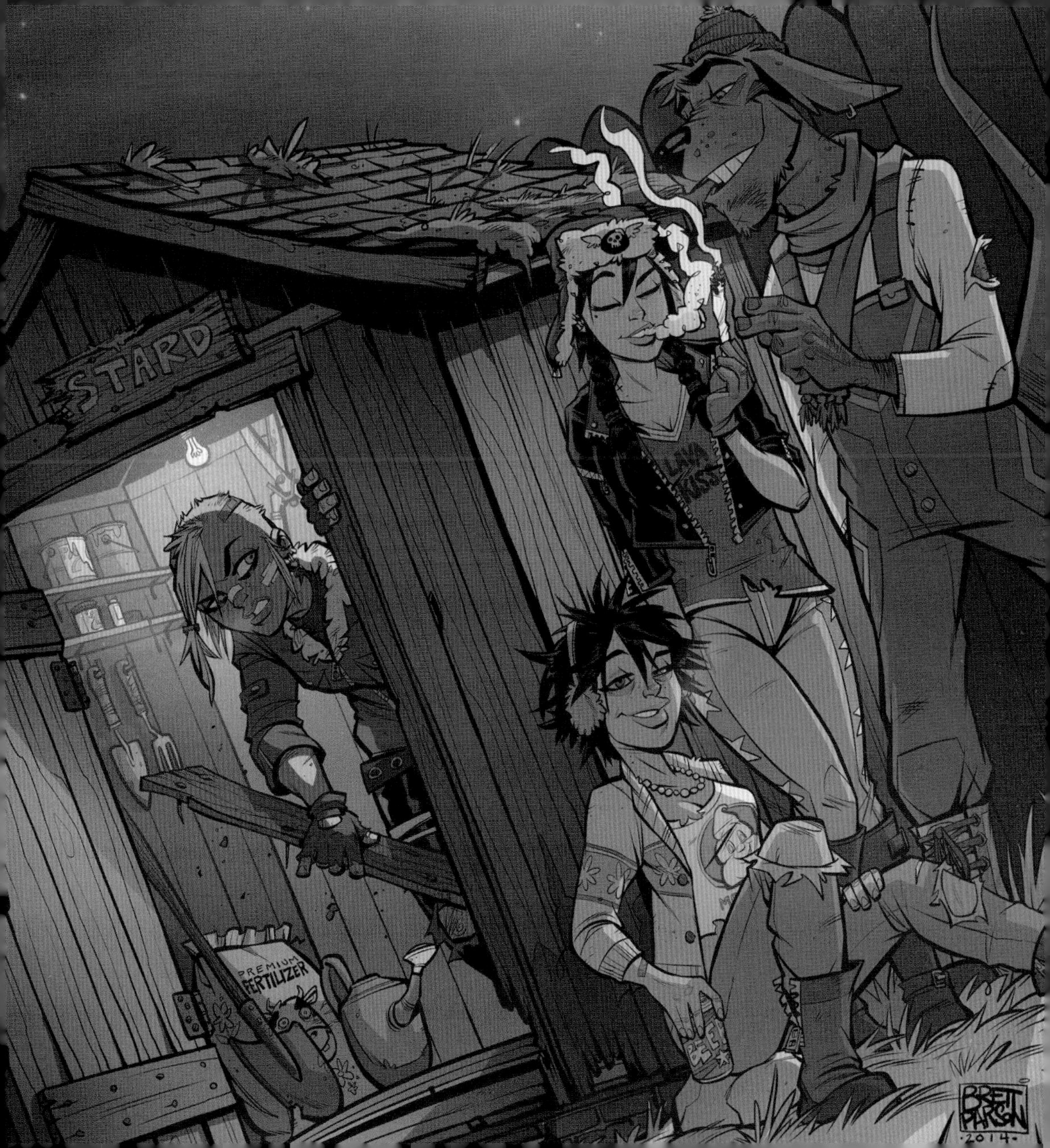
STARD
PREMIUM
FERTILIZER
BRETT PARSON
·2014·

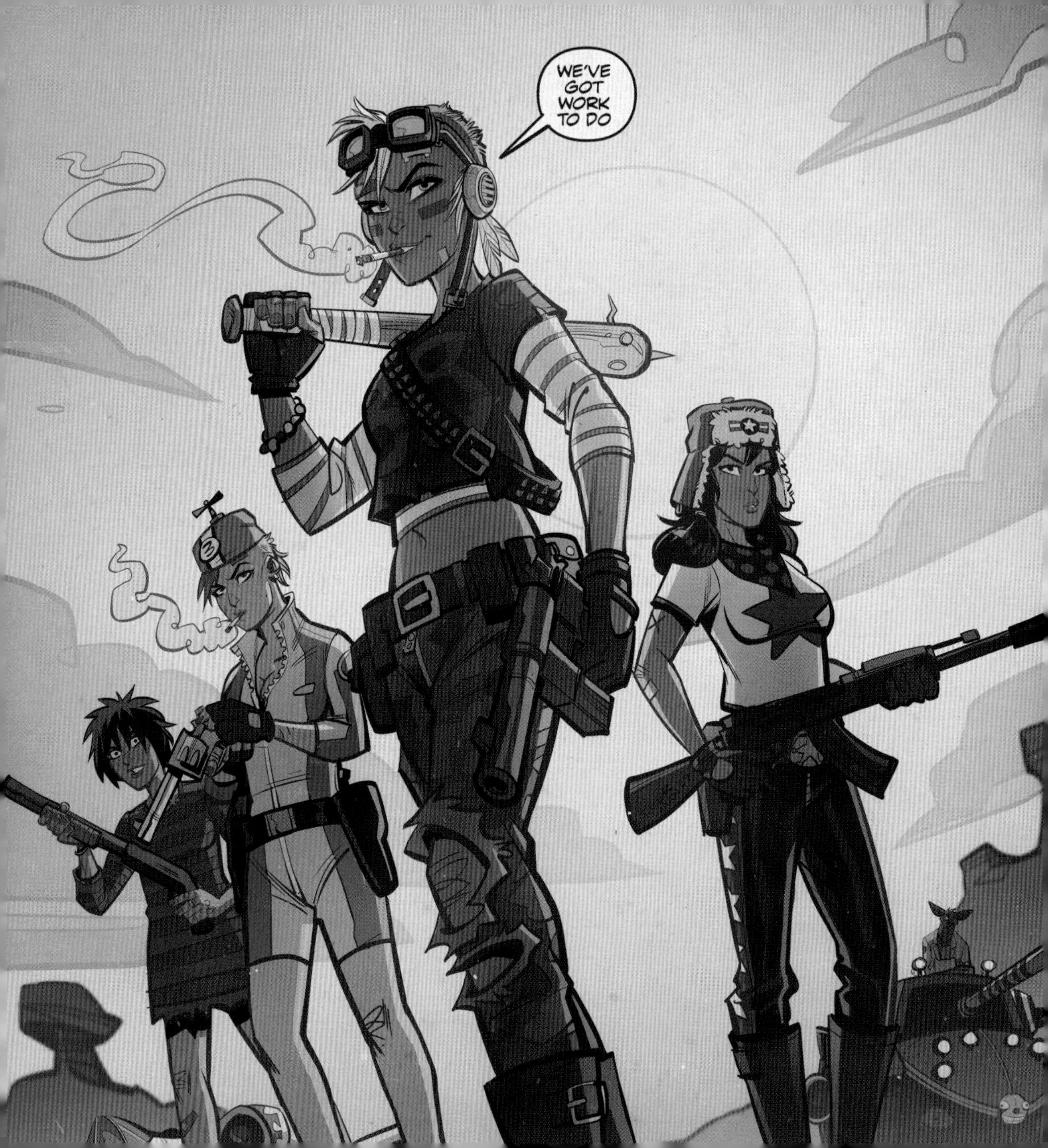
WE'VE GOT WORK TO DO

TOO HIP FOR SPIELBERG!

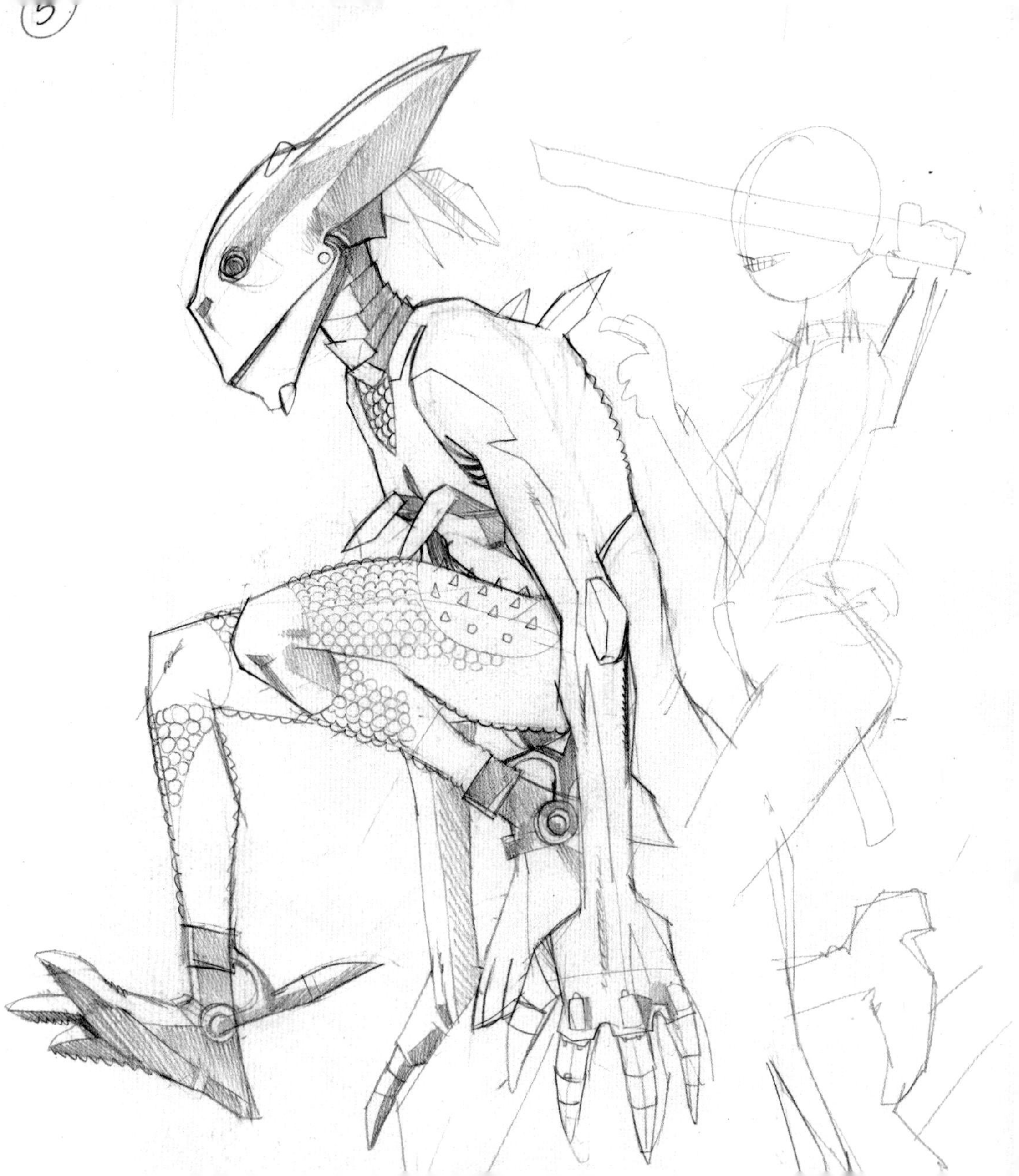
5

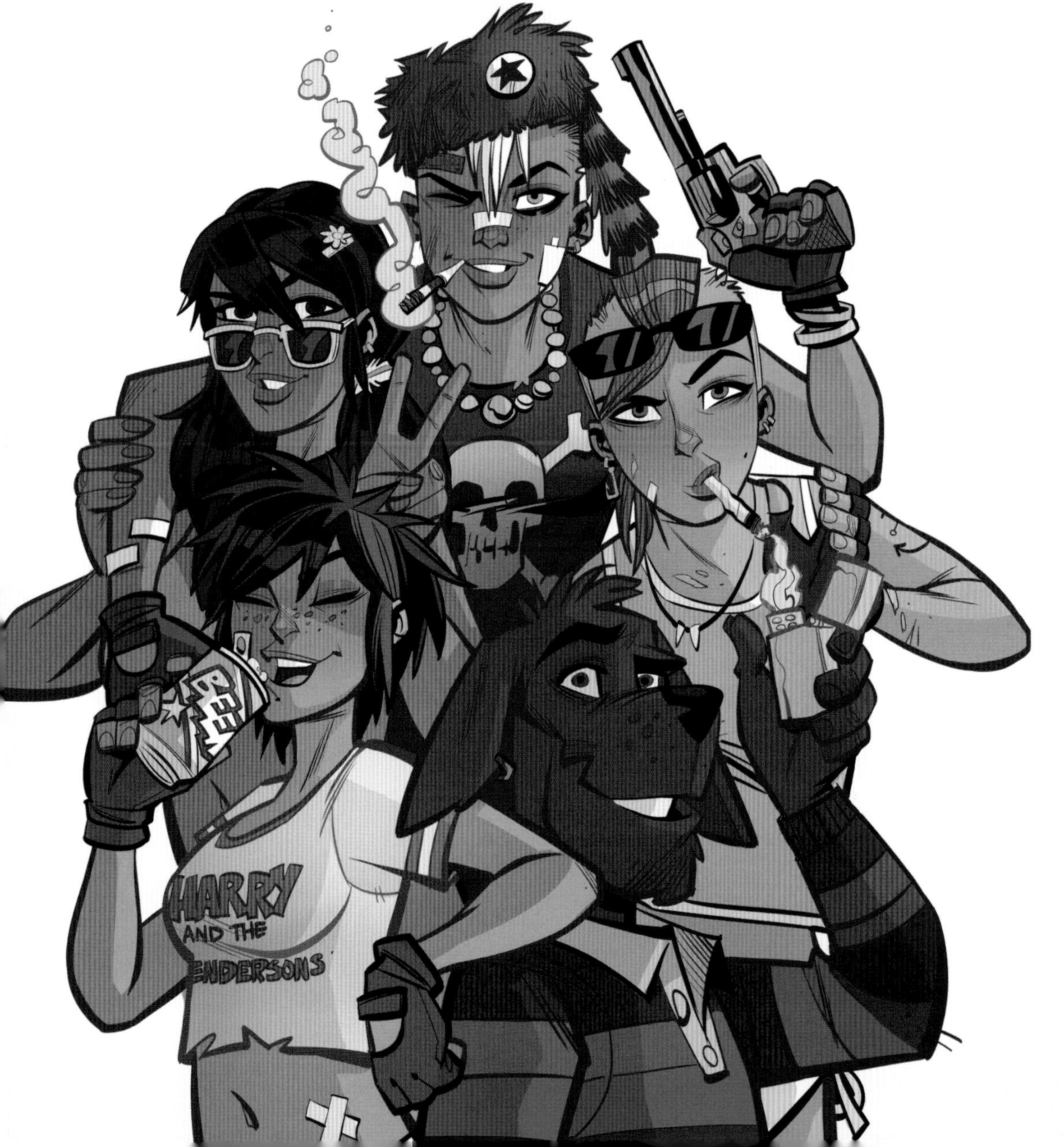
HARRY
AND THE
ENDERSONS

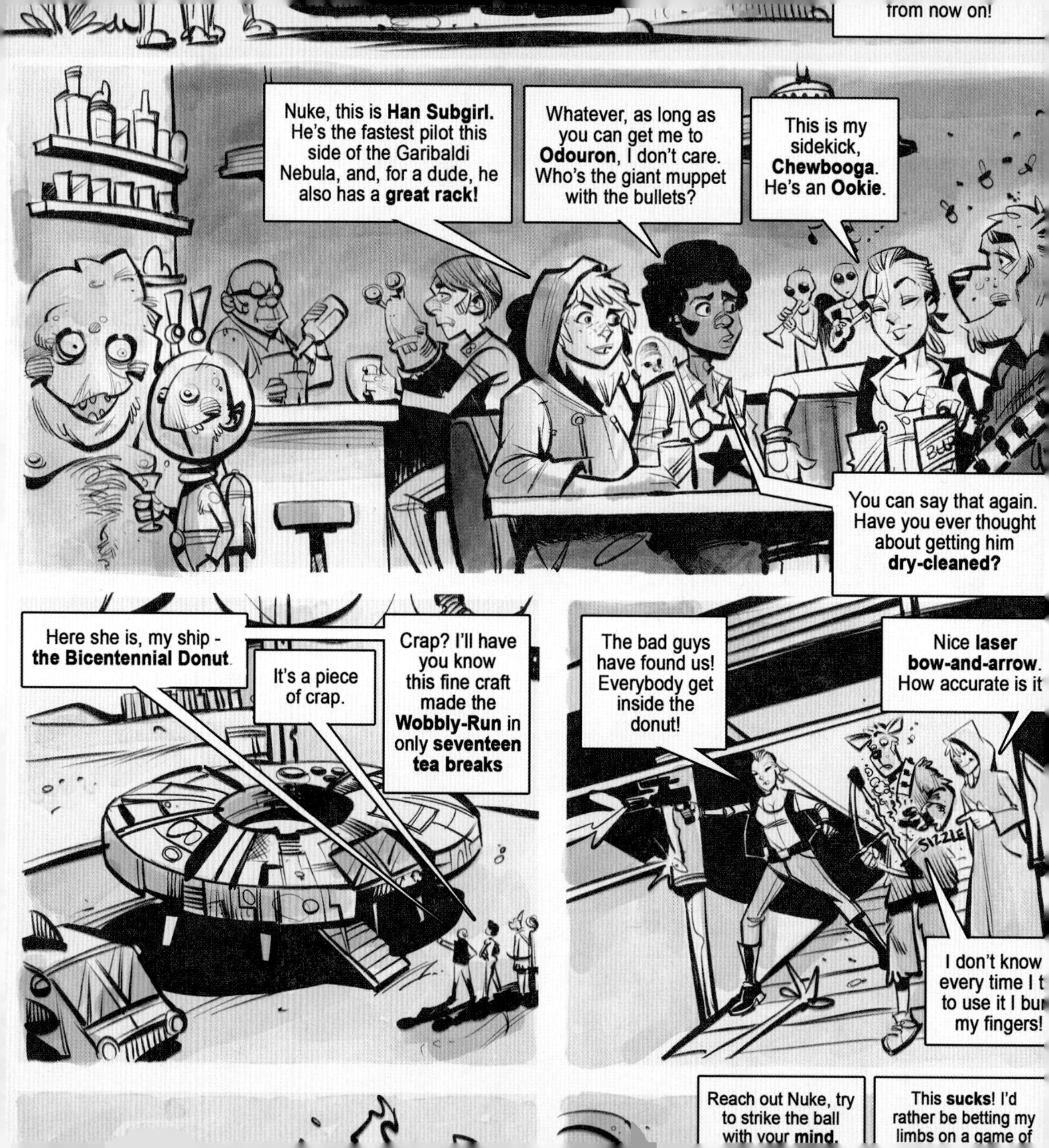

from now on!
Nuke, this is **Han Subgirl.** He's the fastest pilot this side of the Garibaldi Nebula, and, for a dude, he also has a **great rack!**
Whatever, as long as you can get me to **Odouron**, I don't care. Who's the giant muppet with the bullets?
This is my sidekick, **Chewbooga**. He's an **Ookie**.
You can say that again. Have you ever thought about getting him **dry-cleaned?**
Here she is, my ship - **the Bicentennial Donut**.
It's a piece of crap.
Crap? I'll have you know this fine craft made the **Wobbly-Run** in only **seventeen tea breaks**
The bad guys have found us! Everybody get inside the donut!
Nice **laser bow-and-arrow**. How accurate is it
SIZZLE
I don't know every time I t to use it I bu my fingers!
Reach out Nuke, try to strike the ball with your **mind.**
This **sucks**! I'd rather be betting my limbs on a game of

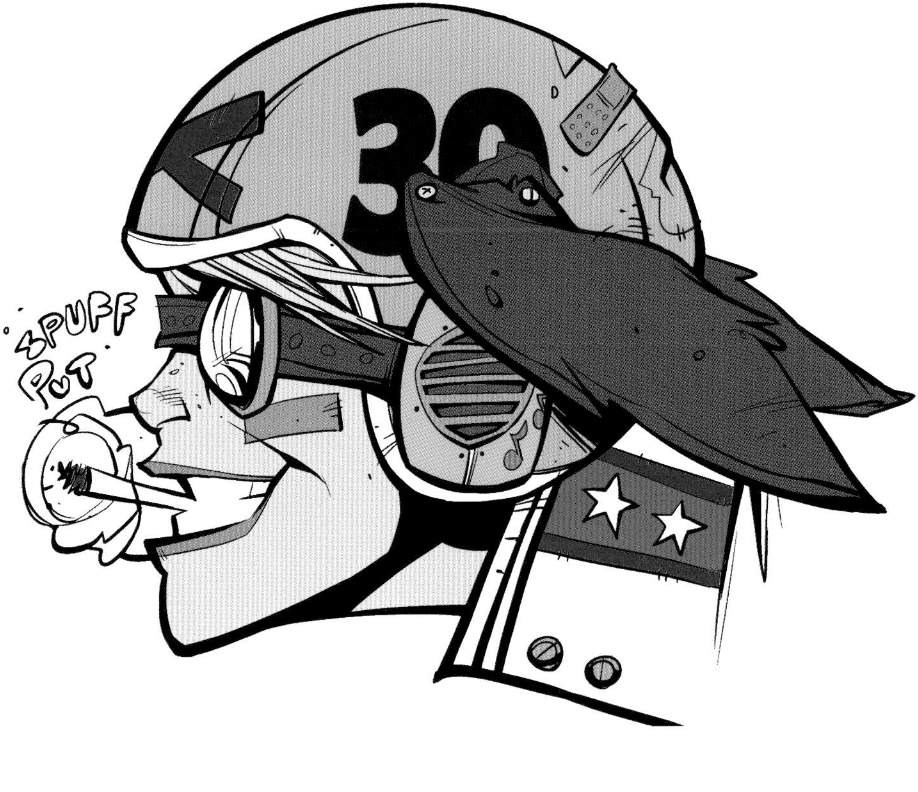

30
PUFF
PUT

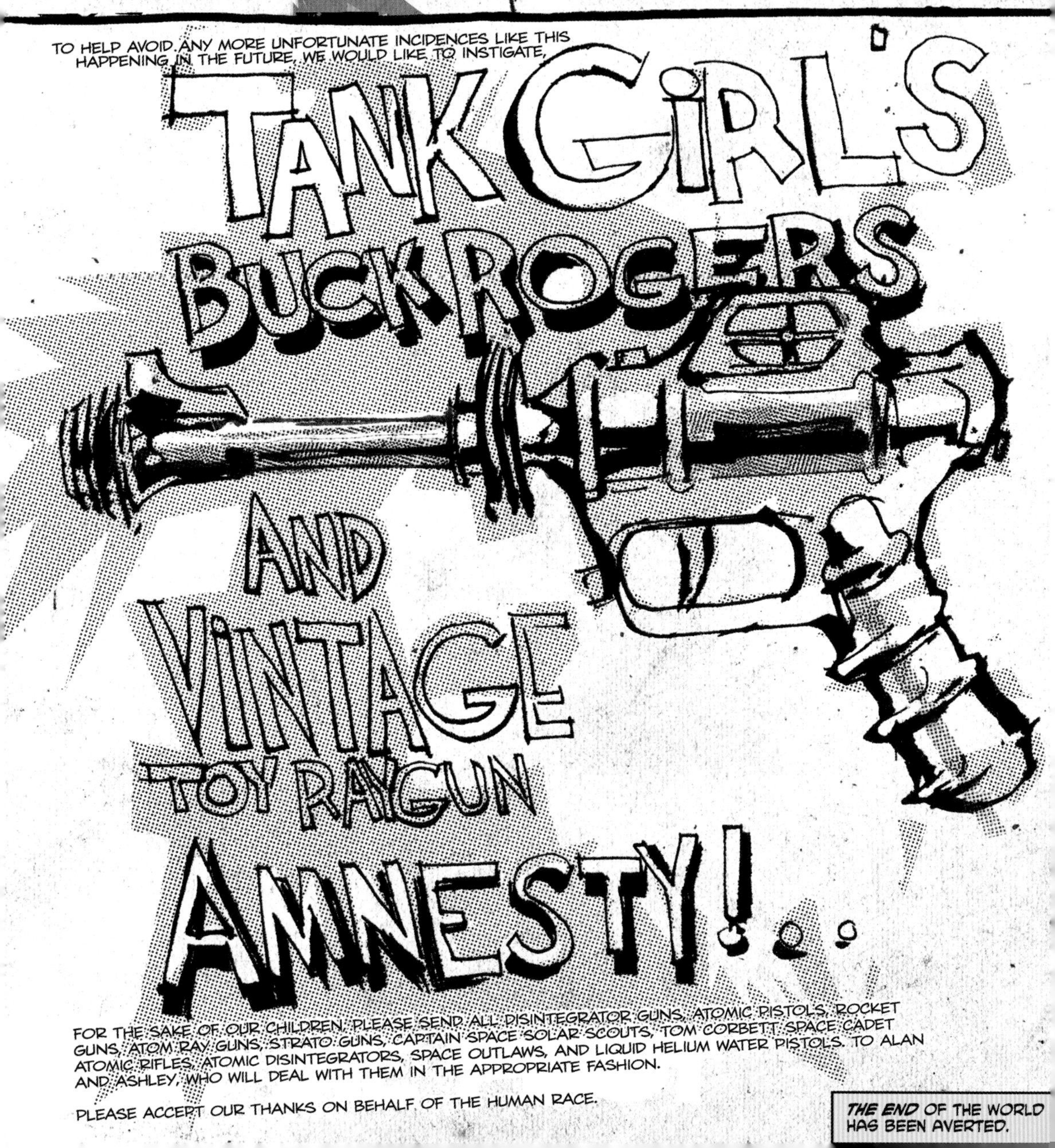
TO HELP AVOID ANY MORE UNFORTUNATE INCIDENCES LIKE THIS HAPPENING IN THE FUTURE, WE WOULD LIKE TO INSTIGATE,
TANK GIRL'S
BUCK ROGERS
AND
VINTAGE
TOY RAYGUN
AMNESTY!...
FOR THE SAKE OF OUR CHILDREN, PLEASE SEND ALL DISINTEGRATOR GUNS, ATOMIC PISTOLS, ROCKET GUNS, ATOM RAY GUNS, STRATO GUNS, CAPTAIN SPACE SOLAR SCOUTS, TOM CORBETT SPACE CADET ATOMIC RIFLES, ATOMIC DISINTEGRATORS, SPACE OUTLAWS, AND LIQUID HELIUM WATER PISTOLS. TO ALAN AND ASHLEY, WHO WILL DEAL WITH THEM IN THE APPROPRIATE FASHION.
PLEASE ACCEPT OUR THANKS ON BEHALF OF THE HUMAN RACE.
THE END OF THE WORLD HAS BEEN AVERTED.

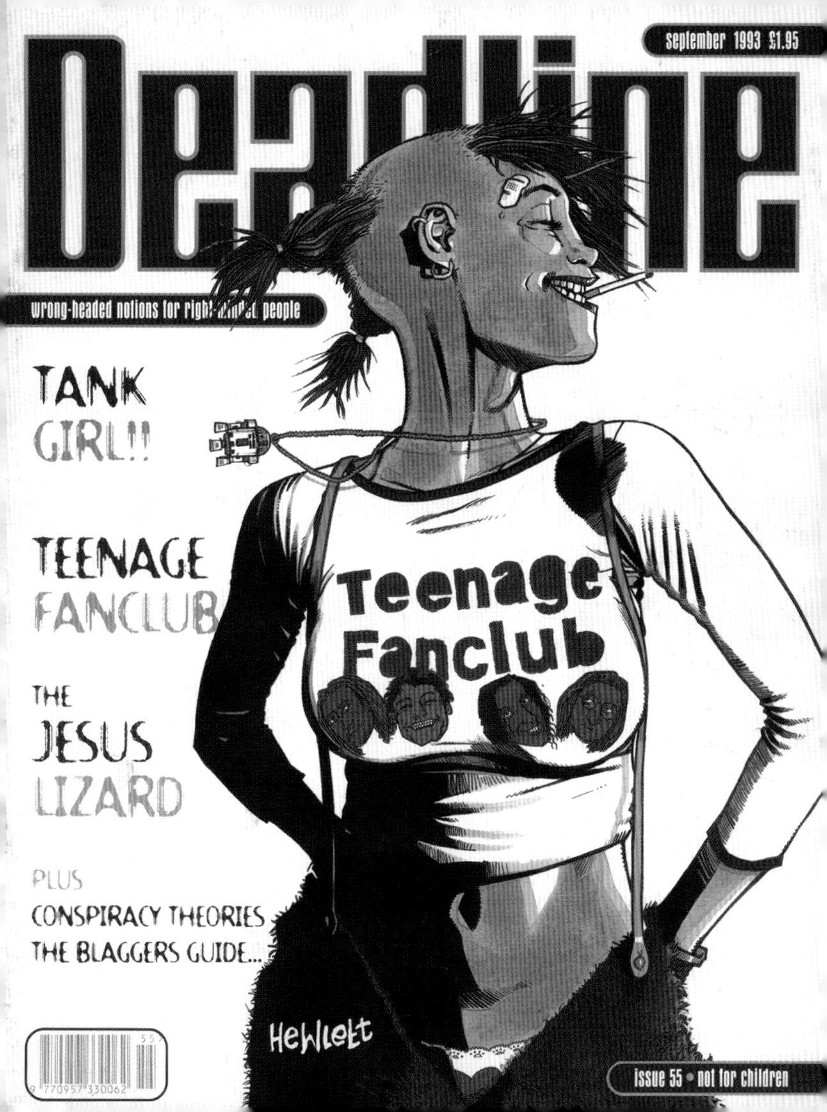
Deadline
september 1993 £1.95
wrong-headed notions for right-minded people
TANK GIRL!!
TEENAGE FANCLUB
THE JESUS LIZARD
PLUS
CONSPIRACY THEORIES
THE BLAGGERS GUIDE...
Teenage Fanclub
HEWLETT
9 770957 330062
issue 55 • not for children

YOURS AYE

I am
completely
utterly
devastatingly
brilliantly
hopelessly
endlessly
crazily
steadfastly
robotically
resolutely
remotely
immeasurably
madly
constantly
fantastically
absolutely
stupidly

truly

fucking

yours

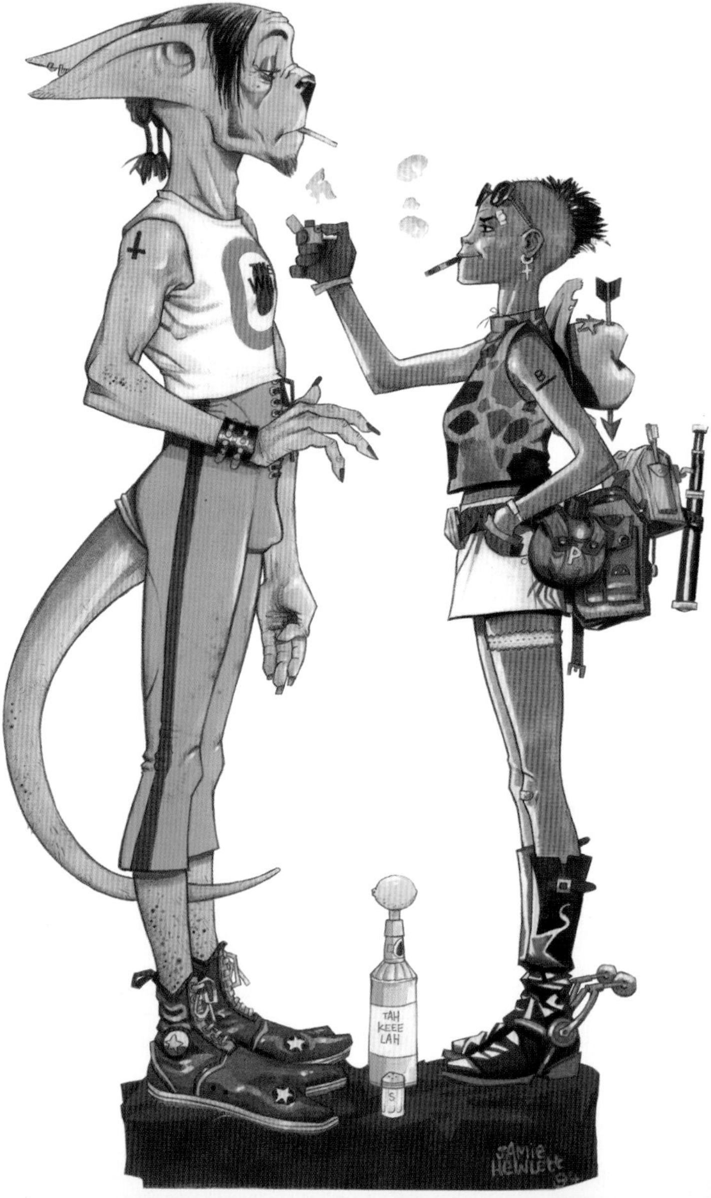
TAH
KEEE
LAH
JAMIE
HEWLETT

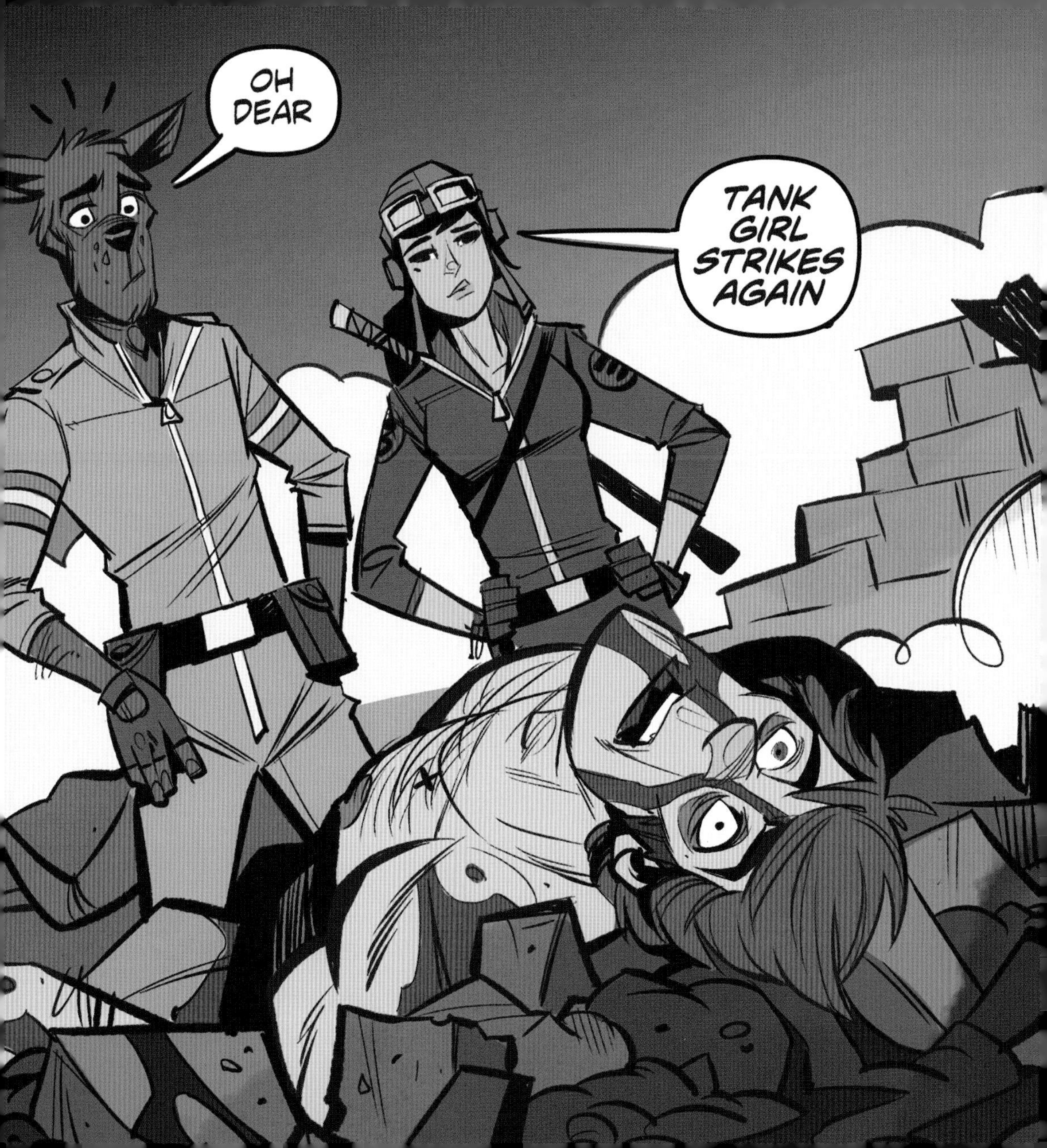
OH DEAR
TANK GIRL STRIKES AGAIN

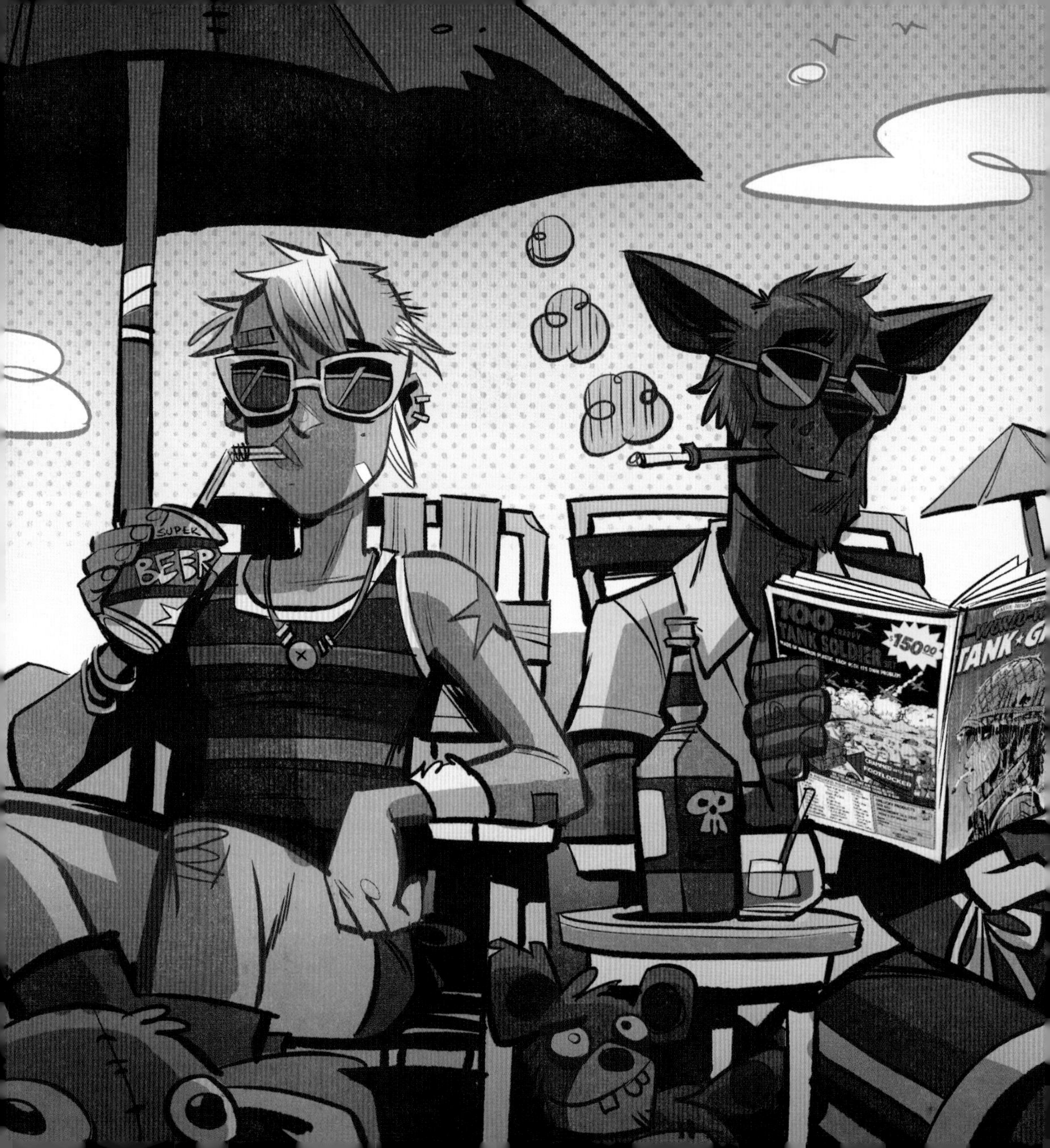
SUPER
BEER
100 CRAPPY TANK SOLDIER SET
$150.00
FOOTLOCKER
TANK

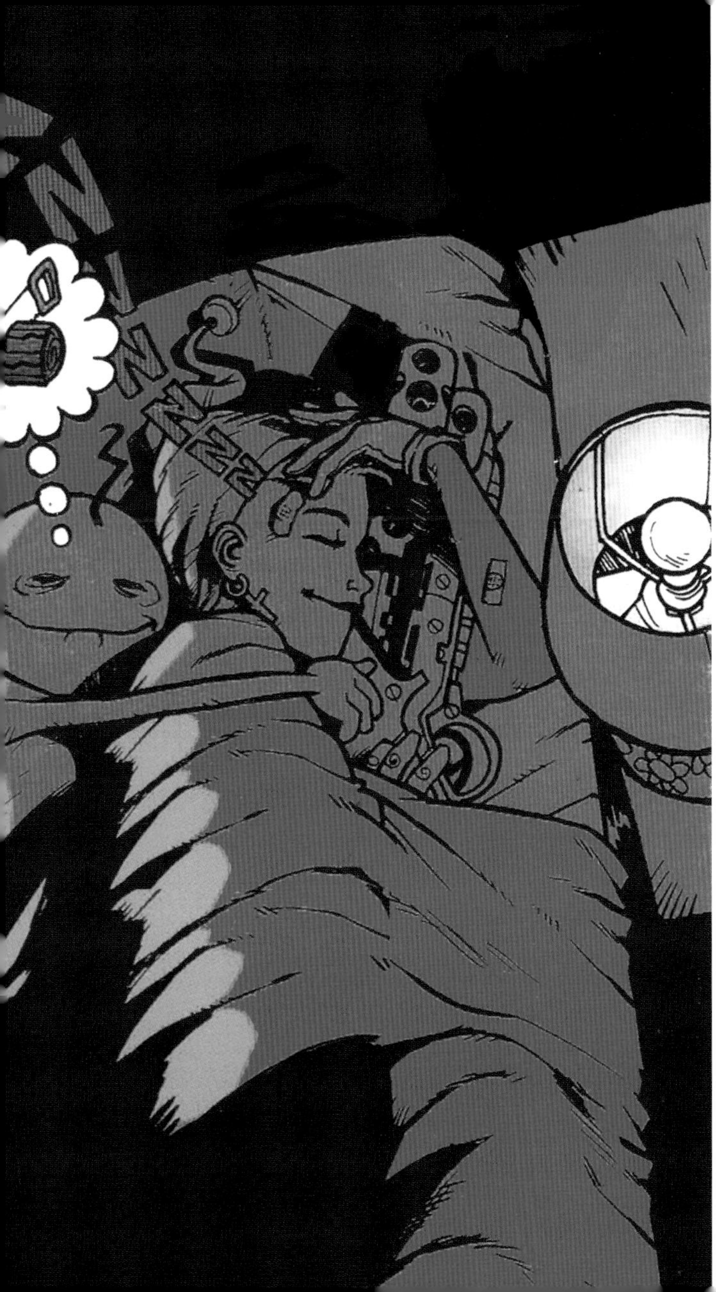

MINE MINE MINE

I lost you in the playground
I lost you near the swings
I was distracted by the
Helter Skelter
and all the chaos
that it brings

I lost you in a crowd of kids
too many faces
too many screams
you jumped out of my pocket
like an errant glove
slipped from my hands
like melting ice cream

but now I'm binding you to me
with an idiot string
I'm pegging you by your ears
to the washing line

and I'm sewing my name
inside you

because you're mine

mine

mine

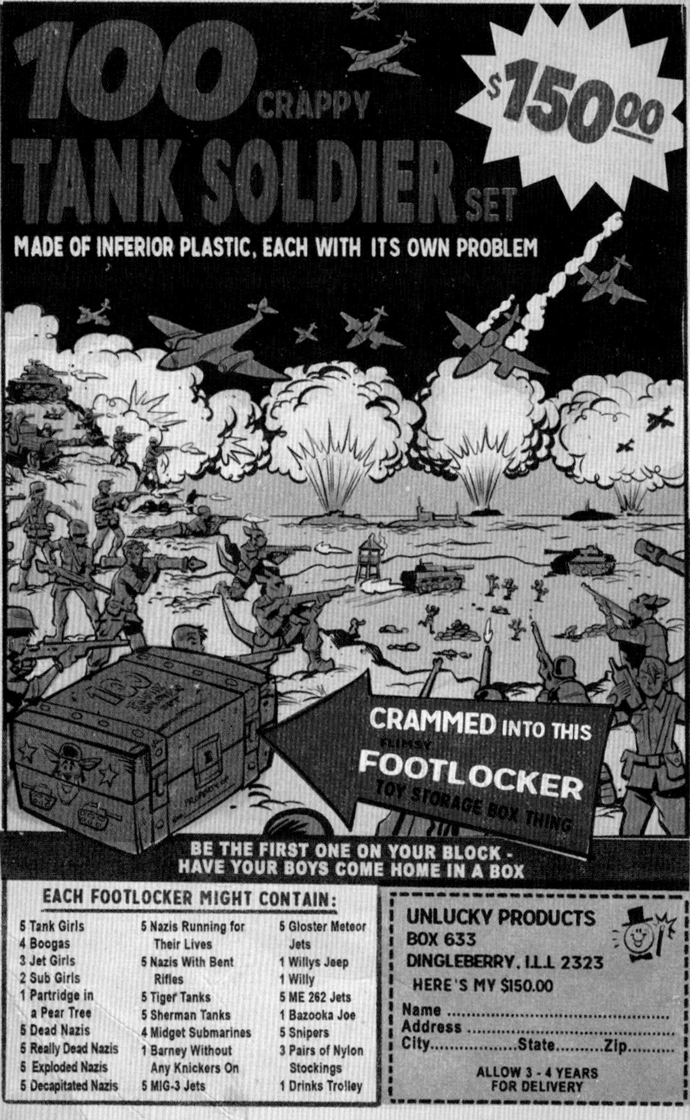
100 CRAPPY
TANK SOLDIER SET
$150.00
MADE OF INFERIOR PLASTIC, EACH WITH ITS OWN PROBLEM
CRAMMED INTO THIS
FLIMSY
FOOTLOCKER
TOY STORAGE BOX THING
BE THE FIRST ONE ON YOUR BLOCK -
HAVE YOUR BOYS COME HOME IN A BOX
EACH FOOTLOCKER MIGHT CONTAIN:
5 Tank Girls
4 Boogas
3 Jet Girls
2 Sub Girls
1 Partridge in a Pear Tree
5 Dead Nazis
5 Really Dead Nazis
5 Exploded Nazis
5 Decapitated Nazis
5 Nazis Running for Their Lives
5 Nazis With Bent Rifles
5 Tiger Tanks
5 Sherman Tanks
4 Midget Submarines
1 Barney Without Any Knickers On
5 MIG-3 Jets
5 Gloster Meteor Jets
1 Willys Jeep
1 Willy
5 ME 262 Jets
1 Bazooka Joe
5 Snipers
3 Pairs of Nylon Stockings
1 Drinks Trolley
UNLUCKY PRODUCTS
BOX 633
DINGLEBERRY, I.L.L 2323
HERE'S MY $150.00
Name
Address
City State Zip
ALLOW 3 - 4 YEARS FOR DELIVERY

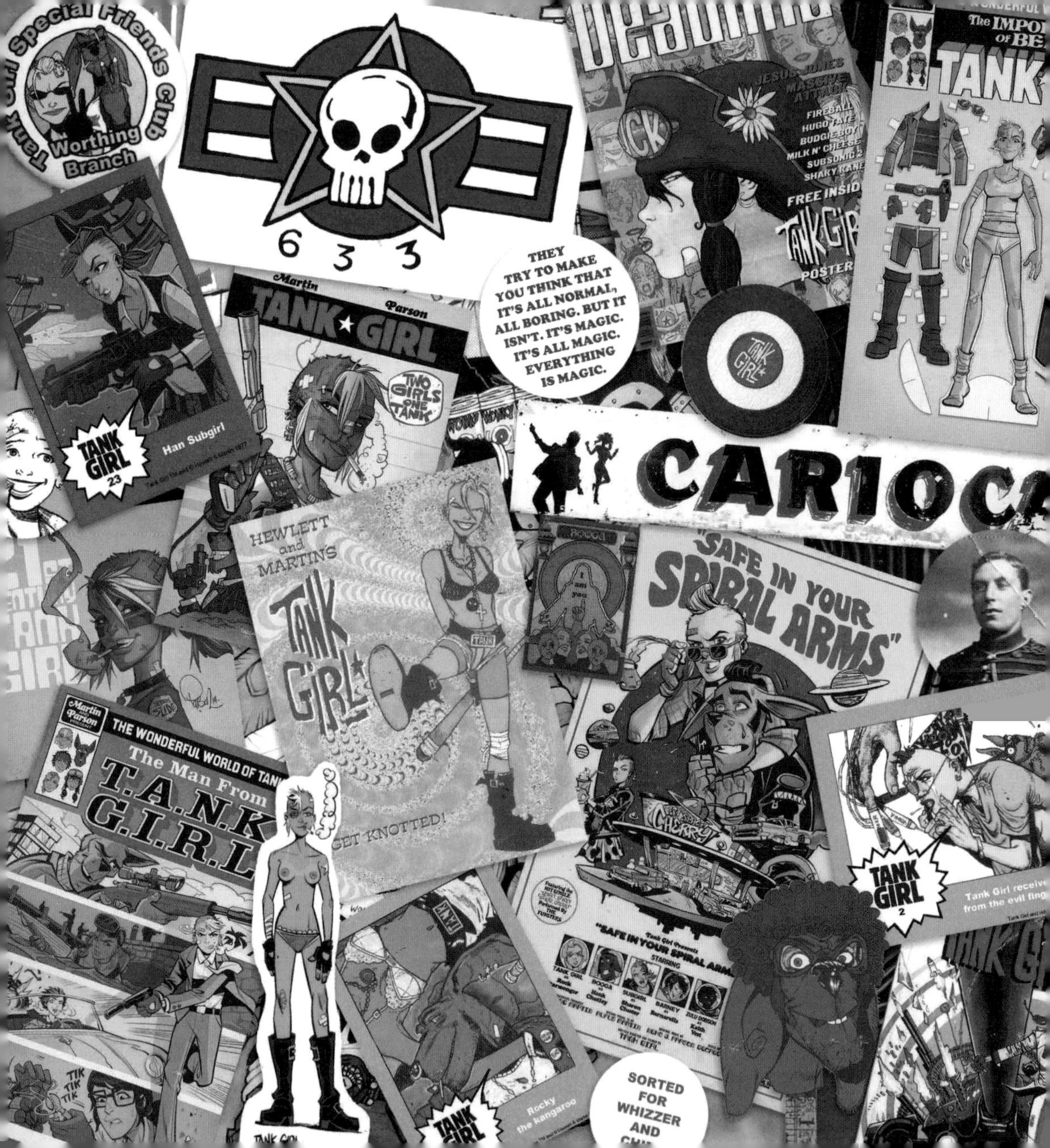

Special Friends Club
Worthing Branch
633
THEY TRY TO MAKE YOU THINK THAT IT'S ALL NORMAL, IT'S ALL BORING. BUT IT ISN'T. IT'S MAGIC. IT'S ALL MAGIC. EVERYTHING IS MAGIC.
JESUS JONES
MASSIVE ATTACK
FIREBALL
HUGO TATE
BUDGIE BOY
MILK N' CHEESE
SHAKY KANE
POSTER
TANK GIRL
Martin
TANK★GIRL
Parson
TWO GIRLS ONE TANK
TANK GIRL 23
Han Subgirl
CARIOCA
HEWLETT and MARTIN'S
TANK GIRL
GET KNOTTED!
"SAFE IN YOUR SPIRAL ARMS"
"SAFE IN YOUR SPIRAL ARMS"
Martin and Parson
THE WONDERFUL WORLD OF TANK
The Man From
T.A.N.K.
G.I.R.L.
TIK TIK TIK
TANK GIRL 2
Rocky the kangaroo
SORTED FOR WHIZZER AND